BREAD

By Beth Hensperger

Photography by
Victor Budnik

Designed by
Thomas Ingalls

CHRONICLE BOOKS
SAN FRANCISCO

Thanks to my Assistants of Photography
Caroline Cory, Denise Cannon.

To Food Stylist Karen Hazarian, for her keen eye.

For her support and beautiful canvas
backgrounds, thanks to Dianne McKenzie.

Painted finishes and backgrounds were done by
Sherry Phelan Wright.

To Thomas Ingalls, many thanks for his attention
to detail and great design of the book.

And to the talent of Gail Grant and
Amanda Bryan.

Printed in Japan.

Library of Congress Cataloging-in-Publication Data
Hensperger, Beth.
    Bread / by Beth Hensperger; photographs by Victor
    Budnik. 000 p. 00 cm.
    Includes index.
    ISBN 0-87701-472-8. ISBN 0-87701-443-4 (pbk.)
    1. Bread. I. Budnik, Victor. II. Title.
TX769.H44 1988
641.8′15—dc19   87-29620

Editing: Carolyn Miller
Photography: Victor Budnik
Book and cover design: Thomas Ingalls + Associates
Designers: Amanda Bryan, Thomas Ingalls

Distributed in Canada by
Raincoast Books
112 East 3rd Avenue
Vancouver, B.C.
V5T 1C8

10 9 8 7 6

Chronicle Books
275 Fifth Street
San Francisco, CA 94103

INTRODUCTION   2

Ingredients   5

  Grains for Breadmaking   6

  Leaveners   9

  Other Basics   10

Equipment   13

  Tools   14

  Ovens   15

  Work Space   17

Techniques   19

Yeasted Breads   27

  White Breads   28

  Whole-Grain Breads   38

  Vegetable and Herb Breads   54

  Picnic Breads   63

  Little Savory Breads   69

  Sweet Breads   79

  Little Sweet Breads   89

Quick Breads   96

  Muffins   97

  Biscuits   105

  Quick Loaves   109

  Coffee Cakes   112

The Art of Glazing   114

Embellishments and Special Techniques   116

Spreads   117

  Butters   118

  Olive and Nut Spreads   120

  Cheese Spreads   121

  Mustards   122

  Jams   123

The Art of Melba   126

Bread and Spirits   130

Bread and Food   133

Menu Suggestions   135

Index   136

Introduction

A GOOD LOAF OF BREAD radiates beauty at every stage of its creation: the fresh yeasty odor of fermenting dough; its smooth, slightly blistered surface after kneading on a scrubbed wooden board; and the spongy texture of dough that has risen to the top of your yellow ceramic bread bowl. A handmade loaf of bread is a source of pride for anyone who likes to cook. Cooks who never attempt bread will always have a sense of "something missing" from their repertoire.

Today we are experiencing a revival of the old home crafts once necessary for survival. Despite nationwide dependence on store-bought bread, we have a long-standing appreciation for the home-baked, hand-hewn loaf. The tradition of the Western-style loaf is centuries old. You owe yourself the opportunity to develop an appreciation for this elegantly simple product of flour, water, salt, and yeast.

There is little doubt that women were the first agriculturalists, or "overseers of grain." All the ancient grain divinities were female. Certainly the home hearth was stoked and the stove was kept hot by the woman in the family. But men were the first commercial bakers, and bread was the first foodstuff to be prepared outside the home. It is still a male-dominated field—partly because it involves heavy manual labor, despite all the mechanical innovations over the centuries.

The United States boasts a wide variety of traditional breads. Groups of immigrants began to arrive here directly following the American Revolution, bringing with them their favorite breads: fluffy potato loaves from Germany, Danish pastry, *croissants* from France, buckwheat *blini* from Russia, hearty ryes and flat breads from Scandinavia. Many commercial bakeries in this country have founded their success on the country loaves of Italy and France. Our Southern heritage gave us corn breads and delicate biscuits. Native ingredients such as corn, pecans, blueberries, and cranberries have resulted in uniquely American breads.

Now is the time to retrieve Grandmother's old bread bowl from the back cupboard, roll up our sleeves, and turn on the oven. Breadmaking is not a skill bakers were born with or an obscure art taking years of disciplined training to master. Though you may not get a perfect loaf the first time, with a dash of effort and good humor, you can be sure to get a good loaf within a very few tries. Let your personal likes and dislikes in regard to flavor, texture, and choice of nutritional additives guide you to recipes that will work for you.

What makes a good baker? Patience in practicing the time-honored breadmaking techniques. The basics run true from recipe to recipe. Gradually you will learn what works, and what does not, and how to be comfortable with your mistakes. Become familiar with interpreting recipes so you can find the ones that work for you. A recipe is like sheet music: the interpretation of it is very personal. Breadmaking is an artistic endeavor.

The beginner has a tendency to be timid with bread dough. Only experience can tell you how much is "enough flour," the "right temperature," or when the dough has been kneaded "enough." The dough will tell you what it needs—once you learn the language.

Breadmaking is physical and spiritual at the same time. It is a meditative procedure, calling on inner awareness as well as acquired skill. Most breadmakers I know, even professional ones mixing large amounts of dough, become quiet and introspective while working. This attention produces a loaf that is highly personal even when much of the process is aided by machine. There is great satisfaction in sculpting a loaf where hours before none existed.

In our fast-paced culture in America today, we have developed "faster yeast" to produce faster breads. But to get the absolute best bread in the world, the one element that is imperative is time—and lots of it. A home kitchen can produce a loaf with a charming hand-wrought shape, a superior flavor, and a moist texture. This is due to good, fresh, hard-wheat flours, long rests to develop the dough, and your own unique touch in allowing the ingredients to blend in harmonious alchemy.

Whether you enjoy a simple daily bread with some sweet butter and jam, butter-rich *croissants*, or the subtle flavor of tomato bread with saffron, keep your ingredients pure. They will speak for themselves, and you will have a loaf of bread that is impossible to reproduce in a commerical bakery.

Ingredients

GRAINS FOR BREADMAKING

WHEAT

There are three varieties of wheat: hard, soft, and durum. Hard wheat, used for **bread flour,** is the highest in protein and the most desirable for breadmaking. Bread flour may be used interchangeably with all-purpose flour. Soft wheat is finer, with less protein, and is excellent for pastries and cakes. Durum wheat, or semolina flour, is a high-protein variety used for pasta making. It is also used in certain bread recipes, where it adds a strong wheat flavor and texture. **All-purpose flour** is a combination of 80 percent hard wheat and 20 percent soft wheat and can be used successfully in all types of baking. I prefer to use unbleached flour, as bleached flour is whitened by a chemical agent.

Flour contains gluten, a combination of two proteins that become stretchy in the presence of moisture and warmth. After kneading, the stretchy quality becomes a meshlike network of starch strong enough to support the growing yeast communities, giving bread its characteristic shape, smell, and texture. Hard wheat contains the highest amount of protein (about 13 percent) and gives lightness and increased workability to flours with little or no gluten, such as rye. Wheat and rye are the only grains that contain gluten and are thus able to make our familiar "loaf." There are many specialty flours on the market such as rice, corn, barley, millet, soy, buckwheat, and oat. These flours generally have high nutritive value and a variety of earthy flavors, but when used alone in baking, they produce dense and crumbly breads. Large amounts of bran will inhibit the rising of bread, so it must be used in moderation. To make a light, palatable loaf, use approximately 1 cup or less of specialty flour to 5 cups of wheat flour.

There are no standards for all-purpose flour or milling techniques, so flours grown in different geographical areas vary greatly; therefore, your baking successes may also differ from one area to another. Take this in stride and not as a reflection of your baking skill. Many bakers grind their own grains as a method of controlling the variables in baking. Unground grain keeps indefinitely, making storage easier. Home electric mills are moderately priced, do not generate heat, use little energy, and grind a wide variety of grains that will give your bread more nutritional benefits. Small hand mills are some work, but nice for grinding small amounts.

Stone-ground whole-grain flours are milled by a slow process using granite stones, which disperses the wheat bran evenly through the flour and allows the flour to stay much cooler than when ground with steel rollers. "Water ground" means the millstones are powered by water. Stone-ground white flour is generally unavailable from small mills, as the space needed for steaming, storing, and drying is enormous, but it is almost a mystical goal among bread devotees to search out this fine flour. There is a trend now to renovate and put back in operation old American mills, to make more high-quality fresh-milled flours and cereals available.

Large commercial flour mills use heat, moisture, and huge steel rollers for grinding grain. Fresh-ground white flour is naturally yellow due to the pigment in the wheat, and unbleached flour is aged and whitened naturally by exposing the flour to air over a few months' time. A shortcut to whitening the flour is to treat the flour with chlorine, which reduces expensive storage time. This flour is called "bleached." **Unbleached flour** is refined, but has no added chemicals or preservatives. If unbleached flour has had the aging process accelerated by potassium bromate, the packaging will be labeled "bromated." It makes excellent bread. Store unbleached flour in a cool, dry place in closed containers, as flour absorbs strong odors and moisture easily. Whole-wheat flour is milled from the whole grain, and since the bran and germ are included, it must be stored in the refrigerator to prevent the oils from becoming rancid. All whole-grain flours, such as corn and rye, should be refrigerated also. Whole-grain flours absorb more moisture than unbleached flour, and the dough is much stickier to the touch. Whole-wheat flour contains more nutritional assets than white flour, such as B vitamins, and has a rougher, more abrasive texture due to its high fiber content.

The quantity of flour used in any bread is approximate. I use the amount of flour called for in a recipe as a guide, but this amount will vary slightly in its absorbancy due to climatic conditions and the type of flour. It is a quality you cannot judge until you begin working the dough. For example, on a humid or rainy day, you may need ¼ to ½ cup less flour than if you were making the bread on a warm, windy day. Also, flours grown in the winter with lots of rain absorb less moisture than flours grown in dry summer weather. These are variables you cannot control, but you can deal with them by paying attention to the dough.

Pastry flour is milled from soft wheat and has a protein content of about 8 percent, making it unsuitable for breadmaking. It has the ability to hold a lot of fat, however, so it is ideal for pastry and cake making. **Cake flour** is finer still, at 6 percent protein, and is used for making lovely, light cakes. Never use **self-rising flour**, unless it is specifically called for in a recipe, as it contains bicarbonate of soda and salt.

Wheat berries are whole-wheat grains or kernels before grinding. They are sprouted or cooked before being added to bread dough. A good proportion is about ½ cup per loaf. The entire kernel is surrounded by a layer of **bran**. Bran is the outer husk of the wheat grain and a by-product of refining. It is used to supplement diets lacking in roughage. The outermost layer over the bran is called the hull. It is inedible and is removed during threshing.

Wheat germ is the seed, or embryo, of the wheat kernel and very high in nutrients, such as B vitamins. Keep refrigerated, as it contains a high percentage of oil, which will turn rancid with exposure to heat and light. The germ is surrounded by starch, known as the *endosperm*, which would nourish the seed if sprouted. The endosperm is ground into flour. *Bolting* is the process that separates the bran and germ from the endosperm.

Gluten flour is starch removed from the wheat berry by a washing process, then dried and milled. Gluten flour is added as a lightening agent for breads low in gluten. It is 40 percent protein and can be used in some allergy diets.

Whole-wheat flour is ground from the entire kernel, leaving lots of nutrients and a sweet, nutty flavor. Whole-wheat flour can be ground from fine to coarse, and your bread's texture will vary accordingly. The finest grind is known as **whole-wheat pastry flour**, which is used in quick breads and pastries.

Cracked wheat is a fine, medium, or coarse cut of the wheat kernel.

Bulgur wheat is cracked wheat that has been parboiled and dried for faster cooking.

Graham flour is named for the pioneer Sylvester Graham, who argued the merits of whole-grain bread as a dietary necessity in the United States earlier in this century. Although it can be used interchangeably with whole-wheat flour, graham flour is milled differently: the whole grain is ground very coarse with some flecks of bran left in, giving it a rich, sweet flavor.

Durum wheat flour is a high-protein, cold-weather strain of wheat. It is creamy golden in color and is used for the highest-quality pastas. It is a delightful flour for bread. **Semolina** has had the bran layer removed and the rest of the durum wheat kernel (including the bran) ground. The cut grains are known as *couscous* (which is also made from millet) and *farina*. When using for bread, be certain to buy a fine grind of **semolina flour**.

Triticale flour is a hardy, hybrid cross of wheat and rye grains. It is high in protein but low in gluten.

Mixed-grain cereals are very popular, especially in a six-grain or nine-grain blend. Nine-grain cereals often consist of wheat, rye, barley, triticale, corn, oat, flax, millet, and soy grits.

RYE

Rye is an earthy, strong-flavored grain similar to wheat. Rye grows wild in eastern Europe, thriving on the cold winters and poor soil. It contains some gluten. **Rye berries** are the whole grain before grinding. **Medium rye flour** is a mixture of light and dark flours and is the best for all-purpose rye breadmaking. It is the rye flour found on supermarket shelves. The lightest rye breads incorporate some wheat flour. **Pumpernickel**, or dark rye flour, is a coarse grind with much of the bran left in, which makes a very dense bread.

BARLEY

Barley is an ancient grain and is extremely high in minerals. It is a grain grown mostly for brewing, as a source of malt, but it makes a sweet and crumbly bread. It should be soaked overnight before boiling. **Pearl barley** is the whole grain with the outer, indigestible husk removed. It cooks quickly, about 1½ hours without soaking. It is a well-known addition to Scotch broth. **Barley flakes** are cooked as a cereal or added to bread. **Barley flour** is ground for bread from pearl barley and is sometimes lightly toasted to improve flavor.

OATS

Oats have always been cultivated by man. They are the grain richest in proteins and minerals. **Oat groats** are the cleaned and hulled whole grain. **Steel-cut oats** are cut from the hulled groat. **Rolled oats** are groats that have been hulled, steamed, and flattened into the familiar flake form. Quick-cooking oats are rolled from cut groats. You can use quick and old-fashioned rolled oats interchangeably. Oat flakes can be ground into a coarse meal for use in breadmaking. **Oat flour** is fine ground for bread from the groats. Oats have a creamy, sweet, well-loved flavor.

CORN

From the Mexican highlands comes the indigenous North American grain, corn, also known as *maize*, or Indian corn. It is a popular grain with a sweet flavor and is the ingredient in tortillas and johnnycake. **Hominy** is the American Indian name for hulled white corn with the germ removed. It is ground into coarse **grits**, a traditional Southern porridge. **Cornmeal** is ground from white or yellow corn. **Polenta** is a coarse grind of yellow corn and very popular as an Italian porridge. **Masa harina** is fine cornmeal ground from white corn soaked in lime water before being dried. It is the main ingredient in tortillas. All grinds of cornmeal can be used in breadmaking. **Corn flour** is finely ground from the whole corn kernel. It is delicious in breads. **Cornstarch** is the silky ground heart of the corn kernel. It is very fine and is used as a thickening agent or in very small quantities to lighten flour for pastry baking, as in shortbread. Popcorn is a specific variety containing a lot of hard starch. Sweet table corn is another variety, eaten immature, when it is tender and juicy.

RICE

One-third of the earth depends on rice for food. It is commonly eaten as a cooked whole grain. **Brown rice** is hulled, but still retains its outer bran covering, which contains natural B vitamins. It comes in short, medium, and long grain, as do the familiar hulled varieties of white rice. Brown rice is very filling and has a long cooking time. It is delicious in breads, adding a sweet, nubby flavor and chewy texture. **Converted rice** is steam treated before hulling, leaving the same nutrients as are found in brown rice. It was developed for quicker cooking. **Basmati rice** is a long-grain Asian variety. It has a superior flavor and is one of the world's finest rices. It needs to be washed well before cooking. **Arborio rice** is a short-grained variety grown in Italy. It is white to creamy yellow and can absorb a lot of liquid without becoming soft. It is good for *paella* and is the ingredient in *risotto*. **Rice flour** is ground from brown or white rice. It is an excellent thickener and well known in bread and pizza making as the best flour for dusting, as it absorbs moisture slowly. **Wild rice** is not rice, but the seed of an aquatic wild grass, which needs long cooking. It is a grain native to North America.

SOY

Soy flour is ground from toasted soybeans and contains 40 to 50 percent protein. It is the famous ingredient in the Cornell nutritional formula for enriching bread. A musty-flavored grain, it may be an acquired taste. Soy flour is fifteen times richer in calcium and iron than wheat.

MILLET

Millet was originally a wild African grass that was first cultivated in Spain. It must be hulled to be digestible. When cooked, its perfectly round grains swell to five times their original size. It is eaten like rice and can be added to bread whole and raw for a delightful crunch and extra nutrition. Millet is a subtle grain that is easy to digest. **Millet flour** is ground from whole millet and produces bread with a crumbly texture.

BUCKWHEAT

Buckwheat is a grass belonging to the sorrel family, which includes rhubarb. It is known as "Saracen corn" and is grown in the rocky soil and cold climates of northeastern Europe and Siberia. **Buckwheat groats**, or *kasha*, are toasted in a skillet with a beaten egg to keep the grains separate before steaming. **Buckwheat flour** is ground from the triangular groat to make a pungent, earthy flour. Buckwheat was brought to America by the Dutch settlers as livestock feed. It is the main ingredient in *blini*, a small pancake, and Japanese *soba* noodles. It also makes wonderful bread when used in small amounts with wheat flour.

Other specialty flours used in breadmaking are **acorn flour**, used by the American Indians, sweet **chestnut flour**, beloved in France and Italy, and **potato flour**, used in Spanish cooking as an excellent thickener.

LEAVENERS

YEAST

Yeast is a one-celled natural wild plant, scientifically known as *Saccharomyces cerevisiae*. It is the soul of bread. To be activated and multiply, yeast needs food in the form of sugar, moisture, warmth, and air. It is important to know that yeast can be killed by too much heat, about 140° or above. It goes into a suspended state below 50°, allowing dough to be refrigerated or frozen for periods of time. Maximum activity happens between 80° to 90°. Yeast eats the sugars and complex carbohydrates in the flour, and, instantly, activity begins in the form of bubbles—a process called fermentation. The by-product of this is alcohol, the beerlike or heady, yeasty smell in raw dough, and CO_2, which is trapped within the stretchy meshlike gluten structure of the dough. The heat of the oven kills the yeast, burns off the alcohol, and sets the porous pattern, creating the familiar texture of bread.

Yeast is sold to the consumer in four different forms: active dry yeast, compressed fresh cake yeast, quick-rise yeast, and instant dried yeast. Nutritional yeasts, such as brewer's and torula, are not leavening agents.

Active dry yeast is sold in a dated ¼-ounce flat foil-wrapped packet, in a three-packet strip, 4-ounce jars, or in bulk from your local health food store. One scant tablespoon of dry yeast is equal to a ¼-ounce premeasured package or a .06-ounce cube of fresh cake yeast. Dry yeast is not activated until first dissolved in warm liquid (about 105° to 115°). It is advisable to invest in a good yeast thermometer to be certain of your liquid temperatures until you can recognize the exact warmth by feel. Without a thermometer, test the water by dripping a few drops on the inside of your wrist. It should feel warm without being uncomfortably hot, as for baby formula. If the water is too cool, the yeast will be slow to activate. If the water is too hot, the yeast will be killed, failing to produce the characteristic foamy effect, and the dough will not rise. Keep dry yeast in the refrigerator in a tightly covered container. If properly stored, dry yeast can remain fresh for up to about one year. But, to be certain, always proof your yeast if there are long lapses between your baking sprees, and do not buy packages that have exceeded their pull date.

Compressed fresh cake yeast is known for its dependability, excellent rising ability, and, some claim, superior flavor. It is sold in .06-ounce and 2-ounce cakes and 1-pound blocks, sometimes available from your local bakery. The 1-pound professional size is absolutely the best yeast available. The smaller cakes sold in the deli case of your grocery are stabilized with starch to prolong shelf life, which also tends to decrease potency. Fresh yeast is highly perishable, must be refrigerated, and will keep for about 2 weeks. When fresh, it is an even tan-gray with no discoloration and breaks with a clean edge. Compressed yeast should be dissolved in lukewarm liquid (about 95°) before adding to the dry ingredients. Compressed yeast may be successfully frozen for several months, but its potency seems to decrease.

Quick-rise yeast is a new development in yeast technology, and there are numerous American brands on the market. It is a new strain of low-moisture yeast that raises dough 50 percent faster than regular yeast. It works best when added directly to the dry ingredients and when the liquid added is about 120°. Follow the manufacturer's instructions, as dough temperature and rising times are different than for general breadmaking. I find there is some loss of flavor and keeping quality, due to the very fast rising. Use a bit less quick-rise yeast in a recipe where a slower, more normal rising time is desired. It is available in ¼-ounce packages, sold in a three-package strip.

Another relative newcomer to the yeast family is **instant dried yeast** from Europe, which is dried to a very low percentage of moisture. It is combined with an emulsifier and a form of sugar, enabling the yeast to activate immediately upon contact with warm liquid. With three times as many yeast cells as active dry yeast, this strain cannot tolerate a lot of sugar, as in sweet dough recipes, or long, slow proofing temperatures, because it is just constantly rising. This yeast enables a dough to be baked without any rising period.

Yeast doughs are affected by high elevation, beginning at about 3,500 feet above sea level. The yeast reproduces at an accelerated rate, so decrease the yeast required by one-third. For example, if the recipe calls for 1 tablespoon of yeast, reduce it to 2 teaspoons. The rising times will also be shorter. To keep a good developed flavor, allow the dough to fully double two times before forming it into loaves. Dough may also tend to dry more quickly, calling for a bit more liquid or a bit less flour, as you feel fit. Many bakers also increase their oven baking temperature by 25°.

BAKING SODA AND BAKING POWDER

Baking soda and/or baking powder are the leavening agents that make quick breads rise and give them a light texture. The leavening is mixed thoroughly with the dry ingredients before coming in contact with the liquid ingredients. In the presence of liquid, the leavening gives off carbon dioxide, which forms the bubbles you see in the batter after mixing. In the presence of heat, the flour and egg proteins set around the bubbles, creating the cooked texture. CO_2 expands more quickly at high altitudes, producing greater leavening power. For baking over 3,500 feet, decrease baking soda/powder amounts by half.

Bicarbonate of soda, known as **baking soda**, is water soluble and neutralizes acids. Breads made with only baking soda tend to have a flatter, more spread-out appearance due to its weaker rising properties, in contrast to baking powder, which gives a higher loaf. When acid ingredients are present in the batter, baking soda, which is an alkali, is needed to create a chemical balance. Acid ingredients include buttermilk, yogurt, sour cream, citrus, molasses, and fruits such as cranberries. Baking soda adds a distinctive flavor that is associated with many quick breads, such as soda bread.

Double-acting **baking powder** is a mixture of bicarbonate of soda and a mild acid such as calcium phosphate or sodium aluminum sulphate. Foods with this ingredient are not recommended for any sodium-restricted diet. Baking powder reacts twice, once when the liquid is added into the batter and again in the presence of heat. The batter may sit for days in the refrigerator and the end product will still be light textured. Single-acting baking powder begins leavening as soon as the dry and wet ingredients become combined. When single-acting baking powder was the only leavening of its kind on the market, recipes instructed bakers in strong words to bake quick breads immediately after mixing. Single-acting baking powder is a product of the past and is no longer commercially available, but the instructions for immediate baking are still part of baking vocabulary.

Too much baking soda or powder has a bitter effect on finished baked goods, so measure judiciously; a little goes a long way. A good proportion guideline is 1½ teaspoons leavening to 1 cup flour. To double or triple a recipe, reduce the total amount of leavening by one-quarter. For more information on baking muffins, biscuits, quick loaves, and quick coffee cakes, see the Quick Bread section.

OTHER BASICS

LIQUIDS

Yeast needs warm liquid in which to be dissolved and activated. Flour needs liquid in order for its gluten to be absorbed. Liquids should be about 105° to 115°F, or feel comfortably warm on the back of your hand.

A loaf made with **water** makes a heavy, crisp crust and a chewy texture, as in French breads. **Milk** is very popular for breads, giving a light, even texture and a thin brown crust, and adding fat to keep bread fresh longer. Instant nonfat dried milk is also excellent. Milk no longer needs to be scalded and cooled for making bread, as it is pasteurized and homogenized, eliminating any enzymes that would slacken the gluten. **Buttermilk**, fresh and dried, and **yogurt** make a fine-textured bread with a sour tang. **Potato water** makes a moist,

dense loaf. Yeast thrives on potato starch. Other liquids for making breads are **beer, wine, broth,** and fruit and vegetable **juices,** depending on the flavor you want and available ingredients.

SWEETENING

Granulated sugar, brown sugar, honey, maple sugar and syrup, molasses, barley malt, and sorghum feed the yeast, give color to the crust, and sweeten the dough. They are used in small amounts, although different sweetenings can change the flavor of a loaf. To substitute honey and other liquid-based sweeteners for granulated-type sugars use ¾ cup honey per each cup of sugar and reduce the total liquid used in the recipe by ¼ cup. In recipes where there is no liquid required, compensate by adding an extra ¼ cup flour.

FAT

Butter, vegetable shortening, oil, and lard give a moist, rich-tasting soft loaf. Breads with fat stay fresh longer; French breads, with no fat, will begin to stale within a few hours. For cholesterol-free diets, substitute cold-pressed vegetable oils.

EGGS

Eggs give a wonderful, golden color and add a tender cakelike texture to bread. One whole egg may be substituted for 2 egg yolks and vice versa in baking recipes. One large egg equals ¼ cup liquid measure; the white equals 3 tablespoons and the yolk is equal to 1 tablespoon. Use duck or quail eggs, if you should have an abundance, for variety of color and flavor.

SALT

Salt is a flavor enhancer. It is optional in bread, but a lack of salt is very noticeable. Too much salt leaves a bitter quality and can inhibit yeast activity. Too little salt leaves the bread tasting flat and causes dough to feel slack during kneading. Iodized and fine sea salt can be used interchangeably. Coarse salt must be ground before using in dough or may be sprinkled on top of breads, such as *focaccia* and bagels, before baking.

Equipment

TOOLS

Breadmaking is a culinary art requiring very little equipment: a bowl, a spoon, and an oven. But there are very nice tools that help make breadmaking easier and more enjoyable.

Choose a work surface in the kitchen that is a comfortable height and is large enough for working with dough. Lay a clean wood, marble, or plastic work surface on the counter for easy clean-up. Keep your work board just for making bread and pastry, as strong odors are hard to scrub off and can impart a taste to dough.

An 8- or 12-cup ceramic, glass, aluminum, or plastic mixing **bowl** with a wide rim is best for combining dough by hand. Ceramic and glass hold heat well. A **heavy-duty electric mixer** or a **food processor** is helpful for heavy or sticky doughs. A set of small bowls is needed for proofing yeast, mixing glazes, etc. Use standard **liquid and dry measures** for accurate measuring. A **kitchen scale** is helpful for certain recipes, large-quantity baking, and weighing out bulk compressed yeast. Get a good set of **yeast and oven thermometers** to check the temperature of liquids and to control oven temperature. A rapid-response type is best for yeast. A **balloon whisk** is perfect for mixing liquid batters. Use a sturdy **wooden spoon** for mixing in flour. Get a whisk and spoon that fit comfortably in your hand and are not too heavy for your wrist. Use a **plastic dough scraper** with a curved side as a hand extension while kneading a wet dough, scraping bowls, and cleaning dough film from work surfaces. A **metal dough scraper** is a good cutting edge for dividing dough. Cover rising dough with **wide plastic wrap**, which also retains precious moisture with an airtight seal. Use a heavy ball bearing-type **rolling pin** to roll out dough, and a **kitchen tape measure** for measuring when cutting and shaping.

Baking sheets of a good-quality aluminum or stainless steel are necessary for free-form loaves and rolls. If the baking sheet is thin or the bottoms of the bread are browning too fast, stack two sheets together for protection. Get a size that allows full heat circulation around it. Rather than greasing my baking sheets, I always line them with a single layer of **parchment paper**. It is an uncoated paper specifically for baking, designed for lining pans to reduce sticking and eliminate washing. Do not substitute waxed paper, which is coated with paraffin and flammable, or aluminum foil, which deflects heat. Parchment does not need to be greased and is reusable.

Baking pans come in lots of sizes, shapes, and materials. Aluminum is lightweight and the best conductor of heat for baking bread. The gauge, or thickness, of the pans determines their efficiency. Buy the best grade, heavier-gauge pans, suitable for professional use. Glass and black-tinned pans brown bread faster, needing a 25° lowering of oven temperature. Black tin needs to have the hot loaf removed immediately, or the moisture under the loaf will rust the pan. Wipe with a clean cloth and store in a dry cupboard to prevent rusting. Clay loaf pans need to bake on the lowest oven rack for the heat to conduct properly and the bottom to brown. European tin is a nonstick alloy and should not be washed with soap or in a dishwasher. Season pans to the manufacturer's instructions before baking. Rinse with hot water and dry immediately. Disposable foil pans are good in a pinch.

Standard loaf pan sizes are 9 by 5 inches and 8½ by 4½ inches. There are also various mini loaf pans, from 6½ by 4½ inches down to 4½ by 2½ inches. Heavy steel baguette pans are usually in **strap** form, meaning they are glued together for easy handling. Buy bread straps that will fit in your oven. Professional equipment is designed to fit in professional ovens.

Specialized baking **molds**, such as fluted *brioche* molds and nonstick decorative *kugelhof* tube pans, are also nice.

Use soft natural-bristle **pastry brushes** from 1 to 3 inches wide for applying glazes, pizza sauces, and dusting off delicate doughs. Clean with hot, soapy water and let dry or place in the dishwasher. I never wash the ones I use for dusting, to keep the bristles soft. Use **unglazed quarry tiles** or a **baking stone** specifically designed for breadmaking to line the oven for the evenly radiated heat necessary for loaves with crisp crusts. Scrub off any accumulated dough with a coarse brush. After baking, the stone will be very hot; let it cool in the oven slowly with the door ajar. Use a **baker's paddle**, sometimes called a **pelle**, or a baking sheet to slide unbaked loaves onto the hot stone for baking. The paddle or sheet must be well floured or lined with parchment paper to prevent sticking. Use heavy-duty insulated **oven mitts** for secure handling of hot pans. I like mitts, as they protect the wrist and part of the upper arm from burns.

Metal or wooden **cooling racks** allow even circulation around a loaf. Racks come in small to very large sizes. A **cutting board** for serving bread is nice, but certainly optional. A **serrated bread knife** is designed to cut bread without squashing or tearing. If used only for bread, the edge will stay perfect and never need resharpening.

OVENS

The first closed oven was invented by the Egyptians, and the same type is still in use today: the beehive oven. It is convenient in warm climates, as it is separated from the living quarters. In colder climates, the first ovens were built behind the fireplace hearth at waist level; later ovens were moved to one side of the fireplace for easier access.

When bread is baked in a closed wood oven, a hardwood fire is built on the oven's brick floor. When the very hot fire has burned down to coals and the temperature for baking is reached (which sometimes take all day), the coals are removed with a shovel and the floor swept clean. Fresh leaves or ground meal is spread on the floor to prevent the bread from sticking. The inside top of the oven is brushed with a wet broom to cool the temperature slightly and to remove any stray ashes. Steam is created by this moisture.

This ritual for baking has not changed over the centuries, and the bread that is produced by these ovens is the standard to which all present-day bread is compared. Professional bakers in Europe still turn out large, dark, thickly crusted loaves with regional variations. Unfortunately, the brick ovens in San Francisco no longer turn out the myriad brands of sourdough bread I remember being able to choose from even twenty years ago; it became too expensive in time and labor for the number of loaves produced. With the renewed interest in home-baked breads, many bread devotees are building small beehive ovens in their backyards. Many Early American historical societies in the east and south have organized demonstrations in fireplace and beehive oven baking at restored Colonial sites. Some sites have all the original kitchen facilities intact.

There are several styles of modern closed ovens from which to choose, depending on the types of food you prepare most often: large professional ovens, fan-forced convection ovens, and conventional gas-heated home ovens, to name a few. New innovations are combination ovens, such as convection/microwaves. All ovens bake differently, and the type of oven you choose is a matter of personal preference. Until recently, all bread recipes were created for use in a conventional oven. Remember that bread requires a stronger heat than cakes and pastries to bake properly and can tolerate a bit of unevenness in temperature. All models have an override (top temperature), which produces an uneven heat. Most ovens do not bake at the exact same temperature you have set on the thermostat. An oven that is 10° to 20°·off can make a difference in your baking times. Besides trial and error, an oven thermometer will help guide you.

In gas and electric ovens, the heating element is located on or under the oven floor. Unglazed clay quarry tiles or a baking stone can help radiate this bottom heat more evenly in a small household oven, simulating a wood-fired oven. Lay the tiles or stone on the middle or lowest rack at least 2 inches away from the oven wall for the heat to circulate, and preheat them at 450° for about 20 to 30 minutes before baking. Many bakers line both the top and bottom rack with tiles, attempting to reproduce as closely as possible the crusty country loaves. Compared to newer models of ovens, the conventional oven is time-consuming and long periods of baking will heat up the kitchen, but I still like it best for bread.

Convection ovens, introduced in the late 1970s, boast an even, very dry, fan-forced heat throughout the entire oven, which is why professional bakers can bake on all their racks at the same time. The home models are much smaller, but they produce the same even, golden color in baked goods. The general rule in converting from a standard oven to a convection oven is to drop the heat 50° and reduce the baking time by a full third. Always keep at least a full inch of space all around each pan for the hot air to circulate properly.

Microwave ovens, which turn electricity into microwave energy, are not used for baking yeasted or quick breads, as the internal method of cooking produces a bread that is dense, tough, and uneven with no crust. This is because microwave baking is done with the absence of hot air. Microwaves can assist in cooking whole grains for hearty breads, however. The stove-top cooking time for wheat and rye berries is usually about 1 hour. With the microwave, the cooking time is reduced to 15 minutes. Many bakers also use the microwave to speed the dough's first rising time by about half. This is called the **micro-rise method**: Place kneaded dough into a large greased microwave-proof bowl and turn once to grease top. Place the bowl in a larger microwave-proof baking dish and cover the dough loosely with plastic wrap or a clean cotton towel. Let it stand in the oven 10 minutes. Add 2 cups hot water to the baking dish. Microwave at 10 percent power for 5 minutes. Any higher power will result in a very heavy, dense loaf. Let it rest again in the oven for 10 minutes with the power off. Microwave again for 5 minutes. Press your finger gently into the top of the dough. If the indentation remains, the dough is ready. If not, let the dough rest at room temperature until fully doubled. Dough may be gently deflated at this point and formed into loaves. If placed in greased Pyrex loaf pans, the dough may have its second rising in the microwave. Check the dough after each rise with a rapid-response yeast thermometer. The dough temperature should never exceed 100°F. Use recipes specifically designed to this kind of oven to yield best results. Finish baking in a conventional oven.

Use your senses to check your bread for doneness: the degree of browning, a hollow sound when the bottom of the loaf is tapped, and a lack of alcohol smell are the indicators. I use the baking times in recipes as a guide, setting my timer 10 to 15 minutes earlier to check the bread and make my own evaluation of the baking process. If the bottom of a loaf is pale and not cooked enough in the required baking time, remove the loaf from the pan and place directly on the oven rack for an additional 5 to 10 minutes. If the top of the bread is browning too fast, place a piece of aluminum foil loosely over the loaves to inhibit browning. If your bread is baking too slowly, raise the heat 25°. If the bottom of a loaf is too brown or burned within the dictated baking time, place an extra baking sheet under the bread pans, line your oven rack with unglazed clay tiles or a baking stone to diffuse heat, or move your oven rack higher in the oven.

WORK SPACE

The preparation of food can be a source of great pleasure. Contributing to that end are a scrupulously clean work area and utensils. Rely on classically shaped pots, pans, bread pans, whisks, wooden spoons, and wide-mouthed bowls. Keep your knives sharp and stored in a place away from the general work area where vigorous kneading and shaping will be done. Keep bread boards, whether wood, plastic or marble, scrubbed clean and, if possible, use only for pastry and breadmaking. Clean up as you go along. Keep the oven as clean as possible. Accumulated residues, especially burnt sugar and meat grease, can release strong odors in the presence of heat, which are easily absorbed by bread and delicate pastry.

Techniques

There are three methods of making yeasted bread. The first and most common method involves proofing the yeast, then mixing it into the wet ingredients and the flour. Most of the recipes in this book use this method. Some recipes use the sponge method, which involves making a spongy substance with the yeast, some liquid, and some of the flour. After this has risen, the remaining ingredients are added. The rapid mix method is used a few times in the book: yeast and some dry ingredients are mixed with hot liquid, then the remaining ingredients are added. Any yeasted bread recipe can be made by any of these three methods.

Most of the yeast breads in this book are **kneaded breads**. Enough flour must be used to form a dough stiff enough to be kneaded. Lean doughs, such as those for French and country breads, have little or no fat added. Rich doughs have fat added and are used to make sweet doughs such as *babka*, and breads such as *challah*.

A **rolled bread** undergoes a double leavening process: once with yeast in the initial mixing and again with the dough being folded or layered (usually with butter), as in *croissants* and Danish pastry. The moisture in the butter evaporates during baking to create steam between the delicate layers of dough.

In **batter bread**, the ingredients are combined and beaten with a wooden spoon or electric mixer to make a soft, sticky dough that is not kneaded. *Brioches, savarins,* and "casserole" loaves are batter breads. Batter breads always need to be baked in a container, such as a loaf pan, as they cannot hold their own shape.

PROOFING THE YEAST

Proofing is a term used by bakers to describe the process of activating yeast. Dry yeast with a dash of sugar is sprinkled, or compressed yeast is crumbled, over warm liquid and stirred gently. Within about 10 minutes, the yeast will become foamy and creamy if it is active. The ideal temperature for activating yeast is between 105° to 115°F. If no thermometer is available, test a drop of the liquid on the inside of your wrist—it should be comfortably warm. If the liquid is too hot, the yeast will be killed and the bread will not rise. If it is too cold, the rise will be slowed. Yeast cells go dormant at 50°F or below and are activated again at 80° to 90°F. At 140°F, the cells begin to die. The only way to kill yeast is with too much heat. One tablespoon or one package of active dry yeast is sufficient to raise 6 to 8 cups of flour. Using more than 2 tablespoons of yeast per that amount of flour imparts a strong yeast flavor, which I find unpleasant.

SPONGE METHOD

Liquid, yeast, sugar, and flour are beaten until smooth, covered loosely, and allowed to rise until foamy and elastic, usually 1 to 4 hours, depending on the kind of bread. A rising sponge forms stretchy gluten strands that will give the bread a very fine texture. The salt and fat required by the recipe are added after the sponge has risen, as they tend to inhibit yeast growth. Other ingredients are then added and the dough is allowed to rise as in any kneaded bread recipe. This is one of the oldest methods for mixing doughs and gives a distinctive flavor to the bread.

For an **overnight sponge**, a sponge is mixed, covered loosely, and allowed to sit overnight at room temperature or in the refrigerator for up to 4 days, allowing it to bubble and ferment longer than a regular sponge. The long time period creates a dough that is finely textured with a tangy flavor, as in Pain de Seigle and Italian Peasant Bread.

RAPID MIX METHOD

This method is the product of the Fleischmann Yeast Test Kitchens, and was developed during the 1960s for their active dry yeast. It is a very popular and fast method of making dough without proofing the yeast in liquid. A portion of the flour and all the other dry ingredients, including the yeast, are thoroughly combined. Hot liquid (120° to 130°F) is added and the dough is mixed vigorously to dissolve the yeast. The rest of the flour is then added. The dough is then kneaded, risen, formed, and baked.

MIXING THE DOUGH

It is not only satisfying to make bread by hand, but it is important to the beginning baker in understanding how bread should feel. As you continue baking, you can choose to make bread by hand, by electric mixer, or by food processor—whichever suits your particular style. Mixing by hand takes about 10 minutes, the mixer about 5 minutes, and the food processor about 1 minute. There seems to be no real difference in the texture or flavor of bread made by these different methods, but it is nice to use a machine to knead sticky and very soft doughs, such as whole grains or *brioches*.

By hand: Place all ingredients as specified by the recipe in a wide-mouthed bowl and beat vigorously with a large whisk for about 3 minutes to create a smooth and creamy liquid. Using a wooden spoon, add flour slowly, *½ cup at a time*, for thorough incorporation before adding more flour. Turn the dough out onto a lightly floured surface to knead when it becomes shaggy and clears the sides of the bowl.

By heavy-duty electric mixer: Place ingredients as specified by the recipe into the work bowl and mix with the paddle attachment at medium to low speed for about 1½ minutes to create a smooth, creamy batter. The whisk attachment can also be used at this stage, if you prefer. Add flour slowly, ½ cup at a time, until a soft dough is formed. The dough will just clear the sides of the bowl and begin to work itself up the paddle. With a plastic dough scraper, remove the dough from the paddle onto a lightly floured surface. The dough will be dry on the bottom of the bowl and wet on the top. Knead by hand to finish the dough. Do not scrape all the dry bits out of the bowl as they will stay very dry lumps in the dough. The dough hook may be used at the very end of mixing, but is not recommended in the early stages of mixing as it cannot blend thoroughly to remove the lumps.

By food processor: This is a very fast method of mixing dough, but it is completely different from the two previous methods. Check your manufacturing instructions for specifics on your machine, as some processors have a motor too weak for bread dough. Small processors can handle about 3 cups of flour and 1½ cups liquid. The standard, or larger, processor can handle 6 to 8 cups of flour and 2½ cups of liquid.

turning until generally smooth. This can take anywhere from 2 to 10 minutes. If the dough sticks to your hands or the surface, flour them. Use the dough scraper to clean off the film of dough that accumulates on the work surface. When adding flour during the kneading process, sprinkle about 1 tablespoon at a time onto the work surface, then knead to ensure full incorporation.

If your dough is stiff and the baked loaf dry, you are adding too much flour. Using too much flour is the most common mistake in making bread. All flours vary slightly in the amount of liquid they can absorb, so don't worry if not all the flour called for in the recipe is used or if some flour is left on the kneading surface. Whole-grain breads can stay sticky or even become more sticky after a long kneading session. Don't worry—pick an arbitrary spot and stop. If your dough is too soft after rising, knead in a bit more flour. The amount of flour used in a recipe is a *guide*, not a constant. Because of atmospheric, emotional, and technical variables, bread is unique with every mixing. This is where experience will eventually come in and guide you. Doughs made with all bread flour will require a bit more kneading

than doughs made of all-purpose flour. Under-kneading is far more common, giving the dough a slack appearance and feel. A soft dough, such as *brioche* or casserole bread, should be very sticky and will not retain its own shape. Chilling the dough is required for handling.

A medium-stiff dough will barely retain its shape and has a tacky quality. It is important for whole-grain doughs to not go beyond this point. The moisture left in this dough contributes to a moist and light baked bread, as in Country Bread with Golden Raisins and Walnuts and Italian Whole-Wheat Bread.

A stiff dough will be firm and smooth and begin to have a slightly unyielding, but resilient tension. All white-flour doughs are in this category. Whole-grain doughs mixed to this point will be dry and crumbly.

Using the plastic yeast blade or steel blade (it doesn't seem to make a difference), dissolve the yeast and sugar in half the total amount of liquid called for. Add the remaining amount of liquid and half the total flour. Use cold liquid at this stage, as the processor itself will heat up the dough. Process for the time directed and then add the remaining flour. Process to just form a ball of dough. Adjust dough consistency now, if needed, by adding more flour or liquid. I always give a few kneads by hand to "feel" the dough consistency. There are many excellent publications that are entirely devoted to making bread in the processor.

KNEADING

Kneading thoroughly integrates the wet and dry ingredients. The proteins in the flour, called gluten, become elastic and create a structure that contains the CO_2 gas manufactured by the yeast. There are schools of hard kneaders and soft kneaders—your own nature will dictate your particular style. Neither style seems to make a difference in the texture of the finished loaf.

Lightly flour your hands and the work surface. Turn the shaggy dough mass onto the surface, using a plastic dough scraper to clear the sides of the bowl. Gently bring the far edge of the dough forward and fold it over itself. With the *heel* of your hand, push the dough away from you, give the dough a quarter turn, and repeat, folding and

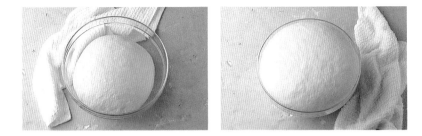

RISING

I like 3- and 4-quart deep plastic containers with lids for raising dough, although any large bowl will do. I tend to avoid metal bowls, as they conduct heat easily and can "cook" the dough if it rises in too warm a spot, such as over a pilot light. I also like dough to rise up in containers with vertical sides rather than in a wide shallow bowl where it rises horizontally and forms a big puddle. Grease the container and place the ball of dough in it, turning the dough once to grease the top. Plastic wrap is good for a cover, helping to retain the precious moisture and to inhibit the formation of a thick skin. Mentally note or mark where the dough will be when risen to double.

It is difficult to predict an exact rising time. Rising time depends on the temperature of the dough, the amount of yeast used, and the general atmospheric conditions. Drafts will cause a dough to rise slowly and unevenly. Whole-grain doughs take longer than white-flour doughs, and doughs high in fats and fruits take longer than leaner doughs. Generally, a dough will take 1 to 2 hours to rise initially to the classic "doubled in bulk" at 75° to 80°F. Test a risen dough by poking two fingers into it. If the indentations remain, the dough is adequately risen. If the marks fill in, re-cover and leave the dough 15 to 30 minutes longer before testing again.

Most of the recipes in this book specify letting the dough rise in a warm place, as in the following suggestions:

- Turn the oven to 150°F for 3 minutes. Turn off heat and allow the dough to sit in oven with the door ajar.
- Allow the dough to rise over a gas pilot on the stove top, or inside the oven, or on top of the dryer while drying clothes.
- Place the bowl in or over a pan of warm water away from drafts.
- A nice ride around town in the back of a car. Dough loves the gentle motion and warmth of a car.

If you have the time, a longer rise makes a delightful, tasty loaf. I like to leave my dough either at a cool-to-warm room temperature for however long it takes to rise or leave it out overnight, as dough activity at room temperature decreases by over half at night. To slow a dough further, I let it rise in the refrigerator 8 hours to overnight, covered tightly with plastic wrap to retain moisture. Dough that has been refrigerated must come back to room temperature to resume its rising process, so count on about 4 to 6 extra hours for the dough to sit at room temperature. I might add, do not discard a slow-rising dough, no matter how long it takes.

COOL RISE METHOD

Some recipes use the "cool rise" or "refrigerator" method. Developed by the Robin Hood Consumer Test Kitchen in the Midwest, this method allows the baker to prepare the dough one day and bake it the next. Mix and knead the dough per recipe instructions. Let the dough rest, loosely covered, about 30 minutes. Divide and shape the dough for loaves, place in greased pans, and cover loosely with plastic wrap to allow for dough expansion. Refrigerate 2 to 24 hours. The dough will continue to rise as it cools, to about 1 inch above the rim of the pan. Remove to bake at any convenient time. Let the pans stand at room temperature while preheating the oven for 10 to 15 minutes. The dough will still be quite cold as it goes into the oven. Also check to be certain your bread pan can take the fast changes in temperature. This method can be used for any bread recipe, and is especially nice for sweet rolls.

DEFLATING THE DOUGH

At this time, the dough should be light, spongy, and delicately domed. There is the exciting realization that homemade bread is imminent. When the dough is doubled, I turn it out onto my lightly floured work surface. The act of turning out the dough naturally deflates it, releasing the large gas pockets, so I don't need the aggressive act of "punching down," although it is a gratifying old bread ritual. I only knead the dough now if I wish to add more flour in case the dough is too soft, as kneading activates the gluten, giving the dough a springy tension that can make it difficult to sculpt. Otherwise, I go straight to dividing the dough to shape my desired loaves. If the dough resists you, cover it and let it rest for 10 minutes; it will relax and you will be able to continue.

Add any embellishments at this time: pat the dough into a large rectangle, sprinkle with fruits and nuts as directed in your recipe, and fold the dough into thirds, sprinkling on more food as necessary. Knead the dough gently to distribute the added ingredients. This technique quickly and efficiently adds any heavy ingredients not added to the dough during mixing.

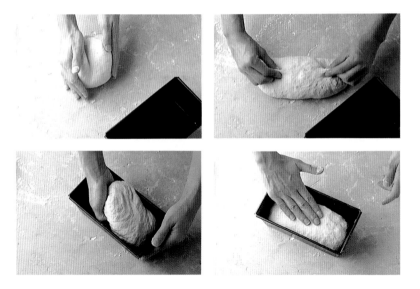

FORMING A LOAF

Pat the dough portion into a rough rectangle with the heel of your hand and your fingertips. Tightly roll the dough towards you, rotating it to make a rectangle, oval, or round shape. The shaping of loaves is highly individual and takes practice. All sorts of bread authorities have complicated instructions for forming a loaf that I have never been able to follow. Have faith—you will find your own way. The main objective is to produce a tight surface tension and a smooth top. Pinch seams together to close. Try not to reshape. Once the loaf is formed and the gluten is activated, it will have to sit about 15 minutes for the dough to relax before it can be reshaped. Place on greased or parchment-lined baking sheets or in well-greased pans, seam side down. Solid fats (butter or shortening) work better for greasing than vegetable oil, as vegetable oil is absorbed quickly into the bread, which may cause some sticking. The dough should fill a full half to two-thirds of the pan. Any less and you will have a flat loaf; any fuller and you will have an overflowing loaf that looks top-heavy. Trial and error should be your guides. Reduce heat by 25° for glass pans and black-tinned pans, as they increase baking time. Black-glazed pans give a dark crust and earthenware pans an even golden crust.

SECOND RISE

Let the dough rise with plastic wrap or a damp tea towel loosely draped over it, in a warm place away from cool drafts of air. The main concern is not to inhibit the delicate rising form of the loaf. The dough is ready when doubled, or about 1 inch above the pan rim. This takes half the amount of time of the initial rise, approximately 30 to 45 minutes. Meanwhile, preheat the oven to the required temperature.

Before being placed in the oven, most loaves are cut with decorative slashes, which allows for the dough to expand during baking. Usually the slashes are no deeper than ¼ inch, and are made by a quick motion with a sharp or serrated knife. The patterns you use are your choice and can become your trademark. Then glaze, which protects the crust during baking and gives a finished look (see page 115 for glaze recipes).

BAKING

Place pans in a preheated oven, on the center to lower (third) shelf (unless the recipe states otherwise), with 2 inches of space between pans for heat circulation. Rolls on baking sheets are best baked in the center of the oven, one sheet at a time. Set the timer. I check the bread at least 10 minutes earlier than the recipe says it will be done, for signs of early or uneven browning. You may need to remove the bread sooner, or shift the pans in the oven to even the browning. It is reassuring to know that after the first 10 minutes of baking, except for allowing heat to escape, you can peek at the bread as much as you like without affecting its shape. Bread will not collapse like a cake with temperature fluctuations. Baking stops the fermentation of the yeast by raising the internal temperature past 140°F and evaporating the alcohol. Within the first 10 minutes, the rapidly expanding gas will reach its limit (this is called "oven spring"), and you can see the shape your finished loaf will be. The heat then sets the gluten cells.

If the dough didn't rise enough before baking, the loaf will be small and compact. If it rose too much, the loaf may collapse in the oven. Every baker I know has seen both of these classic mistakes at least once. It is part of the process.

Generally, lean doughs (without fat), such as French and Vienna, are baked at high temperatures of 400° to 425°F; and rich, more cakelike doughs with butter, fruits, and nuts bake at 350°F. Each recipe will be specific on this point.

Practice using all of your senses to determine if a loaf is done: your sense of smell to determine if all the alcohol is evaporated; your sight to decide if a crust is browned to your specifications; your hearing to test the bottom of the loaf for a hollow sound. And remember—homemade bread is supposed to look homemade. Appreciate the irregularities!

COOLING AND SLICING

Remove the bread immediately from pans to cool on racks before slicing. Technically bread has not finished baking until it is cool and the excess moisture has evaporated. French breads and rolls beg to be eaten immediately, but richer cakelike breads, such as *brioches*, should be cooled completely and then reheated. The delicate texture and rich flavor of bread cannot fully be appreciated until it is completely cooled.

A serrated bread knife is designed for slicing bread without squashing or tearing. Slice loaves on a bread board with a sawing motion. Bread needs to cool slightly before slicing, unless specifically noted in the recipe. Warm bread is easiest to slice turned on its side.

Store bread in the refrigerator or at room temperature in plastic wrap.

FREEZING

Wrap in plastic wrap when completely cooled. Then wrap in foil. Freeze up to three months. Label and date loaves, if possible. Glaze, ice, or dust with powdered sugar after thawing, if called for in the recipe.

REHEATING

Bread may be reheated, thawed or unthawed, in a 350° oven. Place an unsliced loaf au naturel or wrapped in foil in a preheated oven for 15 to 30 minutes to crisp the crust and heat through. Sliced breads and rolls reheat best wrapped. To reheat bread in a microwave oven, place the unwrapped loaf or slice on a paper towel. Microwave on high only until slightly warm, about 15 seconds. If bread or rolls are overheated, they will become hard and tough as they cool.

Yeasted Breads

BUTTERMILK-HONEY BREAD

*T*his is where every American loaf begins: the breadmaker's "little black dress." A beautiful bread to grace any table, to toast to your heart's content, and to give as a gift. All the yeast breads in this collection have their roots in this recipe. For your very first loaf, please begin here.

Yield: 2 round or 9-by-5-inch loaves

1 package (1 tablespoon) active dry yeast
1 teaspoon sugar
¾ cup warm water (105° to 115°)
1½ cups buttermilk, warmed to just take off the chill
2 tablespoons unsalted butter, melted
3 tablespoons honey
1 tablespoon salt
6 to 6¼ cups unbleached all-purpose or bread flour
Rich Egg Glaze, page 115

1. Sprinkle yeast and sugar over warm water in a small bowl. Stir to combine and let stand to proof until foamy, about 10 minutes.
2. Combine buttermilk, butter, honey, and yeast mixture in a large bowl. Add salt and 2 cups flour. Whisk hard to combine. Add remaining flour, ½ cup at a time, beating with a wooden spoon after each addition, until a shaggy dough is formed.
3. Turn out onto a lightly floured surface and knead about 5 minutes, adding flour 1 tablespoon at a time as necessary, until dough is smooth and satiny. Place in a greased bowl, turn to grease top, and cover with plastic wrap. Let rise until doubled in bulk, about 1 to 1¼ hours in a warm area.

4. Gently deflate dough, turn out on a lightly floured surface, and divide into 2 equal portions. Form into round or standard loaves. Place in two 9-by-5-inch greased pans or on a greased or parchment-lined baking sheet. Cover lightly with plastic wrap and let rise until fully doubled in bulk, 30 to 45 minutes.
5. Brush bread with egg glaze and bake in a preheated 375° oven for about 45 minutes, or until loaf is nicely browned and pulls away from sides. Remove from pans to cool on racks before eating.

CHALLAH

*T*his recipe was shared with me by my first bread guru, Barbara Hiken. She would always find the best recipes at potluck suppers and church bazaars or in little-known recipe books and then graciously pass them on. It was she who taught me to have no secrets as far as breakmaking was concerned and to share what I had learned. This egg bread is a Jewish specialty—almost a cross between cake and bread, and a cousin to brioche. Everyone who has tasted this bread says it is the best challah he or she has ever eaten. You can make your reputation on it. The method of mixing the yeast with the dry ingredients is known as rapid mix (see page 20). It is fast and very easy.

Yield: 2 large braided breads

2 packages (2 tablespoons) active dry yeast
½ cup sugar or honey
1 tablespoon salt
5½ to 6 cups unbleached all-purpose or bread flour
1¾ cups hot water (120°)

4 eggs, slightly beaten
½ cup (1 stick) unsalted butter, melted
Rich Egg Glaze, page 115
Poppy or sesame seeds

1. Place yeast, sugar, salt, and 2 cups of flour in a large bowl. Add water, eggs, and butter. Beat hard with a whisk until smooth, about 3 minutes. Scrape sides of bowl occasionally.
2. Add remaining flour ½ cup at a time with a wooden spoon. Continue beating until dough is too stiff to stir. Turn shaggy mass out onto a lightly floured board. Adding flour, 1 tablespoon at a time as necessary, knead until dough is smooth and elastic and a layer of blisters shows under skin. The dough needs to be a bit firm for free-form loaves.
3. Place dough in a greased bowl, turning once to grease top. Cover with plastic wrap and let rise in a warm place until doubled, about 1 to 1½ hours.
4. Gently deflate dough, turn out onto a lightly floured surface, and divide into 6 equal portions. Roll each section into a strip and lay 3 strips side by side. Braid each 3 strips from middle to taper ends. Pinch ends and tuck them under. Place on a greased or parchment-lined baking sheet. (Challah also makes nice braided loaves in standard bread pans, if you like.) Cover loosely with plastic wrap and let rise until almost doubled, about 30 to 40 minutes. Because of the eggs, this loaf does not need to completely double. It will rise a lot in the oven.
5. Brush dough with glaze and sprinkle with seeds. Bake in a preheated 350° oven for 40 to 45 minutes, or until a deep golden brown. Carefully lift braids off baking sheet with a spatula to cool completely before slicing.

Cinnamon Challah

Before braiding, roll 6 sections of dough in ¼ cup ground cinnamon, completely coating all surfaces. Braid as directed. The bread will bake with a delicate swirl pattern and make a fine cinnamon bread.

FRENCH BREAD

*T*he *pain ordinaire*, or everyday bread, for much of the Western world. The elements—flour, water, salt, and yeast— are basically the same as they were eight thousand years ago. This versatile bread can be eaten with a thick slab of bacon cooked over an open fire, or alongside the most delicate *beurre blanc* sauce.

French bread should have a crackly crust, a chewy texture, lots of uneven holes, a long side crack from expansion in the oven, and a grainy taste. It's best eaten hot, straight out of the oven, for as it cools, it begins to stale.

1½ packages (1½ tablespoons) active dry yeast
1 tablespoon sugar
2 cups warm water (105° to 115°)
3 cups unbleached bread flour
1 tablespoon salt
3 cups unbleached all-purpose flour
Cornmeal for dusting
Egg Glaze, page 115

1. Sprinkle yeast and sugar over water in a large bowl. Stir until combined. Let stand until dissolved and foamy, about 10 minutes.
2. Add 2 cups bread flour and salt. Beat hard with a whisk for 3 minutes, or until smooth. Add remaining bread and unbleached flour ½ cup at a time with a wooden spoon. The dough will form a shaggy mass and clear sides of bowl.

3. Turn dough out onto a floured surface and knead, adding flour 1 tablespoon at a time as necessary, until dough becomes soft, silky, and resilient, about 5 minutes. It will not be sticky.
4. Place dough in a greased bowl and turn once to grease top. Cover with plastic wrap and let rise in a cool area of the kitchen until tripled in bulk, 1½ to 2 hours. If you have time, punch dough down and allow it to rise again, about 1 hour. The dough may also rise in the refrigerator overnight.
5. Gently deflate dough, turn out onto a lightly floured surface, and divide into portions for desired loaves. Knead in more flour now, if necessary. Place 4 inches apart on a greased or parchment-lined baking sheet sprinkled with cornmeal.
6. *Quick Method*: Directly after forming loaves, slash tops diagonally with a serrated knife and brush with glaze. Place in a cold oven on the middle or lower rack. Turn oven temperature to 400° oven for 35 to 40 minutes or until crusty.
7. *Standard Method*: Loosely cover loaves with plastic wrap and let rise until puffy and doubled, about 30 to 40 minutes. Preheat a baking stone at 450° for at least 20 minutes, if desired. Reduce heat to 400° to bake, or preheat at 400° if not using a stone. Slash tops of loaves diagonally and brush with glaze. Spray a mist of water into oven or throw a few ice cubes onto oven floor to crisp crust, if desired. Bake until crusty (see time chart, below). Eat immediately or cool on a rack.

YIELDS AND BAKING TIMES FOR ONE RECIPE OF FRENCH BREAD

6 ficelles	20 minutes
4 baguettes	25 to 30 minutes
1 pain de campagne	45 to 50 minutes
6 champignons	20 to 25 minutes
2 bâtards	35 to 40 minutes
4 l'épis	30 to 35 minutes
4 petits pains	15 to 20 minutes
4 boules	25 to 30 minutes

To Make Baguettes and Ficelles: Cut dough into 4 or 6 even pieces. Flatten each into a rectangle with the palm of your hand. Starting at long end, roll up jelly-roll fashion, using your thumbs to roll tightly. Pinch seams to seal. Roll back and forth on work surface to adjust dough to a length that will fit your baking sheet. Slash tops 3 or 4 times diagonally. *Ficelles*, or "strings," are about 1½ inches thick in diameter when baked. Baguettes, or "rods," are about 2 inches in diameter and about 16 inches long.

To Make Pain de Campagne (round country bread): Roughly pat dough into an uneven circle. Pull up sides and knead into center of loaf to create a tight round ball. Slash top in a tic-tac-toe pattern.

To Make Champignons (little "mushrooms"): Divide dough into 6 even pieces. Divide each piece into 2 uneven portions. Form larger piece into a tight round. Form smaller piece into a round and place atop larger ball. With a floured finger, poke a hole in center of 2 rounds to help them adhere to each other. Let rise only about 15 to 20 minutes, as the mushroom shape becomes less defined the more it rises.

To Make Bâtards: Divide dough into 2 even portions. Pat each into a rectangle and roll up as for baguettes, but shape each loaf into a 12-inch-long elongated oval with tapered ends. Slash top 3 times diagonally or make one long slash down the middle of each loaf.

To Make l'Épis (shafts of wheat): Cut dough into 4 even portions and form each into a 12-inch baguette. Holding kitchen shears at a 45-degree angle, cut halfway into dough from top. With other hand, turn cut piece to one side. Cut at 3-inch intervals, turning pieces to alternate sides to resemble a head of wheat. Let rise 25 minutes before baking.

To Make Petits Pains (little breads or French rolls): Divide dough into 15 equal portions. Form each into small rounds or ovals. With ovals, pinch ends to form an almost spindle shape. Slash top once down middle. Let rise 15 minutes before baking.

To Make Boules (small round loaves): Divide dough into 4 equal portions. Form each into a tight round loaf as for Pain de Campagne. Slash an X on top.

FRENCH BREAD MADE IN THE FOOD PROCESSOR

Please read the section on making bread in the food processor on pages 21–22.

1. Using plastic yeast blade, dissolve in processor bowl:
   1 cup warm water (105° to 115°)
   1½ packages (1½ tablespoons) active dry yeast
   1 tablespoon sugar
2. Let stand 10 minutes.
3. Add 1 cup cold water (processor will heat up dough).
4. Add 1 tablespoon salt and 2 cups flour. Process 15 seconds.

5. Add the remaining 4 cups flour and process just to form a ball of dough. Test dough and add more flour or water if necessary. Process 60 seconds. Remove dough from work bowl and knead by hand just to form a smooth ball, about 10 times. Proceed as in basic recipe.

ITALIAN PEASANT BREAD

I love very simple breads. The more uncomplicated the flavor of the bread, the more dramatic it tastes. This loaf is a fragrant Italian-style homemade bread. It can be baked on a baking stone, and the decrease in temperature halfway through baking reproduces a wood-burning oven with heat descending as the fire dies. The cornmeal and whole-wheat flours are added to reproduce the texture of less refined flours. The sponge, or "mother," gives the grain a chance to develop its own taste.

Yield: 1 large round loaf

Sponge
½ package (1½ teaspoons) active dry yeast
1 cup milk
2 tablespoons malt syrup
¼ cup cornmeal
½ cup whole-wheat flour
½ cup unbleached all-purpose or bread flour

Dough
Sponge, above
½ package (1½ teaspoons) active dry yeast
1 cup warm water (105° to 115°)
1 tablespoon salt
2 tablespoons unsalted butter, melted
3 to 3½ cups unbleached all-purpose or bread flour

Extra cornmeal or coarse semolina for dusting

1. Prepare the sponge: In a large bowl, whisk together yeast, milk, malt syrup, cornmeal, and whole-wheat and all-purpose flours. Beat hard until creamy and smooth. Cover loosely with plastic wrap and let sponge rise at room temperature 12 to 24 hours.
2. Pour sponge into large bowl of a heavy-duty mixer fitted with a paddle. Add yeast, water, salt, butter, and 1 cup flour. Beat at medium speed for 3 minutes, or until smooth. Add remaining flour at low speed ½ cup at a time until a soft dough is formed. The dough will just clear sides of bowl. Stop immediately so dough will remain very moist. This dough can also be made by hand, but the mixer is helpful due to tacky quality of dough.
3. Turn dough out onto a lightly floured surface and knead 5 to 7 minutes to form a soft, silky dough, adding flour 1 tablespoon at a time as necessary. Do not add too much flour. The dough should barely hold its own shape. Place in a greased bowl, turning once to coat entire surface. Cover with plastic wrap and let rise in a warm place until tripled, about 2 hours, or overnight at a cool room temperature.
4. Gently deflate dough, turn out onto a lightly floured surface, and form into a tight round or oblong loaf. Roll lightly in flour and place on a cornmeal or semolina-sprinkled baker's paddle or baking sheet, rough side down. Cover loosely with plastic wrap and let rise until puffy, about 40 minutes. If dough seems very soft, it is a good idea to place a piece of parchment under loaf while it is rising. Preheat a baking stone in a 450° oven for 20 to 30 minutes, if desired.
5. Slash top of loaf decoratively with one long swift motion of a serrated knife. Slide onto hot stone, if used, with a quick

motion of the wrist. If loaf is on parchment, leave it on. It will come off easily later after baking.

6. Bake in a preheated 450° oven for 10 minutes, 400° for 15 minutes, and 325° for 20 to 30 minutes. The loaf is done when it is lightly domed and browned. Cool on a rack before eating.

YOGURT FRENCH BREAD

*T*he beauty of this simple loaf never ceases to delight my aesthetic sense: a moist, chewy interior; a developed tang in taste and aroma; a crisp, cracked crust; and a highly domed uneven round. An earthy daily bread, California sourdough style. This bread stays fresh wrapped in plastic for 3 days. It makes wonderful croutons for salads when a few days old. This loaf is best baked on a baking stone.

Yield: 1 large or 2 medium rounds, or 10 rolls

Sponge
2 packages (2 tablespoons) active dry yeast
1 teaspoon sugar
1½ cups warm water (105° to 115°)
1½ cups unbleached all-purpose or bread flour

Dough
Sponge, above
1 package (1 tablespoon) active dry yeast
3 tablespoons corn oil
1 cup (8 ounces) plain yogurt
1 tablespoon salt
3 to 3½ cups unbleached all-purpose or bread flour

Cornmeal for sprinkling

1. First prepare the sponge: Sprinkle yeast and sugar over water in a large bowl and whisk to combine. Let stand 5 minutes until dissolved. Whisk in flour until creamy and smooth. Cover tightly with plastic wrap and let stand at room temperature overnight or longer, 12 to 36 hours. The sponge can be stored 3 days in refrigerator before using.

2. The next day, place sponge in bowl of a heavy-duty mixer and add following dough ingredients to sponge with a paddle attachment: yeast, oil, yogurt, salt, and 1 cup flour. Beat at medium speed for 3 minutes, or until smooth. Gradually add the flour at low speed ½ cup at a time to make a soft dough. This will take about 3 minutes. When dough has just cleared sides of bowl, turn out onto a lightly floured surface. The dough may also be mixed by hand, but the mixer is helpful due to the tacky quality of the dough.

3. Turn dough out onto a lightly floured surface and knead vigorously to create a rather soft, moist, yet springy and elastic dough, about 5 to 7 minutes, adding flour 1 tablespoon at a time as necessary. Use a dough scraper to clean up film of dough that accumulates on work surface. The dough will be quite tacky.

   Place dough in a bowl greased with more corn oil, turn once to grease top, and cover with plastic wrap. Let stand at room temperature until doubled or tripled in bulk, about 1½ to 2 hours. If sponge is cold, it might take longer. Gently deflate dough and let rise again 1 hour, if possible. This second rise develops taste and texture a bit more, but bread will be beautiful with just one rise.

4. Gently deflate dough and turn out onto a lightly floured surface. Form into 1 or 2 round, oblong, or oval loaves, or 10 rolls. Place loaves on a baker's paddle or baking sheet liberally sprinkled with cornmeal, seam side down. Place rolls 2 inches apart on a greased or parchment-lined sheet. Cover loosely with plastic wrap. The dough, being soft, may spread a bit, but resist the temptation to touch it. It is a good idea to place a piece of parchment under bread while it is rising. Preheat a baking stone in oven at 450° for 20 minutes, if desired.

5. Slash top of loaves or rolls and slide onto hot baking stone, if used. Place in a preheated 450° oven; reduce oven temperature to 400°. Bake loaves 45 minutes, rolls 20 to 25 minutes, or until brown. Leave bread on parchment. It can be removed easily after baking.

   Cool on a wire rack for ½ hour, and serve warm with butter.

Honey and Seed Bread

A glorious golden loaf with a lot of crunch for lovers of seeds. It's good as a base for an open-faced grilled cheese sandwich. The combination of seeds can vary with your mood and what's available on the shelf. This bread makes excellent toast (second only to raisin bread).

Yield: Two 9-by-5-inch loaves

1½ packages (1½ tablespoons) active dry yeast
1 teaspoon sugar
¾ cup warm water (105° to 115°)
1½ cups warm milk (105° to 115°)
2 tablespoons unsalted butter, melted
2 tablespoons honey
5½ to 6 cups unbleached all-purpose
  or bread flour
1 tablespoon salt
2 tablespoons raw whole millet
1 tablespoon fennel seed
1 tablespoon poppy seed
1 tablespoon raw sesame seed
Rich Egg Glaze, page 115 (optional)

1. Sprinkle yeast and sugar over water in a small bowl. Stir to dissolve and let stand until foamy, about 10 minutes.
2. In a large bowl, combine milk, butter, honey, and yeast mixture with a whisk. Add 2 cups flour, salt, millet, and seeds. Beat hard until smooth, about 3 minutes. Add remaining flour ½ cup at a time with a wooden spoon until a shaggy dough is formed.
3. Turn out onto a lightly floured surface and knead until smooth and silky, about 5 minutes, adding flour a tablespoon at a time as needed. Place in a greased bowl, turning once to grease top, and cover with plastic wrap. Let rise in a warm area until doubled, about 1 to 1½ hours.
4. Gently deflate dough, turn out onto a lightly floured surface, and divide into 2 equal portions. Shape into 2 loaves and place in greased 9-by-5-inch pans, seam side down. Cover loosely with plastic wrap and let rise to 1 inch above rims of pans, about 45 minutes. Brush with egg glaze, if desired, for a dark and glossy crust.
5. Bake in a preheated 375° oven for 40 to 45 minutes, or until golden brown. Remove from pans and cool on a rack before slicing.

Gruyère Pullman Loaf

The rectangular loaf known as a pullman or a *pain de mie* is characterized by its even slices and has little or no crust. The pullman pan for home baking comes in a traditional 9-by-5-inch size and a larger 11-by-5-inch size. Both have a fitted lid that slides into place and helps shape the loaf by containing its rising, producing bread with a dense crumb suited to thin slicing for toast, oven-dried melba toast, and fancy English tea sandwiches. The grated cheese makes the flavor of this bread exceptional.

Yield: 1 large or 2 small pullman loaves,
  or two 9-by-5-inch loaves

2 packages (2 tablespoons) active dry yeast
1 teaspoon sugar
⅓ cup warm water (105° to 115°)
1¾ cups warm milk (105° to 115°)
4 tablespoons unsalted butter, melted
1 tablespoon salt
5 to 5½ cups unbleached all-purpose
  or bread flour
1¼ cups grated Gruyère cheese, mixed with
  2 tablespoons flour to prevent clumping

1. Combine yeast, sugar, and water in a small bowl. Stir to dissolve and let stand 10 minutes until foamy.
2. In a large bowl, combine milk and butter. Add yeast mixture, salt, and 2 cups of flour. Stir with a whisk until smooth. Continue to add flour, using a wooden spoon, until stiff. Add cheese.
3. Turn out onto a lightly floured surface and knead until smooth, about 5 minutes, adding flour 1 tablespoon at a time as necessary. Place in a greased bowl, turn once to grease top, cover with plastic wrap, and let rise in a warm area until doubled, about 1 to 1½ hours.
4. Punch dough down, turn out onto a lightly floured surface, and roll to form a 10-by-15-inch rectangle. Roll up tightly in jelly-roll fashion, pinch seam, and place seam side down in a greased large pullman loaf pan, 2 small pullman pans, or two 9-by-5-inch loaf pans.

    The dough will fill pans from one-third to one-half full. Cover with plastic wrap and let rise to fill pans four-fifths full, about 30 minutes. Cover pullman loaves with their greased covers. Use a metal baking sheet, with one side greased, to cover dough in standard loaf pans. Weight down baking sheet with a brick.
5. Bake in a preheated 400° oven for 25 minutes. Remove lids and bake another 15 minutes, or until bread is brown and solid to the touch. Remove from pans and cool completely on rack before slicing.

Bread Sticks
Divide dough into 4 equal portions. Divide each into 10 to 12 portions. Roll each portion with your palms into a stick about 1 inch in diameter. Let rest for 5 minutes, then roll to ½ inch in diameter. Place sticks on a greased or parchment-lined baking sheet and bake in a preheated 375° oven for 25 to 30 minutes, or until golden brown.

BRIOCHE

*E*very European country has its egg bread, but French *brioche* is the queen. It is one of the great pastries of the world, a cross between cake and bread. It is a rich but unpretentious bread. This classic recipe comes from the French cooking academy, Cordon Bleu.

Brioche is now one of the simplest breads to make, with the aid of a heavy-duty electric mixer, although it can be made by hand, if you prefer. The dough is very soft and moist, and needs to stay as cold as possible, even while you are forming the loaves, to prevent the butter from separating from the dough. A good *brioche* has a close, even crumb and is not greasy or crisp. Make it in a classic fluted or plain mold, with or without its jaunty topknot.

This recipe is good with jam for brunch. It needs no butter. For a *bonne bouche*, tuck a teaspoon of Roquefort cheese under each topknot before baking or toss ⅓ cup chopped fresh herbs into the dough. Serve toasted or fresh. *Brioche* is also excellent made in the traditional loaf shape and used for sandwiches and spreads such as Mushroom Butter, page 118.

Yield: 16 *petits brioches à tête* (individual size)

4½ cups unbleached all-purpose flour
1 package (1 tablespoon) active dry yeast
¼ cup sugar
2 teaspoons salt
½ cup hot water (120°)
6 eggs, at room temperature
1 cup (2 sticks) unsalted butter, cut into small pieces and softened
Rich Egg Glaze, page 115

1. In bowl of a heavy-duty mixer fitted with a paddle attachment, combine 1 cup flour, yeast, sugar, and salt. Add hot water and beat at medium speed for 2 minutes, or until smooth.
2. Add eggs one at a time, beating well after each addition. Gradually add 2 cups more flour.
3. When well blended, add butter a few pieces at a time. Beat just until completely incorporated. Gradually add exactly 1½ cups more flour slowly at low speed for about 2 minutes. Beat until thoroughly blended and creamy. The dough will be very soft and have a batter-like consistency.
4. Scrape with a spatula into a greased bowl. Cover tightly with plastic wrap and let rise at a cool room temperature until doubled, about 3 hours.
5. Gently deflate dough with a spatula, cover tightly, and refrigerate 12 hours or overnight. The dough may be frozen at this point for up to 2 weeks. When ready to use, place in refrigerator to thaw for a day.
6. Turn chilled dough out onto a lightly floured surface. Divide dough in fourths. Roll each portion into a rope about 12 inches long and 1 inch in diameter. Divide each into four 2-inch pieces and four 1-inch pieces. Round pieces with fingers to make 16 larger balls and 16 small ones. Do not worry if rolls vary slightly in size. Place in well-buttered 3½-inch fluted molds or standard muffin tins. Place larger balls in molds and snip an X on top of each with scissors. Push your finger through the middle of dough to bottom. Place a small topknot in each center. Brush with egg glaze. Let rise at a cool room temperature until doubled, about 45 minutes. The butter will separate from the dough if it is risen in the traditional "warm place" called for in regular bread recipes.
7. Bake in a preheated 400° oven for 10 to 15 minutes, or until golden brown. Remove from molds to cool completely on a rack before eating. *Brioche* is best when reheated.

LARGE BRIOCHE À TÊTE

Yield: Two 8-inch *brioches*

*D*ivide the preceding *brioche* dough into halves. Divide each piece in 2 unequal pieces as for the *petits*, shape into rounds, and follow directions as for *petits brioche à tête*, preceding. Place in 2 greased 8-inch fluted molds, charlotte pans, or round baking dishes. Glaze and let rise until doubled. Bake in a preheated 375° oven 35 to 40 minutes, or until good and brown. Remove from pan and cool completely. Slice in wedges and serve with a compound butter or fruit preserves. Note: If using the *brioche* for a *croustade*, bake the day before it is needed.

YIELDS AND BAKING TIMES FOR ONE RECIPE OF BRIOCHE

16 to 18 *petits brioches à tête* (3½-inch mold)	400°	10 to 15 minutes
8 *petits brioches* (5½-inch mold)	375°	20 to 25 minutes
2 *gros brioches à tête* (8-inch mold)	375°	35 to 40 minutes
Two 9-by-5-inch loaves	375°	35 to 40 minutes
Six 6-by-3-inch loaves	375°	20 to 25 minutes
1 large 12-inch braid, *kugelhof,* or 9-inch cake	375°	50 to 60 minutes
2 *mousselines* (1-pound coffee cans or cylinder mold)	350°	35 to 40 minutes
1 *couronne* (crown)	375°	35 to 40 minutes

BRAN-MOLASSES SUNFLOWER BREAD

*T*his is the bread that started my baking career. The customers in the restaurant where I worked demanded brown bread, so I took a white bread recipe and added bran. A few years later, I received a large bag of sunflower seeds by accident, they appeared in the bread. In the presence of heat, sunflower seeds exude their flavorful and nutritious oil into bread. The whole-grain nutty flavor and aroma are intoxicating. If you find your bread a bit too heavy, cut back on the bran until you get the texture of your perfect loaf.

Yield: 2 round or 9-by-5-inch loaves

1 package (1 tablespoon) active dry yeast
2 tablespoons sugar
¾ cup warm water (105° to 115°)
1½ cups warm milk (105° to 115°)
4 tablespoons unsalted butter, melted
⅓ cup molasses
1¼ cups bran
1 tablespoon salt
½ cup raw sunflower seeds
About 5 cups unbleached all-purpose
    or bread flour

1. Combine yeast, sugar, and water in a small bowl. Stir to dissolve and let stand until foamy, about 10 minutes.
2. Combine milk, butter, molasses, bran, salt, and seeds in a large bowl, stirring hard with a whisk. Add 2 cups flour and yeast mixture. Beat with a whisk until smooth and creamy, about 3 minutes.
3. Add flour ½ cup at a time, using a wooden spoon, until dough is stiff. Knead on a lightly floured surface until smooth, about 5 minutes, adding flour 1 table-spoon at a time as necessary. Place in a greased bowl, turn once to grease top, cover with plastic wrap, and let rise in a warm area until doubled, about 1 to 1½ hours.
4. Punch dough down gently, turn out onto a lightly floured board, and divide into 2 portions. Form each into a round or 9-by-5-inch loaf. Place seam down on a greased or parchment-lined baking sheet or in greased pans. Cover loosely with plastic wrap and let rise until doubled, about 45 minutes.
5. Bake in a preheated 375° oven for 45 minutes, or until nicely browned. Remove from pans immediately and cool on racks.

BROWN RICE BREAD WITH DUTCH CRUNCH TOPPING

I've always loved the classic Dutch crunch topping made from rice flour, but the breads underneath seemed terribly plain. Not any more. Here is a delicious toasting bread with a nubby texture. Serve with homemade blueberry jam (see Berry Jam, page 123).

Yield: Two 9-by-5-inch loaves

2 packages (2 tablespoons) active dry yeast
1 teaspoon sugar or honey
1 cup warm water (105° to 115°)
1 cup warm buttermilk (105° to 115°)
½ cup honey
¼ cup vegetable oil
1 tablespoon salt
2 cups cooked short-grain brown rice
5½ to 6 cups unbleached all-purpose
    or bread flour
Dutch Crunch Topping, following

1. Sprinkle yeast and sugar over warm water in a small bowl and stir until dissolved. Let stand until foamy, about 10 minutes.
2. Combine buttermilk, honey, oil, and salt in a large bowl with a whisk. Add rice and beat until smooth. Add yeast mixture and 2 cups flour. Beat hard for 3 minutes, or until smooth. Add flour ½ cup at a time with a wooden spoon until a soft, bulky dough is formed.
3. Turn dough out onto a lightly floured surface and knead until smooth and springy, about 5 to 7 minutes, adding flour 1 tablespoon at a time as necessary. This dough will be slightly sticky. Place in a greased bowl, turn once to coat top, cover with plastic wrap, and let rise in a warm area until doubled, 1½ to 2 hours.
4. Gently deflate dough, turn out onto a lightly floured surface, and divide into 2 portions. Form into loaves and place in 2 greased 9-by-5-inch bread pans. Let rest 15 minutes while preparing Dutch Crunch Topping. Coat top surface of each loaf with a thick layer of topping. Let stand, uncovered, 20 minutes, until dough is level with tops of pans.
5. Bake in a preheated 375° oven for 45 to 50 minutes or until brown. Cool on a rack completely before slicing.

Dutch Crunch Topping
2 packages (2 tablespoons) active dry yeast
1 cup warm water (105° to 115°)
2 tablespoons sugar
2 tablespoons vegetable oil
½ teaspoon salt
1½ cups rice flour (not sweet rice flour)

Combine all ingredients with a whisk and beat hard to combine. Let stand 15 minutes.

CORNMEAL-HONEY BREAD

*C*ornmeal in a yeast-bread dough makes a moist, sweet, and grainy textured loaf. This one lends itself to a cheery holiday meal, accenting cranberries and sweet potatoes. Better yet, serve for a summer barbecue, featuring chili and artichokes with *aïoli*, or make thick-sliced toast with Pecan-Honey Butter, page 119.

Yield: 2 round loaves

1 package (1 tablespoon) active dry yeast
¾ cup warm water (105° to 115°)
1½ cups warm buttermilk (105° to 115°)
2 tablespoons unsalted butter, melted
⅓ cup honey
1 tablespoon salt
1 cup yellow cornmeal, fine or medium grind
4½ to 5 cups unbleached all-purpose
  or bread flour

1. Combine yeast and water in a small bowl and stir to dissolve. Let stand until bubbly, about 10 minutes.
2. In a large bowl, combine buttermilk, butter, honey, and salt. Add cornmeal. Beat with a whisk until smooth, about 3 minutes, and add yeast mixture. Add ½ cup flour at a time with a wooden spoon until dough is stiff.
3. Turn dough out onto a lightly floured surface and knead until smooth and springy, about 5 minutes, adding flour 1 tablespoon at a time as necessary. Place in a greased bowl, turn once to grease surface, and cover with plastic wrap. Let rise in a warm place until doubled, about 1 to 1¼ hours. Gently deflate dough, turn

out onto a lightly floured board, and divide into 2 loaves. Form into rounds and place on a greased or parchment-lined baking sheet. Cover loosely with plastic wrap and let rise until doubled, about 40 minutes.
4. Bake in preheated 375° oven for 40 minutes or until browned. Place on a rack and cool before slicing.

PISTACHIO-HONEY OAT BREAD

*C*alifornia grows beautiful pistachio nuts. The nut meat is a grayish white and its half-open shell an appealing earthy beige. The tradition of dyeing them red began when they were sold at carnivals in the forties. Avoid red nuts for cooking. Pistachios are easy to shell, and add another dimension to the everyday oat loaf. This bread is also good with almonds or without nuts at all. Oat bread makes great cinnamon toast and grilled cheese sandwiches.

Yield: 2 or 3 round loaves

2 packages (2 tablespoons) active dry yeast
1 teaspoon sugar
½ cup warm water (105° to 115°)
2 cups warm milk (105° to 115°)
½ cup honey
4 tablespoons unsalted butter, melted
5 to 5½ cups unbleached all-purpose
  or bread flour
1 tablespoon salt
2 cups rolled oats
1 cup shelled pistachios, skinned and dried
  (see page 116)
Oatmeal for sprinkling

1. Sprinkle yeast and sugar over warm water in a small bowl. Stir to dissolve and let stand until foamy, about 10 minutes.
2. Combine milk, honey, and butter in a small bowl.
3. Combine 1 cup flour, salt, and oats in a large bowl. Add milk and yeast mixtures. Beat with a whisk until smooth. Add pistachios and more flour ½ cup at a time, using a wooden spoon, until a soft dough is formed.
4. Turn dough out onto a lightly floured surface and knead until smooth and springy, about 5 to 7 minutes, adding flour 1 tablespoon at a time as necessary. The dough will retain a tacky quality. Push back any nuts that fall out of dough. Place in a greased bowl, turn once to grease top, and cover with plastic wrap. Let rise in a warm place until doubled, about 1½ hours.
5. Gently deflate dough, turn out onto a lightly floured surface, and divide into 2 or 3 portions. Form into round loaves and roll entire loaf in oats, completely coating its surface. Place on a greased or parchment-lined baking sheet. Cover loosely with plastic wrap and let rise until doubled, about 45 minutes.
6. Bake in a preheated 375° oven for about 45 minutes, or until brown. Cool on a rack before slicing. Serve with Homemade Butter, page 118.

FRENCH NUT BREAD

*T*his dense, moist brown bread is one of the great peasant breads of Europe. A yeasted nut bread is a unique flavor treat, good with St. André cheese and figs. It can also be made with walnuts, pecans, macadamias, almonds, or a mixture of nuts on hand.

Yield: 2 round loaves

2½ cups hazelnuts, lightly toasted and skinned (see page 116)
2½ cups whole-wheat flour
2 packages (2 tablespoons) active dry yeast
¼ cup brown sugar
1¼ cups warm water (105° to 115°)
1 cup warm milk (105° to 115°)
½ cup walnut oil
2½ teaspoons salt
About 3 cups unbleached all-purpose or bread flour

1. Grind 1¼ cups nuts and 1 cup whole-wheat flour to the consistency of fine meal in a blender or food processor. Set aside.
2. Sprinkle yeast and and a pinch of brown sugar into ¼ cup warm water in a small bowl. Stir until dissolved and let stand until foamy, about 10 minutes.
3. Combine remaining 1 cup water, milk, oil, sugar, and salt in a large bowl with a whisk. Add yeast and nut mixtures. Add remaining whole-wheat flour 1 cup at time, mixing with a wooden spoon. Add unbleached flour ½ cup at a time until a soft dough is formed.
4. Turn dough out onto a well-floured surface and knead until firm yet still springy, about 5 to 7 minutes, adding flour 1 tablespoon at a time as necessary. Because of the whole-grain flour, dough will retain a tacky quality. Do not add more flour than required, as dough will get hard and bread will be very dry. Place in a greased bowl, turn once to grease top, and cover with plastic wrap. Let rise in a warm place until doubled, about 1 to 1½ hours. Do not worry if it takes longer.
5. Gently deflate loaf, turn out onto a lightly floured board, and knead in nut pieces. They will tend to keep falling out, but just push them back in. Divide dough into 2 pieces and form round loaves. Place on a greased or parchment-lined baking sheet and cover loosely with plastic wrap. Let rise about 40 to 50 minutes, or until doubled in bulk.
6. Slash 3 or 4 parallel gashes on tops with a serrated knife and bake in a preheated 375° oven until brown, 45 to 50 minutes. Cool on a rack.

ITALIAN WHOLE-WHEAT BREAD

*T*his is a spectacular bread when made into a large loaf and baked on a hot stone to produce a crisp crust and delicate inner crumbs. If this is the only bread you make out of this book, you will still be hailed as a master baker. The baked goat cheese is so enticing a complement that it should be not overlooked. This loaf is best eaten the same day it is baked. Serve with champagne, a salad with a squeeze of fresh lemon, and the warm marinating oil from the cheese.

Yield: 1 large loaf, 2 medium loaves, or 8 large rolls

Sponge
1 package (1 tablespoon) active dry yeast
1 teaspoon sugar
⅔ cup warm water (105° to 115°)
1 cup cool water
1 cup whole-wheat flour
1½ cups unbleached all-purpose or bread flour

Dough
Sponge, above
2½ teaspoons salt
1½ cups unbleached all-purpose or bread flour

Cornmeal for dusting
Baked Marinated Goat Cheese, page 121 (optional)

1. Prepare the sponge: Sprinkle yeast and sugar over warm water in a large (3- or 4-quart) bowl and stir until dissolved. Let stand until foamy, about 10 minutes. Add cool water, whole-wheat flour, and unbleached flour. With a whisk, beat until smooth. Cover loosely with plastic wrap and let stand at room temperature 4 hours to overnight. This sponge can be stored 1 week in the refrigerator before using, if necessary.
2. Add salt and ½ cup unbleached flour to sponge. Beat hard with a whisk for 10 minutes, or 5 minutes in a mixer with a paddle attachment. With a wooden spoon, add remaining flour as needed to make a soft dough.
3. Turn dough out onto a lightly floured surface and knead vigorously to create a soft, moist, elastic dough that will still feel sticky, 5 to 7 minutes, adding flour 1 tablespoon at a time as necessary. Use a dough scraper to clean off film of dough that accumulates on work surface as you go along. Take care not to add too much flour; this dough should just hold its shape and have a definite tacky quality.

4. Cover dough and let it rest 20 minutes on work surface. Shape dough into desired shapes and place on a greased or parchment-lined baking sheet dusted with cornmeal. Cover loosely with plastic wrap and let rise at room temperature until tripled in volume, about 1 hour. Meanwhile, preheat a baking stone in the oven at 450° for 20 minutes, if desired.

5. Slide shaped and risen loaf gently onto a baker's paddle or baking sheet heavily sprinkled with cornmeal. Gently slash top of loaf and slide into oven onto hot stone, if used, with a quick motion of the wrist. Place in a preheated 450° oven, reduce temperature to 425°, and bake loaf 35 to 40 minutes (20 minutes for rolls).

6. The bread is done when bottom is tapped and you hear a hollow sound. It will not be very dark brown due to the wheat flour and small amount of sugar. Cool on a rack before cutting and serving with goat cheese, if you like.

WHOLE-WHEAT
EGG BREAD

*T*his exceptional recipe makes a very beautiful and flavorful bread. It is a good beginning whole-grain recipe. I like to classify this as an "everyday" bread, one you can make week after week, year after year. Do not be put off by the small amount of pastry flour—it is only to help lighten and tenderize the bread. If whole-wheat pastry flour is not available, use all whole-wheat flour. Whole-wheat pastry flour is *not* like white pastry flour, and they are not interchangeable. Whole-wheat pastry flour has a considerably higher protein content, so it can be used for breadmaking. White pastry flour is too soft for anything but cakes and pastries.

Yield: 1 medium-sized braid

1 package (1 tablespoon) active dry yeast
Pinch sugar
²/₃ cup warm water (105° to 115°)
1¹/₂ cups whole-wheat pastry flour
2¹/₂ teaspoons sea salt
¹/₄ cup maple syrup
¹/₄ cup corn oil
3 eggs
1¹/₂ to 1³/₄ cups whole-wheat flour
Rich Egg Glaze, page 115
Oats for sprinkling

1. In a small bowl, stir yeast and sugar into water until dissolved and let stand for 10 minutes, or until foamy.

2. Place whole-wheat pastry flour and salt in bowl of heavy-duty mixer. Add yeast mixture, maple syrup, oil, and eggs. Beat with a paddle attachment on medium speed for 2 minutes, or until smooth. Add whole-wheat flour ¹/₂ cup at a time until a soft dough is formed that clears sides of bowl. This bread can be made by hand, if you prefer.

3. Turn dough out onto a lightly floured surface and knead until smooth yet slightly sticky, about 5 to 7 minutes, adding flour 1 tablespoon at a time as necessary. Do not add too much flour, dough will retain a very sticky consistency. Shape dough into a ball, place in a greased bowl, and turn to grease top. Cover with plastic wrap and let rise in a warm area until doubled, about 1 hour.

4. Gently deflate dough, turn out onto a lightly floured surface, and divide into 3 equal portions. With the palms of your hands, form each strand into a rope about 14 inches in length. Lay 3 strips side by side on a greased or parchment-lined baking sheet. Alternating outside ropes, lay left strand over middle, then right over middle. Continue, making a a 3-strand braid; pinch ends and tuck them under. Cover loosely with plastic wrap and let rise until doubled, about 30 minutes. Brush braid with glaze and sprinkle with sesame seeds.

5. Bake in a preheated 375° oven for 30 to 35 minutes, or until lightly browned and a cake tester comes out clean. Remove from baking sheet to cool on a rack.

COUNTRY BREAD WITH GOLDEN RAISINS AND WALNUTS

*T*he *cloche* baking dish is really a clay oven in miniature. A dish with a domed cover, it has a porous surface that ensures moist, evenly radiated heat. It creates a rugged country loaf in any modern oven. The best loaves for a *cloche* are low in fat and sugar, which can burn and adhere to the clay. One large loaf is produced per baking, and heavy-duty oven mitts are recommended for secure handling. One bite into the crisp crust and soft texture and you will know why this method of baking has rave reviews. This bread will bake nicely on a baking stone in the absence of a *cloche*. Serve with St. André Butter, page 121, and fresh pears or apples.

Yield: One 10-inch loaf

1½ packages (1½ tablespoons) active dry yeast
Pinch sugar
2½ cups warm water (105° to 115°)
2 tablespoons walnut oil
1 tablespoon salt
¾ cup rye flour
¼ cup bran
¾ cup whole-wheat flour
½ cup golden raisins
½ cup coarsely chopped raw
   or lightly toasted walnuts
4 to 4½ cups unbleached all-purpose
   or bread flour
Cornmeal for sprinkling

1. Sprinkle yeast and sugar over ½ cup warm water in a small bowl. Stir until dissolved and let stand until foamy, about 10 minutes.
2. In the bowl of a heavy-duty mixer with a paddle attachment, combine remaining 2 cups water, oil, salt, rye flour, bran, and whole-wheat flour. Beat 3 minutes at medium speed, or until smooth. Add yeast mixture and beat to combine. Add raisins and nuts. This bread can be made by hand, if you prefer.
3. Add unbleached flour ½ cup at a time until a soft dough is formed. Turn out onto a lightly floured surface and knead to form a soft, springy dough, about 5 minutes, adding flour 1 tablespoon at a time as necessary. The dough will retain a slight stickiness due to the whole grains. Place in a greased bowl, turning to coat top. Cover with plastic wrap and let rise in a warm place until doubled, about 1½ hours.
4. Gently deflate dough. Turn out onto a lightly floured surface and shape into a round by kneading and pulling ends lightly together on the bottom to create surface tension.
5. Sprinkle *cloche* dish with yellow or white cornmeal. Place dough in dish, seam side down. Move dough around to cover entire bottom and part of the sides with meal. It is okay to have extra meal left in pan. Slash top with serrated knife. This will allow steam to escape and give dough room to expand. Cover with *cloche* dome and let rest 20 minutes, no more.
6. Before placing in oven, rinse inside of *cloche* dome with water. Drain off excess drips. A bit of water dripping does not matter. Place dome on dish and place in center of a preheated 450° oven.
7. After 10 minutes, lower oven to 400° and set a timer for 20 minutes. After 20 minutes, remove dome and allow loaf to brown thoroughly, about 15 minutes longer.
8. Remove loaf to cool on a rack before serving.

NOTE: To clean *cloche*, tap out excess cornmeal after dish has cooled completely. With a dry brush, scrub off any bits of dried dough stuck to clay. Wash out with plain water only, as any soap will be absorbed into porous texture of clay, giving bread a soapy taste.

HONEY WHOLE-WHEAT BREAD

*T*his is the recipe you've been looking for: a real everyday loaf—nutty, slightly sweet, crusty whole-wheat bread. A sure success for beginning bakers, it uses 40 percent whole-grain flour and is made in a heavy-duty mixer for easier handling of the dough. Serve with softened fresh cream cheese mixed with chopped dried apricots, a few golden raisins, and chopped toasted almonds.

Yield: Two 9-by-5-inch loaves

2 packages (2 tablespoons) active dry yeast
Pinch sugar or honey
1 cup warm water (105° to 115°)
1 cup warm milk (105° to 115°)
½ cup honey
3 tablespoons unsalted butter
2½ cups whole-wheat flour
1 tablespoon salt
1 egg
3½ to 4 cups unbleached all-purpose
   or bread flour

1. Combine yeast and sugar in water in a small bowl and let stand until foamy, about 10 minutes.
2. Combine milk, honey, and butter in a small bowl.
3. Combine whole-wheat flour and salt in bowl of a heavy-duty mixer with the paddle attachment. Add milk mixture, egg, and yeast mixture. Beat at medium speed for 3 minutes, or until smooth. Add unbleached flour ½ cup at a time until a soft dough is formed. This bread can be made by hand, if you prefer.
4. Turn dough out onto a lightly floured surface and knead until smooth and elastic, about 5 to 7 minutes, adding flour 1 tablespoon at a time as necessary. Dough will retain a slightly sticky quality. Place in a greased bowl, turn once to grease top, and cover with plastic wrap. Let rise in a warm place until doubled, 1 to 1½ hours.
5. Gently deflate dough. Turn out onto a lightly floured surface and divide into 2 equal portions. Form into oblong loaves and place in greased 9-by-5-inch pans. Cover loosely with plastic wrap and let rise until level with tops of pans, about 30 minutes.
6. Place in a preheated 375° oven and bake 35 to 40 minutes, or until crusty and golden. Turn out of pans to cool on a rack before slicing.

CRACKED-WHEAT BREAD

*C*racked wheat gives a special nutty texture and extra nutrition to this homey loaf. Bulgur wheat can be used interchangeably with cracked wheat. This bread is good with Sesame-Peanut Butter, page 120, a high-protein and very flavorful spread.

Yield: 3 medium round loaves

1½ cups boiling water
¾ cup cracked wheat or bulgur
1½ packages (1½ tablespoons) active dry yeast
Pinch sugar
¼ cup warm water (105° to 115°)
1 cup warm buttermilk (105° to 115°)
¼ cup molasses
1 tablespoon honey
4 tablespoons unsalted butter, cut into pieces
1 tablespoon salt
¼ cup raw sesame seeds
2 cups whole-wheat flour
2½ to 3 cups unbleached all-purpose
   or bread flour
2 tablespoons melted butter for brushing loaves

1. Pour boiling water over cracked wheat in a bowl and let stand 1 hour to soften.
2. In a small bowl, sprinkle yeast and sugar in warm water. Stir to dissolve and let stand until foamy, about 10 minutes.
3. Combine buttermilk, molasses, honey, and butter in a small bowl.
4. In a large bowl, combine salt, sesame seeds, and whole-wheat flour. Add milk and yeast mixtures and beat with a whisk until smooth, about 3 minutes. Drain cracked wheat and add.
5. Add unbleached flour ½ cup at a time until a soft dough forms, using a wooden spoon. Turn dough out onto a floured surface and knead until soft and springy to the touch, about 5 minutes, adding flour 1 tablespoon at a time as necessary. The dough will remain quite tacky.
6. Place dough in a greased bowl, turn to grease top, and cover with plastic wrap. Let rise in a warm area until doubled, about 1 hour and 15 minutes.
7. Gently deflate dough, turn out onto a lightly floured surface, divide into 3 equal portions, and shape into round or oblong loaves. Place on a greased or parchment-lined baking sheet. Brush tops with melted butter and cover loosely with plastic wrap. Let sit until doubled in bulk, about 30 minutes. Brush tops again with melted butter.
8. Bake in a preheated 350° oven for 35 to 45 minutes, or until brown. Cool on racks.

CELESTE'S SUNFLOWER-OATMEAL BREAD

*C*eleste was my baking assistant for years. She is a sculptor, has the temperament of a true artist, and makes outstanding bread. She was inspired to make this bread one day. I loved the subtle blend of grains and wrote the ingredients down. It is one of the best breads in this collection.

Yield: 3 small round loaves

1 package (1 tablespoon) active dry yeast
Pinch sugar
1¼ cups warm water (105° to 115°)
1¼ cups warm buttermilk (105° to 115°)
¼ cup honey
2 tablespoons molasses
2 tablespoons unsalted butter
1 cup whole-wheat flour
1 cup rolled oats
¾ cup raw sunflower seeds
1 tablespoon salt
1 egg, lightly beaten
About 4 to 5 cups unbleached all-purpose
  or bread flour
Rich Egg Glaze, page 115
Oats for sprinkling

1. In a small bowl, combine yeast, sugar, and warm water and stir to dissolve. Let stand until foamy, about 10 minutes.
2. Combine buttermilk, honey, molasses, and butter in a small bowl.
3. In a large bowl, combine whole-wheat flour, oats, sunflower seeds, and salt. Add buttermilk mixture, yeast, and egg. Whisk hard for about 3 minutes. Add unbleached flour about ½ cup at a time with a wooden spoon until a soft dough is formed.

4. Turn dough out onto a lightly floured surface and knead for about 5 minutes, adding flour 1 tablespoon at a time as needed to produce a smooth and springy dough. Place in a greased bowl and turn once to grease top. Cover with plastic wrap and let rise in a warm place until doubled in volume, about 1½ hours.
5. Gently deflate dough, turn out onto a floured surface, and divide into 3 round loaves. Place on a greased or parchment-lined baking sheet sprinkled with oats. Cover loosely with plastic wrap and let rise for about 30 minutes, or until doubled. Brush with Rich Egg Glaze and sprinkle with oats.
6. Bake in a preheated 375° oven for 40 minutes. Loaves are done when brown and bottoms sound hollow when tapped. Cool on racks before slicing.

GRAHAM BREAD

*T*his Swedish bread was brought to my home for a potluck dinner years ago by my friend, Judy Larsen. In those first years of serious breadmaking, Judy and I had a lot of conversations about bread over cups of tea. The recipes she shared with me from her mother in Minnesota gave me a standard by which I could judge all others. She was also helpful with the myriad questions I always seemed to have as a beginning breadmaker. Scandinavians are notoriously good bakers, gifted in working with the tempermental whole grains. Graham flour is technically whole-wheat flour, but has a much richer, nutty flavor. This loaf is the essence of a comforting, wholesome winter bread. Note that this is a large recipe, yielding 4 standard loaves.

Yield: Four 9-by-5-inch loaves

2 tablespoons (2 packages) active dry yeast
1 cup brown sugar
4½ cups warm water (105° to 115°)
1⅔ cups instant nonfat dried milk
½ cup (1 stick) unsalted butter, melted,
  or vegetable oil
¾ cup molasses
1 tablespoon plus 1 teaspoon salt
4 eggs, lightly beaten
3 cups graham flour
9 to 10 cups unbleached all-purpose
  or bread flour
Rich Egg Glaze, page 115

1. Combine yeast, a pinch of brown sugar, and ½ cup warm water in a small bowl and stir to dissolve. Let stand until foamy, about 10 minutes.
2. Combine remaining 4 cups water, dried milk, remaining brown sugar, butter, molasses, and salt in a large mixing bowl.
3. Add yeast mixture and eggs to liquid ingredients. Whisk to combine. Add graham flour and beat hard until smooth, about 3 minutes. Add flour 1 cup at a time with a wooden spoon until a shaggy dough is formed.
4. Turn out onto a well-floured surface and knead for a full 10 minutes until dough is smooth and very springy, adding flour 1 tablespoon at a time as necessary. Do not add too much flour or dough will become very stiff and hard to work.
5. Place in a greased bowl and turn once to grease top. Cover with plastic wrap and let rise in a warm area until doubled, about 1½ hours. Gently deflate and, if possible, let rise again for 45 minutes. This extra rise helps flavor and texture develop.

6. Gently deflate dough, turn out onto a lightly floured board, and divide into 4 equal portions. Form into loaves and place in 4 greased 9-by-5-inch loaf pans. Cover loosely with plastic wrap and let rise until doubled, or no more than 1 inch above rim of pan, about 30 to 40 minutes. This also makes lovely round free-form loaves, if desired.

7. Brush with egg glaze and bake in a preheated 350° oven until golden brown, about 40 to 45 minutes. Cool bread 5 minutes in pan and turn out to cool completely on a rack, laying bread on its side.

RAIN AND SUN

A light-and-dark braided loaf of buckwheat and cornmeal doughs. Serve with a garden salad, a pyramid *chèvre*, and black grapes.

Yield: 2 braids

Buckwheat Dough
1 package (1 tablespoon) active dry yeast
3 tablespoons brown sugar
½ cup warm water (105° to 115°)
1 cup warm buttermilk (105° to 115°)
3 tablespoons unsalted butter, melted
1 egg, lightly beaten
Grated zest of ½ orange
2 teaspoons salt
½ cup buckwheat flour
1 cup whole-wheat flour
2 to 2¼ cups unbleached all-purpose or bread flour

Cornmeal Dough
1 package (1 tablespoon) active dry yeast
Pinch sugar
½ cup warm water (105° to 115°)
⅔ cup half and half
¼ cup maple syrup
4 tablespoons unsalted butter, melted
2 eggs, lightly beaten
1½ teaspoons salt
⅔ cup yellow cornmeal
3 to 3½ cups unbleached all-purpose or bread flour

Rich Egg Glaze, page 115

1. To make buckwheat dough, sprinkle yeast and a pinch of brown sugar over warm water in a small bowl. Stir to dissolve. Let stand 10 minutes until foamy.

2. In a large bowl, combine buttermilk, remaining brown sugar, butter, and egg. Add orange zest, salt, buckwheat and whole-wheat flours. Beat hard with a whisk for 3 minutes, or until smooth. Add yeast mixture and beat well. With a wooden spoon, add unbleached flour ½ cup at time to make a soft dough.

3. Turn dough out onto a lightly floured surface and knead until dough is rather soft and sticky but is elastic and holds its shape, about 5 minutes, adding flour 1 tablespoon at a time as necessary. Place in a greased bowl and turn once to grease top. Cover with plastic wrap and let rise in a warm area until doubled, about 1 to 1¼ hours.

4. To make the cornmeal dough, sprinkle yeast and sugar over warm water in a small bowl. Stir to dissolve. Let stand 10 minutes until foamy.

5. In a large bowl, combine half and half, maple syrup, butter, eggs, salt, and cornmeal. Beat hard with a whisk until smooth, about 3 minutes. Add yeast mixture and beat well. Add unbleached flour ½ cup at a time to make a soft dough.

6. Turn out onto a lightly floured surface and knead until smooth and springy, about 5 minutes. Dough will be grainy in texture and be slightly sticky. Place dough in a greased bowl, turn once to grease top, and cover with plastic wrap. Let rise in a warm area until doubled, about 1 to 1¼ hours.

7. Gently deflate doughs. Turn out onto a lightly floured surface and divide each dough into 3 equal portions. Roll each third into a 16-inch rope. On a greased or parchment-lined baking sheet, lay 2 strands of cornmeal and 1 strand of buckwheat parallel to each other with buckwheat in middle. Braid loaf and tuck under ends. Repeat with other 3 strands, placing cornmeal strand in middle. Cover each loosely with plastic wrap and let rise until doubled, about 30 minutes. Brush tops with egg glaze.

8. Bake in a preheated 375° oven for 40 to 45 minutes, or until brown and crusty. Cool on racks before slicing.

WILD RICE AND THREE-GRAIN BREAD

Wild rice has been called the "caviar of grains." It is native to North America, growing in the central and upper Great Lakes area. Wild rice is higher in protein than wheat, making it an excellent cereal. It has an earthy, assertive flavor and makes a beautiful loaf that will please the heart of the most hardcore health disciples. I like to bake these loaves in clay pans. Serve for breakfast with a white log of Montrachet rolled in fresh-grated orange zest.

Yield: Two 9-by-5-inch loaves

2 packages (2 tablespoons) active dry yeast
Pinch sugar
1¼ cups warm water (105° to 115°)
1 cup warm milk (105° to 115°)
½ cup honey
4 tablespoons unsalted butter, melted
1 tablespoon salt
½ cup oat flour
½ cup rye flour
1 cup whole-wheat flour
1 cup cooked wild rice (⅓ cup raw),
*   see page 116*
3½ to 4 cups unbleached all-purpose
*   or bread flour*
Rich Egg Glaze, page 115
Rolled oats for sprinkling

1. Sprinkle yeast and sugar over ¼ cup warm water in a small bowl and stir until dissolved. Let stand until foamy, about 10 minutes.
2. In bowl of a heavy-duty mixer fitted with a paddle attachment, combine milk, water, honey, and butter and mix at low speed. Add yeast mixture. Add salt, oat, rye, and whole-wheat flours. Beat at medium speed for 3 minutes, or until smooth. Add rice. Add unbleached flour ½ cup at a time until a soft dough is formed. This bread can be made by hand, if your prefer.
3. Turn dough out onto a lightly floured surface and knead until smooth, about 5 to 7 minutes, adding flour 1 tablespoon at a time as necessary. The dough will be sticky and nubby in texture. Place in a greased bowl, turn once to grease top, and cover with plastic wrap. Let rise in a warm area until doubled, 1½ to 2 hours.
4. Gently deflate dough, turn out onto a lightly floured surface, and divide into 2 portions. Form into 2 loaves and place in greased 9-by-5-inch loaf pans. Cover loosely with plastic wrap and let rise until even with tops of pans, about 40 minutes.
5. Brush with egg glaze and sprinkle tops with oats. Bake in a preheated 375° oven for 45 minutes or until crusty. Remove from bread pans and transfer to a rack to cool before slicing.

COUNTRY RYE BREAD

Whole grains add flavor and texture to homemade bread. The addition of potato water in combination with wheat, rye, buckwheat, and oats makes the bread coarse textured and moist. The yeast thrives on the starchy essence of potato, making the loaf high and full. This rustic rye bread speaks of the earth's elements. Serve with Tapenade, an olive spread (page 120), and fresh tomatoes or Cream Cheese with Fresh Herbs, page 121.

Yield: 1 large free-form loaf

Sponge

2 packages (2 tablespoons) active dry yeast
2¼ cups warm potato water (105° to 115°),
*   see note*
¼ cup honey
¼ cup molasses
1 cup whole-wheat flour
1 cup medium rye flour

Dough

3 tablespoons oil
1 tablespoon salt
¼ cup bran
¼ cup buckwheat flour
¼ cup oat flour or rolled oats
Sponge, above
2½ to 3 cups unbleached all-purpose
*   or bread flour, as needed*

Rolled oats and bran for sprinkling

1. Prepare the sponge: In a large bowl, whisk together yeast, water, honey, and molasses. Add flours and beat hard with a whisk until creamy and smooth, about 3 minutes. Cover loosely with plastic wrap and let rise in warm place for 45 minutes to 1 hour.
2. Whisk oil, salt, bran, buckwheat flour, and oat flour into sponge until well combined and smooth. With a wooden spoon, add unbleached flour ½ cup at a time until a soft dough is formed.
3. Turn dough out onto a lightly floured surface and knead to form a soft, springy, yet sticky dough, about 5 to 7 minutes, adding flour 1 tablespoon at a time as necessary. Place in a greased bowl, turning to coat entire surface. Cover with plastic wrap and let rise in a warm area until doubled, about 1½ hours.

4. Gently deflate dough. Turn out onto a lightly floured surface and form into a round or oval loaf. Place loaf on a baker's paddle or baking sheet heavily sprinkled with rolled oats and bran, seam side down. Cover loosely with plastic wrap and let rest at room temperature for 20 to 30 minutes. Preheat a baking stone in a 450° oven for 20 minutes, if desired. Dust top with a bit of unbleached flour.

5. Slash top of loaf decoratively with a serrated knife and slide onto hot stone, if used, with a quick motion of your wrist. Place in a preheated 450° oven, reduce oven heat to 400°, and bake for 10 minutes, then reduce heat to 375° and bake for 30 minutes, or until loaf is brown. Cool on a wire rack before slicing.

NOTE: To make potato water, cut 1 to 2 large scrubbed and unpeeled potatoes into chunks. Place in a medium saucepan, cover with water, and simmer until potatoes are tender, about 15 to 20 minutes. Drain and measure liquid. Let cool to desired temperature for recipe. Mash or puree potatoes for use in recipe, if required. Potato water may be stored a few days in refrigerator until needed. Warm before using.

PAIN DE SEIGLE

*T*his is an earthy French-style sour rye bread that is baked after the dough is fermented in stages for 3 days. It has a chewy, whole-grain texture. The flavor boasts a good tang for sourdough-lovers. Because of the starter, this loaf of rye will stay moist at room temperature for about 3 days. To keep any longer, freeze. Serve with tossed seasonal greens and Seafood Butter, page 119.

Yield: 2 round free-form loaves

Starter
1 package (1 tablespoon) active dry yeast
1 cup unbleached all-purpose or bread flour
1 cup lukewarm water (85° to 100°)

Sponge
2 cups warm water (105° to 115°)
2 tablespoons molasses
Starter, above
1½ cups medium rye flour
1½ cups unbleached all-purpose or bread flour

Dough
Sponge, above
½ package (1½ teaspoons) active dry yeast
3 tablespoons vegetable oil
2 tablespoons molasses
4 teaspoons salt
4 teaspoons caraway seed
½ cup medium rye flour
3 to 3½ cups unbleached all-purpose or bread flour

Rolled rye or coarse cornmeal for sprinkling
Rich Egg Glaze, page 115

1. Day One: Make starter by placing yeast and flour in a deep bowl or 4-quart plastic bucket with lid. Add water and whisk hard until a smooth batter is formed. Cover and let stand at room temperature about 24 hours. Starter will begin to bubble and ferment.

2. Day Two: Make sponge by adding water and molasses to starter. Whisk to combine. Add flours 1 cup at a time to form a smooth batter. The sponge will be very wet. Scrape down sides of bowl, cover, and let rest again at room temperature for about 24 hours.

3. Day Three: To make dough, stir down sponge. Add yeast, oil, molasses, salt, caraway seed, and rye flour to sponge and beat hard with a whisk to combine. Add unbleached flour ½ cup at a time with a wooden spoon until a soft dough is formed.

4. Turn out onto a lightly floured surface and knead strongly for about 7 to 10 minutes, adding flour 1 tablespoon at a time as necessary until dough is soft, springy, and does not stick to work surface. The dough will be smooth, yet retain a bit of stickiness. Place in a greased bowl and turn once to grease top. Cover with plastic wrap and let rise at room temperature until doubled, about 1 hour.

5. Gently deflate dough. Turn dough out onto a lightly floured surface and divide into 2 equal portions. Form into round or oval loaves. Place on a greased or parchment-lined baking sheet sprinkled heavily with rolled rye or coarse cornmeal and coat bottom and some of sides by rolling loaves around. Cover loosely with plastic wrap and let rise at room temperature until puffy and almost doubled, 45 minutes to 1 hour. Preheat a baking stone in the oven at 450°, if desired, for 20 minutes.

6. Slash loaves diagonally no deeper than ½ inch. Brush entire surface of loaf with egg glaze. Place in a preheated 450° oven, reduce oven to 375°, and bake 40 to 45 minutes, or until brown and crusty. Cool completely on a rack before slicing.

FENNEL-ORANGE RYE BREAD

*E*ach Scandinavian and northern European country makes rye bread with its own particular flair. This is a Swedish rye, flecked with orange and savory fennel.

Yield: Two 9-by-5-inch loaves

1 package (1 tablespoon) active dry yeast
Pinch sugar
¼ cup warm water (105° to 115°)
1 cup warm milk (105° to 115°)
1 cup fresh orange juice
½ cup molasses
2 tablespoons vegetable oil
2½ teaspoons salt
1½ tablespoons fennel seeds
2 cups medium rye flour
4 to 4½ cups unbleached all-purpose
*   or bread flour*
Rich Egg Glaze, page 115 (optional)

1. Sprinkle yeast and sugar over warm water in a small bowl. Stir to dissolve and let stand 10 minutes, or until foamy.
2. In a large bowl, combine milk, juice, molasses, oil, and yeast mixture. Add salt, fennel seeds, and rye flour. Whisk hard until smooth, about 3 minutes. Add unbleached flour ½ cup at a time with a wooden spoon until a soft, shaggy dough clears the sides of the bowl.
3. Turn out onto a lightly floured surface and knead until smooth and silky, about 5 to 7 minutes, adding flour 1 tablespoon at a time as needed. Place in a greased bowl and turn once to grease top. Cover with plastic wrap and let rise in a warm area until doubled, about 1 to 1½ hours.
4. Gently deflate dough, turn out onto a lightly floured surface, and divide into 2 equal portions. Shape into loaves and place in 2 greased 9-by-5-inch pans, seam down. Cover loosely with plastic wrap and let rise to 1 inch above rim of pans, about 40 minutes. Brush with Rich Egg Glaze, if desired, for a dark, glossy crust.
5. Bake in a preheated 375° oven for 40 to 45 minutes, or until golden brown. Remove from pans to cool on a rack before slicing.

DIJON RYE BREAD

*D*ijon mustard is made from ground mustard seeds, white wine, vinegar, and spices. It is an excellent seasoning and shows up in the most unlikely places—as in this rye bread. This bread can also be made with grainy mustard, which has had its hull left on, giving a stronger, more piquant flavor. Serve individual loaves of Dijon Rye with cold roast chicken and an endive salad.

Yield: Ten 4½-by-2½-inch loaves

2 packages (2 tablespoons) active dry yeast
Pinch sugar
1½ cups warm water (105° to 115°)
¼ cup vegetable oil
¼ cup molasses
⅔ cup Dijon mustard
1 tablespoon salt
1 tablespoon caraway seeds, ground in
*   a spice mill or food processor*
½ cup bran
1 cup rye flour
3½ to 4 cups unbleached all-purpose
*   or bread flour*

Mustard Glaze
1 teaspoon Dijon mustard
1 tablespoon molasses
2 tablespoons hot water

1. Sprinkle yeast and sugar over ½ cup warm water in a small bowl and stir until dissolved. Let stand until foamy, about 10 minutes.
2. Combine remaining 1 cup water, oil, molasses, mustard, and yeast mixture in a large mixing bowl. Add salt, seeds, bran, and rye flour. Beat hard with a whisk until smooth, about 3 minutes. Add unbleached flour ½ cup at time with a wooden spoon to make a smooth and silky-textured dough. Take care not to add more flour than required, as this is dense, heavy dough.
3. Turn out onto a lightly floured surface and knead until smooth, about 5 to 7 minutes, adding flour 1 tablespoon at a time as necessary. The dough will be a bit sticky. Place in a greased bowl, turn once to grease top, cover with plastic wrap, and let rise in a warm place until doubled, about 1 to 1½ hours.
4. Gently deflate dough, turn out onto a lightly floured surface, and divide into 10 equal portions. Form 10 mini oval-shaped loaves and place in greased mini bread pans. Cover loosely with plastic wrap and let rise until doubled, about 30 minutes. Mix ingredients for mustard glaze and brush it on tops of loaves.
5. Bake in a preheated 375° oven 25 to 30 minutes, or until crusty and brown. Remove bread from pans and transfer to racks to cool completely before slicing.

BLACK RUSSIAN BREAD

*E*very baker should have a dark rye in his or her repertoire. There is immense satisfaction in making a good pumpernickel-style loaf. You can control the density of this bread by varying the proportion of the flours: for a lighter bread add more white flour in place of the whole-grain flours. Cool the bread completely before slicing. It stays fresh at room temperature for several days. Serve sliced thin, with smoked fish or deviled egg salad. Bake in mini loaf pans for cocktail-size slices and spread with Feta Cream Butter, page 121.

Yield: 2 medium round loaves,
or 8 mini loaves

2 packages (2 tablespoons) active dry yeast
Pinch sugar
½ cup warm water (105° to 115°)
2 cups water
¼ cup molasses
¼ cup apple cider vinegar
4 tablespoons unsalted butter
1 ounce unsweetened chocolate
½ cup whole-wheat flour
3 cups medium rye flour
3 cups unbleached all-purpose or bread flour
1 cup bran
2 tablespoons caraway seed
½ teaspoon fennel seed
1 tablespoon salt
1 tablespoon instant espresso powder
1 tablespoon minced shallot
¼ cup cornmeal
1 tablespoon unbleached all-purpose flour
1 teaspoon caraway seeds
Cornstarch Glaze, page 115 (optional)

1. In a small bowl, combine yeast and warm water with sugar. Stir to dissolve and let stand until foamy, about 10 minutes.
2. Heat 2 cups water, molasses, vinegar, butter, and chocolate to 105° to 115°. The butter and chocolate will be melted. Set aside.
3. Combine whole-wheat, rye, and white flours in a large bowl and set aside.
4. In bowl of a heavy-duty mixer fitted with a paddle attachment, combine 2 cups mixed flours, bran, seeds, salt, espresso, and shallot. At low speed, add yeast and chocolate mixtures. Mix until smooth and beat at medium speed for 3 minutes.
5. At low speed, add ½ cup of remaining mixed flours at a time, until dough clears sides of bowl and begins to work its way up paddle. It will be very sticky, but firm. Scrape off paddle and knead in flour to make a springy yet dense dough. Not all mixed flours may be used. Form into a ball and place in a greased bowl. Turn once to grease top. Cover with plastic wrap and let rise in a warm area until doubled, about 1½ to 2 hours. Combine cornmeal, flour, and caraway and set aside.
6. Gently deflate dough. Turn out onto a lightly floured surface, divide into 2 portions, and form into 2 rounds. Place seam down on a greased or parchment-lined baking sheet sprinkled with cornmeal mixture. Cover loosely with plastic wrap. Let rise until doubled and puffy, about 45 minutes to 1 hour. Slash an X into top. Brush with Cornstarch Glaze if a shiny crust is desired.
7. Bake in a preheated 350° oven for 50 minutes, or until loaves are well browned. Remove from baking sheet to cool completely on a rack.

BUTTERMILK-POTATO BREAD

*T*he humble potato ranks as one of the world's most important foods, along with wheat, corn, and rice. It has sustained stomachs during famines, revolutions, and mass migrations. Surprisingly enough, the potato was discovered and brought to Europe by Pizarro in the 1500s. It was a staple food for the Andean Indians living over eleven thousand feet, where corn would not grow. The potato has become a daily food throughout the Western world. Yeast thrives on potato starch, and the bread it produces has a characteristic fluffy texture and rather sweet flavor. As with other vegetables, a recently harvested homegrown potato has no rival. The entire recipe may be formed into one very large round loaf and baked on a stone to produce a magnificent bread.

Yield: Two 9-by-5-inch loaves,
     1 large round loaf,
     or 2 dozen rolls

1 large potato
2 packages (2 tablespoons) active dry yeast
2 tablespoons sugar
1 cup cold buttermilk
2 tablespoons unsalted butter
1 tablespoon salt
6 to 7 cups unbleached all-purpose
     or bread flour
Flour for dusting, or Rich Egg Glaze, page 115,
     and poppy seeds for sprinkling

1. Peel potato and cut into large pieces. Place in a saucepan, cover with water, bring to a boil, and cook until soft. Drain and reserve liquid, adding water as necessary to make 1 cup. Mash potato and set aside.
2. Warm or cool potato water to 105° to 115°. Sprinkle yeast and a pinch of sugar over potato water in a small bowl. Stir to combine and let stand until foamy, about 10 minutes.
3. Warm buttermilk and butter until butter melts. Stir in salt, remaining sugar, and mashed potato. If potatoes are lumpy, beat until smooth, otherwise there will be lumps in the bread. Add yeast mixture.
4. Add yeast and potato mixture to 2 cups flour. Whisk hard for 3 minutes, or until smooth. Add flour ½ cup at a time with a wooden spoon until a soft dough is formed.
5. Turn out onto a lightly floured surface and knead about 10 minutes. Add more flour, 1 tablespoon at a time, as needed to produce a smooth, springy dough. Do not let dough get too dry by adding too much flour. Place in a greased bowl and turn once to grease top. Cover and let rise in warm place until doubled in volume, about 1 hour. Do not worry if it takes up to 2 hours.
6. Gently punch dough down to deflate and turn out onto a lightly floured surface. Divide into 2 equal portions and form into loaves. Place seam down in 2 greased 9-by-5-inch loaf pans. Cover loosely with plastic wrap and let rise about 30 minutes. Dust with flour or top with Rich Egg Glaze and poppy seeds.
7. Bake in a preheated 375° oven for 45 minutes or until loaves are deep brown and have a crisp crust. Remove from pans to cool on racks.

Potato Rolls
After deflating risen dough, pat dough into a rectangle ¾ to 1 inch thick on a lightly floured surface. Dust top of dough lightly with flour. Cut with a sharp knife into pieces about 2 inches square. Place 1 inch apart on a greased or parchment-lined baking sheet. Cover loosely with plastic wrap and let rise in a warm, draft-free place for 20 minutes. The rolls will be puffy. Bake in a preheated 375° oven for 25 to 30 minutes, or until brown.

HERB AND CHEESE BREAD

*B*ecause of its earthy nature, Herb and Cheese Bread is a good loaf to place whole on the table so that pieces can be torn off as the appetite dictates. Revel in the crumbs, the wayward bits of crusty cheese, and the combination of savory herbs.

Yield: Four 10-inch-long, thick free-form loaves

1 recipe French Bread dough, page 30
1 tablespoon each dried basil and chervil leaves
2 teaspoons each dried tarragon, savory, and thyme leaves
1½ teaspoons fresh-ground black pepper
⅓ cup fruity olive oil
1½ cups grated medium or sharp Cheddar cheese
Cornmeal for sprinkling

1. Prepare French Bread dough. While it is rising, combine herbs and pepper with olive oil. Let sit at room temperature 1 hour.
2. Gently deflate dough, turn out onto a lightly floured surface, and divide into 4 equal portions. Roll or pat out 1 section into an 8-by-12-inch rectangle. Using a spatula, spread with one-fourth of herbs and oil. Sprinkle with one-fourth of cheese, leaving a 1-inch margin all around dough. Roll up jelly-roll fashion from the long edge. Pinch seams and ends. Place on a greased or parchment-lined baking sheet sprinkled with cornmeal. Repeat with other 3 sections of dough to fill and form loaves.
3. Let rise, loosely covered with plastic wrap, about 25 minutes, or until doubled. Slash top with a serrated knife or snip at a 45-degree angle with kitchen shears about ¼ inch deep in a few places.
4. Bake in a preheated 400° oven for 35 to 40 minutes, or until crusty and brown. Enjoy hot from oven.

WHOLE-WHEAT BASIL BREAD

*T*he air around a garden patch of basil is very sweet indeed. It is a strongly aromatic herb, and in the foods it graces, no other herb will do. In this wonderful bread, only fresh basil will give the proper pungent flavor, which is paired with a natural mate, the extravagant pine nut. Serve with any food using fresh or cooked tomato to form a natural trinity.

Yield: Two 9-by-5-inch loaves

1 package (1 tablespoon) active dry yeast
Pinch sugar
½ cup warm water (105° to 115°)
1 cup warm buttermilk (105° to 115°)
1 cup warm water (105° to 115°)
¼ cup honey
4 tablespoons unsalted butter, melted
5 to 5½ cups whole-wheat flour
½ cup minced fresh basil
½ cup pine nuts, chopped
2½ teaspoons salt

Oil Wash
1 tablespoon butter
1 tablespoon olive oil
1 garlic clove, crushed
Pinch of cayenne

Parmesan cheese for sprinkling, optional

1. Sprinkle yeast and sugar over warm water in a small bowl and stir until dissolved. Let stand until foamy, about 10 minutes.
2. Mix buttermilk and water in a medium bowl. Stir in honey and melted butter. Place 2 cups flour, basil, nuts, and salt in a large bowl. Add milk and yeast mixtures and whisk about 3 minutes, or until smooth. Add flour ½ cup at a time with a wooden spoon until a soft dough is formed.
3. Turn dough out onto a lightly floured surface and knead until soft, slightly sticky, and very pliable, about 5 minutes, adding flour 1 tablespoon at a time as needed. Keep dough a bit on the soft side, as bread will be lighter this way.
4. Place dough in a greased bowl, turn once to grease top, cover with plastic wrap, and let rise in a warm place until doubled, about 1 to 1½ hours. Don't let this dough rise more than double in volume. Gently deflate dough and let rise again, if you have time. It will take half the time to rise the second time.
5. Gently deflate dough, turn out onto a lightly floured surface, and divide into 2 sections. Form into loaves and place in two 9-by-5-inch greased pans. Cover loosely with plastic wrap and let rise again until doubled, about 30 minutes.
6. Prepare oil wash: in a small pan, melt butter and olive oil. Add garlic and cayenne. Brush loaves with oil wash and sprinkle with a bit of Parmesan cheese, if desired.
7. Bake in a preheated 350° oven for 50 to 60 minutes, or until loaves are brown. Remove from pans to cool on a rack.

OLIVE BAGUETTES

I like my breads simple—to complement my meal and let my palate clearly taste all the elements. And I love to muse on the civilizations that have depended on the olive for culinary, cosmetic, and medicinal uses. The fact that olive trees have a life span of three hundred to six hundred years is enough to make me reach for another large wedge of olive baguette. Eat this loaf directly out of the oven with pasta salad, fresh ripe tomatoes, and a wedge of Gorgonzola cheese. This recipe uses the rapid-mix method (see page 20).

Yield: Two 8-to-10-inch-long loaves

1 package (1 tablespoon) active dry yeast
2 tablespoons olive oil
2 teaspoons salt
3 to 3½ cups unbleached all-purpose
  or bread flour
1½ cups hot water (120°)

Olive Filling
2 large garlic cloves, minced
2 tablespoons minced shallot
2 cups black olives, chopped
Grated zest of ½ lemon
2 tablespoons olive oil

Cornmeal for sprinkling

1. Place yeast, oil, salt, and 1 cup flour in a large bowl. Stir and add the hot water with a whisk. Beat well for about 3 minutes, or until smooth.
2. Add flour about ½ cup at a time with a wooden spoon.

3. Turn out onto a lightly floured surface. Knead for about 5 minutes, or until dough is springy, smooth, and resilient to the touch, adding flour 1 tablespoon at a time as needed. Place in a greased bowl, turn once to grease top, and cover with plastic wrap. Let rise in a warm place until tripled, about 1 hour.
4. Meanwhile, combine ingredients for filling and set aside to let flavors meld while dough is rising.
5. Gently deflate dough, turn out onto a lightly floured surface, and divide into 2 sections. Roll or pat each section into a large rectangle. Spread each with one-half of the filling and roll up jelly-roll fashion from the long edge. Pinch seams and sides. Place on a greased or parchment-lined baking sheet sprinkled with cornmeal.
6. Let rise, covered loosely with plastic wrap, until doubled, about 25 minutes. Slash tops with a serrated knife in 3 places.
7. Bake in a preheated 400° oven for 25 to 35 minutes or until brown.

FRESH-HERB BREAD

T his herb bread is so subtle and delicious, it can't really be described. It is a good, simple loaf wrought with the fresh herbs you have available and the inspiration of the moment. Pick, rinse, pat dry, and toss in. I always include a good measure of parsley for freshness in color and taste. The lemon is the magic accent ingredient.

Yield: Two 9-by-5-inch loaves,
  2 medium rounds,
  or 4 to 6 small loaves

1 package (1 tablespoon) active dry yeast
2 tablespoons brown sugar
¼ cup warm water (105° to 115°)
5½ to 6 cups unbleached all-purpose
  or bread flour
1 tablespoon salt
½ cup chopped walnuts or hazelnuts
Grated zest of 1 lemon
2 cups warm water (105° to 115°)
3 tablespoons walnut oil or melted butter
1 cup chopped fresh herbs (any combination of
  parsley, chervil, oregano, dill, chives, mint,
  caraway, thyme, lovage, marjoram)

1. Sprinkle yeast and a pinch of brown sugar over warm water in a small bowl. Stir to dissolve and let stand until foamy, about 10 minutes.
2. Combine 1 cup flour, remaining brown sugar, salt, nuts, and zest in a large bowl. Add 2 cups warm water, yeast, and oil with a whisk. Beat hard for 2 minutes, or until smooth. Add herbs and remaining flour ½ cup at a time, stirring with a wooden spoon until dough becomes stiff.
3. Turn out onto a lightly floured surface and knead until smooth, about 5 minutes, adding flour 1 tablespoon at a time as needed. Place in a greased bowl, turn once to grease top, and cover with plastic wrap. Let rise until doubled, about 1 to 1½ hours, in a warm place.
4. Gently deflate dough and turn out onto a lightly floured surface to divide into desired loaves. Shape and place in 2 greased 9-by-5-inch pans or on a greased or parchment-lined baking sheet, seam down. Cover loosely with plastic wrap and let rise for about 40 minutes, or until doubled.
5. Bake in a preheated 375° oven for 40 to 45 minutes, or until nicely brown and fragrance is filling kitchen. Cool on racks before slicing and eating with Homemade Butter, page 118.

RED PEPPER–SEMOLINA BREAD

Semolina flour is milled from durum wheat, a high-protein wheat used in pasta making. Available in Italian groceries and natural foods stores, this golden flour makes a crisp, flavorful country bread. Semolina comes in various grinds, some quite coarse, like farina. Be certain you use fine-ground semolina flour in this bread. Sometimes I substitute capers for the roasted peppers to totally change this bread's character. Both versions are very good to serve with cheese, wine, and tomato sauces.

Yield: 2 large round spiral or serpentine-shaped loaves

Sponge
1 package (1 tablespoon) active dry yeast
2 cups warm water (105° to 115°)
2 cups semolina flour

Dough
2 large red bell peppers
Sponge, above
3 1/2 to 4 cups unbleached all-purpose or bread flour
1/4 cup olive oil
1 tablespoon salt

Rich Egg Glaze, page 115
Raw sesame seeds
Cornmeal for sprinkling

1. To make sponge, combine yeast, water, and semolina flour in a large bowl. Beat hard with a whisk until creamy. Cover loosely with plastic wrap and let sponge rise 1 hour at room temperature.

2. Roast peppers under a broiler or over an open flame until completely charred. Wrap the peppers in a paper towel and place in a closed plastic bag until cool. Rub the charred skin off peppers with towel. Core and seed peppers. Dice and set aside.

3. Stir sponge and whisk in 1 cup unbleached flour, oil, salt, and red peppers. Add remaining flour 1/2 cup at a time with a wooden spoon until a soft, shaggy dough is formed.

4. Turn dough out onto a lightly floured surface and knead to form a soft, silky dough, adding more flour, 1 tablespoon at a time, as needed to make a dough that can just hold its own shape. Place dough in a greased bowl, turning once to coat top. Cover with plastic wrap and let rise in a warm place until tripled, about 2 hours.

5. Gently deflate dough, turn out onto a lightly floured surface, and form into 2 tight round spiral or serpentine-shaped loaves. To form the traditional serpentine, roll each piece of dough into a log about 2 feet long. Roll with your palms in an outward motion to elongate and press out air bubbles. Form dough coils from opposite ends, meeting in center to make an inverted S. Brush tops with Rich Egg Glaze and roll in sesame seeds. Place on a baker's paddle or baking sheet sprinkled with cornmeal. Cover loosely with plastic wrap and let rise until doubled, about 30 minutes. Preheat a baking stone in a 450° oven for 30 minutes, if desired.

6. Give the loaves a slash with one swift motion of a serrated knife. Slide onto hot stone, if used, with a quick motion of the wrist.

7. Place in a preheated 450° oven, reduce heat to 375°, and bake for 35 to 40 minutes, or until bread is lightly domed, brown, and crusty. Cool on a rack before eating.

TOMATO-SAFFRON BREAD

Saffron is an herb of the sun, warm and golden. Any food graced by even just a few grains of the most expensive, aromatic spice in the world has its characteristic bright color and pungent aroma. It is an exquisite, subtle addition to bread. Tomato-Saffron Bread complements seafood salads and Mediterranean-style fish stews. It also makes excellent grilled cheese sandwiches or cucumber and watercress tea sandwiches.

Yield: Two 9-by-5-inch braids

1 package (1 tablespoon) active dry yeast
1/2 cup warm water (105° to 115°)
1/8 teaspoon saffron threads or powdered saffron
1 1/2 cups fresh tomato juice, see recipe following (or substitute canned tomato juice)
2 tablespoons tomato paste
3 tablespoons honey
3 tablespoons olive oil or unsalted butter
5 1/2 to 6 cups unbleached all-purpose or bread flour
2 1/2 teaspoons salt
Egg Glaze, page 115
2 tablespoons poppy seeds

1. Sprinkle yeast over 1/4 cup warm water in a small bowl. Stir until dissolved and let stand until foamy, about 10 minutes. Steep saffron in remaining 1/4 cup warm water for 5 minutes.

2. Warm tomato juice in a saucepan and add tomato paste, honey, and oil.

3. In a large bowl, combine 2 cups flour and salt. Add yeast mixture, saffron mixture, and tomato juice mixture and beat with a whisk for about 3 minutes, or until smooth. Add flour ½ cup at a time, using a wooden spoon, until mixture forms a thick, shaggy mass clearing sides of bowl.

4. Knead on a lightly floured surface, adding flour 1 tablespoon at a time as necessary until a smooth, springy dough is formed. Place in a greased bowl, turn once to grease top, and cover with plastic wrap. Let rise in a warm place until doubled, about 1½ hours.

5. Gently deflate dough, turn out onto a lightly floured surface, and divide into 4 equal portions. With your palms, roll each section into a 12-inch log. Twist 2 sections of dough around each other to form a 2-strand braid. Repeat for remaining portions. Place in 2 greased 9-by-5-inch pans. Brush with egg glaze and sprinkle with poppy seeds. Cover loosely with plastic wrap and let dough rise until it reaches tops of pans, about 45 minutes.

6. Bake in a preheated 375° oven for 35 to 40 minutes, or until bottoms are light brown. Remove from pans to cool on racks.

Fresh Tomato Juice

Use very ripe tomatoes. Remove blemishes and cut into chunks. For 1½ cups juice, you will need 3 cups tomatoes. Place in a nonaluminum saucepan, bring to a boil, and simmer about 20 minutes, or until soft and juicy. Put through a food mill or sieve to remove seeds and skin. Let stand and ladle off water that separates on top. Add salt, sugar, or lemon juice to taste.

SEEDED DILL RYE

*T*he umbrella-shaped dill plant is known for the characteristic strong, aromatic flavor it adds to pickled cucumbers and potato salad. Dill is also known as one of the best digestive herbs. It adds an exciting, warm quality to this savory rye bread. I always bake this bread in standard loaves, as it is one of the greatest sandwich breads from the home baker.

Yield: Two 9-by-5-inch loaves

1½ packages (1½ tablespoons) active dry yeast
3 tablespoons brown sugar
2 cups warm water (105° to 115°)
1½ cups rye flour
½ cup instant nonfat dried milk
1 tablespoon dill weed
1 tablespoon dill seed
1 teaspoon caraway seed
2½ teaspoons salt
3 tablespoons unsalted butter, melted
3½ to 4 cups unbleached all-purpose
* or bread flour*
Rich Egg Glaze, page 115 (optional)

1. Sprinkle yeast and a pinch of brown sugar over ½ cup warm water in a small bowl. Stir to dissolve and let stand until foamy, about 10 minutes.

2. Combine rye flour, dried milk, remaining brown sugar, dill weed, seeds, and salt in a large bowl. Add remaining water, butter, and yeast mixture. Whisk hard until smooth, about 3 minutes. Add flour ½ cup at a time with a wooden spoon until a shaggy dough is formed.

3. Turn out onto a lightly floured surface and knead until smooth and silky, about 5 minutes, adding flour a tablespoon at a time as needed. Place in a greased bowl, turn once to grease top, and cover with

plastic wrap. Let rise in a warm place until doubled, about 1 to 1½ hours.

4. Gently deflate dough, turn out onto a lightly floured surface, and divide into 2 equal portions. Shape into loaves and place in 2 greased 9-by-5-inch pans, seam down. Cover loosely with plastic wrap and let rise to 1 inch above rim of pan, about 40 minutes. Brush with Rich Egg Glaze, if desired, for a dark and glossy crust.

5. Bake in a preheated 375° oven for 40 to 45 minutes, or until golden brown. Remove from pans and cool on a rack before slicing.

TAOS PUMPKIN BREAD

*I*n America, pumpkin is usually associated with jack o'lanterns, pies, and desserts. But in Latin America, Africa, and Central Europe, pumpkin is eaten as a vegetable. It can be used interchangeably in other winter squash and sweet potato recipes. The best pumpkin for cooking is a sugar pumpkin, usually about 2 to 6 pounds, which is smaller than the large field pumpkins used for carving at Halloween. Look for a vivid orange color, firm skin, and no soft spots. You can store them in a cool area for a few months, if they're not used immediately. Pumpkin must always be cooked before eating. This earthy, sienna-colored Southwestern bread is baked in an outdoor adobe beehive oven called a *horno*, and is likely to appear for harvest celebrations. Serve with Pine Nut Butter, page 119, baked pinto beans, and large grilled green chilies stuffed with cheese. This bread is also good cut into thick slices and grilled.

Yield: One 10-inch round loaf

1 package (1 tablespoon) active dry yeast
½ cup brown sugar
1½ cups warm water (105° to 115°)
2 eggs
1 cup pumpkin puree, canned or homemade
  (see recipe, following)
1 tablespoon salt
½ cup cornmeal
5½ to 6 cups unbleached all-purpose
  or bread flour
Cornmeal and flour for sprinkling

1. Sprinkle yeast and a pinch of brown sugar over water in a large bowl. Stir to combine and let stand until foamy, about 10 minutes.
2. With a whisk, add eggs and pumpkin to yeast mixture. Add remaining brown sugar, salt, cornmeal, and 2 cups flour. Beat hard with a whisk until smooth, about 3 minutes. Add flour ½ cup at a time with a wooden spoon until a soft dough is formed.
3. Turn out onto a lightly floured surface and knead vigorously for about 5 minutes to create a soft, smooth, and elastic dough. Add enough remaining flour for dough to hold its own shape. Place in a greased bowl, turn once to grease top, and cover with plastic wrap. Let rise at room temperature until doubled, 1 to 1½ hours.
4. Gently deflate dough and turn out onto a lightly floured surface. Form into 1 large country loaf and place on a greased or parchment-lined baking sheet sprinkled with cornmeal and flour. Cover loaves loosely with plastic wrap and let rise 30 minutes, or until doubled. Meanwhile, heat a baking stone in a 450° oven for 30 minutes, if desired. Sprinkle tops of loaves with flour.

5. Slash loaves decoratively with a serrated knife. Slide loaves with parchment onto stone, if used (parchment is easily removed later). Place in a preheated 450° oven, reduce oven temperature to 375°, and bake 45 to 55 minutes, or until loaves are lightly browned. Remove parchment and cool on racks before serving.

Pumpkin Puree

Wash pumpkin and cut off top. Scoop out and discard seeds. Cut in half, then into large cubes, leaving skin intact. Place in a covered baking dish, flesh down, with a little water. Bake at 350° for 1½ hours, or until tender. Drain, cool, then peel off and discard skin. Puree pulp until smooth in a blender or food processor.

CARROT AND POPPY SEED BREAD

A native of Afghanistan, the carrot plant's sweet, edible root comes in a variety of shapes: long and thin, short and thin, globular like a beet, or very stubby with a rounded end. Most American carrots are predictably orange, but varieties range from white to purple. Carrots blend nicely in a bread dough, giving color and sweetness. The poppy seeds, apricot, and hint of citrus here add elegance.

Yield: 3 medium round loaves

1½ packages (1½ tablespoons) active dry yeast
Pinch sugar
½ cup warm water (105° to 115°)
2 cups shredded raw carrots
¼ cup minced dried apricots
2 tablespoons poppy seeds

2 tablespoons sugar
Grated zest of 1 orange or tangerine
2½ teaspoons salt
1½ cups whole-wheat flour
About 4 cups unbleached all-purpose
  or bread flour
1½ cups buttermilk
⅓ cup unsalted butter, melted, or walnut oil

1. Sprinkle yeast and sugar over warm water in a small bowl. Stir to dissolve and let stand until foamy, about 10 minutes.
2. In a large bowl, combine carrots, apricots, seeds, sugar, zest, salt, whole-wheat flour, and ½ cup unbleached flour.
3. In a medium bowl, combine yeast mixture, buttermilk, and butter. Pour into center of dry ingredients and stir briskly with a whisk until combined, about 3 minutes. Add all-purpose flour ½ cup at a time with a wooden spoon until a shaggy dough is formed.
4. Turn out onto a lightly floured surface. Knead, incorporating flour 1 tablespoon at a time as necessary to produce a soft springy dough, about 7 minutes. This dough is a bit bulky and should stay a little on the sticky side. You can knead in more flour after first rising if dough is too soft to support its own shape when formed into loaves. Place in a greased bowl, turn once to coat top, and cover with plastic wrap. Let rise in a warm place until doubled in volume, about 1½ to 2 hours.
5. Gently deflate dough, turn out onto a lightly floured surface, divide into 3 sections, and form into round loaves. Place on a greased or parchment-lined baking sheet. Cover loosely with plastic wrap and let rise about 45 minutes, or until not quite doubled.
6. Bake in a preheated 375° oven for 40 minutes, or until brown. Cool on racks before serving.

ITALIAN-STYLE HERB BREAD

*M*ozzarella is a fresh cow's-milk cheese made with very little rennet, the animal or vegetable enzyme that curdles milk. It is a soft, malleable cheese with a mild, tangy flavor, used widely in cooking because it melts so beautifully. Always use whole-milk rather than skim-milk mozzarella, if possible, for better flavor and texture.

This spicy-sausage-and-cheese-stuffed bread is the epitome of beautiful picnic fare. Serve with a cold pasta salad, fresh fruit, and red wine under the trees.

Yield: 1 large rectangular loaf; serves about 6

1½ teaspoons fresh-ground pepper
2 teaspoons each dried basil, thyme, savory, and chervil
⅓ cup olive oil
1½ packages (1½ tablespoons) active dry yeast
Pinch sugar
1 cup warm water (105° to 115°)
1 cup dry white wine
1 tablespoon sugar
1 tablespoon salt
About 5½ cups unbleached all-purpose or bread flour
1½ pounds sweet Italian sausages, removed from casing and crumbled
1 large yellow onion, chopped
2 garlic cloves, minced
¼ cup chopped oil-packed sun-dried tomatoes
1 tablespoon anise liqueur
8 ounces whole-milk mozzarella, diced
Olive oil for brushing (optional)

1. Combine pepper and herbs in a small bowl with olive oil and let stand at least 1 hour at room temperature.
2. Sprinkle yeast and sugar over warm water in a small bowl. Stir to dissolve and let stand until foamy, about 10 minutes. Combine wine, yeast mixture, sugar, salt, and herb-oil mixture and beat with a whisk until foamy. Add flour 1 cup at a time, stirring with a wooden spoon, to make a soft dough.
3. Knead on a lightly floured surface until dough is springy, smooth, and resilient, about 5 minutes, adding flour 1 tablespoon at a time as needed. Place in a greased bowl, turn once to grease top, and cover with plastic wrap. Let rise in a warm place until doubled, about 1 hour.
4. While dough is rising, combine sausages, onion, and garlic in a large skillet and cook over medium heat until sausage is browned and onions are soft. Stir in tomatoes and liqueur. Let cool to room temperature.
5. Gently deflate dough, turn out onto a lightly floured board, and pat into a 14-by-10-inch rectangle. Spread sausage evenly over center third of dough. Sprinkle with cheese. Fold into a rectangle by bringing the 2 long ends together and pinch to close. Fold each short end over about 1 inch and pinch to close. Lay seam side down on a greased or parchment-lined baking sheet. Snip or slash with a knife 1 inch deep at an angle. Brush with olive oil, if desired. Let rest 10 minutes, then bake in a preheated 400° oven for 40 to 50 minutes, or until brown. This also bakes nicely on a baking stone. Cool completely on a rack before slicing.

SPINACH BRIOCHE

*E*xcellent for a picnic. Savor Spinach Brioche with fruit and a mildly chilled chardonnay. The individual breads are easy to wrap and serve. Serve with Tomato Mustard, page 122.

Yield: Twelve 3½-inch *brioches*

¼ cup minced shallots
2 tablespoons unsalted butter
2½ cups cleaned, chopped, and loosely packed fresh spinach
1 cup grated Muenster cheese
¼ cup coarse-ground pine nuts
Salt and pepper to taste
1 recipe Brioche dough, page 36, risen overnight in refrigerator
Rich Egg Glaze, page 115

1. In a large sauté pan or skillet, sauté shallots in butter until soft and golden, about 5 minutes. Add spinach and toss until just wilted. Cool. Add cheese, nuts, and seasoning.
2. Divide cold dough into 12 equal portions. Divide each portion into 1 small and 1 large portion. Press the larger half into a well-greased 3½-inch fluted *brioche* tin or standard-size muffin tin. Extend dough ½ inch over edge. Fill with 3 to 4 tablespoons filling.
3. Pat small half into a 3-inch circle and place it over the filling, bringing up edges of bottom layer and pinching to seal and enclose filling completely. Shape and fill remaining portions of dough.
4. Cover loosely with plastic wrap and let rise at a cool room temperature 1½ to 2 hours, or until risen a bit above edge of tin. Brush with Rich Egg Glaze and bake in a preheated 375° oven for 20 to 25 minutes, or until brown. Remove from tins, cool slightly on a rack, and serve warm.

PUMPERNICKEL-CURRANT BREAD WRAPPED AROUND BRIE

*C*heck the size of your oven before making this bread. It needs a 2-inch clearance all the way around. Bread wrapped around Brie is a truly wonderful appetizer—beautiful and delicious. Serve it with apples and fresh nuts. The frosted grape garnish appears extravagant, but it takes very little preparation and can be done the day ahead.

Yield: 1 braid wrapped around a
2-pound cheese; serves about
20 as hors d'oeuvres

2 packages (2 tablespoons) active dry yeast
1 teaspoon sugar
2 cups warm water (105° to 115°)
4 tablespoons unsalted butter, melted
¼ cup molasses
2 cups rye flour
¼ cup unsweetened cocoa
1 tablespoon salt
1 tablespoon caraway seed
1 cup currants, soaked in hot water and drained
3½ to 4 cups unbleached all-purpose
* or bread flour*
½ cup white cornmeal for sprinkling
One 2-pound wheel Brie cheese
* (8 inches in diameter)*
Frosted Grapes, page 116

1. Sprinkle yeast and sugar over ¼ cup warm water in a small bowl. Stir to dissolve and let stand until foamy, about 10 minutes.

2. Combine remaining water, butter, molasses, and yeast mixture. Add rye flour, cocoa, salt, seed, and currants. Whisk for about 3 minutes, or until smooth.

3. Add unbleached flour ½ cup at a time with a wooden spoon until dough is stiff. The dough needs to be quite firm to hold its braid nicely. Knead on a lightly floured surface until smooth, about 5 minutes, adding flour 1 tablespoon at a time as needed. Place in a greased bowl, turn once to grease top, cover with plastic wrap, and let rise in a warm place until doubled, about 1 hour.

4. Gently deflate dough, turn out onto a lightly floured surface, and divide into 3 equal portions. Roll each out with your palms to a rope about 24 inches long. Starting in the center, braid loosely to each end. Place on a greased or parchment-lined baking sheet dusted with cornmeal and wrap around a greased 8-inch cake tin. Join ends, stretching if necessary, and pinch to seal. Cover loosely with plastic wrap and let rise for 25 minutes only, until just puffy.

5. Bake in a preheated 350° oven for 25 to 35 minutes, or until a cake tester comes out clean and bottom is brown. Use a knife to loosen braid from cake pan. Lift off baking sheet and cool on a rack, being careful not to crack loaf. It will stay fresh, wrapped well, for 1 day, and up to 1 month if frozen.

6. To serve, place bread on a large board or in a shallow basket lined with fig leaves. Cut a small section of braid into slices. Set cheese in center, spreading braided wreath a bit if necessary to fit cheese in place. Garnish with frosted grapes. Cut the Brie in long thin triangular wedges from center.

CHAMPIGNON BRIOCHE

*T*his is a mushroom-stuffed *brioche* loaf with an elegant name and an elegant taste.

Yield: One 12-inch *couronne*

1 recipe Brioche dough, page 36,
* chilled overnight*

Mushroom Ragout
6 tablespoons unsalted butter
¼ cup minced shallots
1½ pounds cultivated or wild mushrooms,
* coarsely chopped*
⅓ cup chopped fresh parsley
1½ teaspoons chopped fresh tarragon,
* or ½ teaspoon dried tarragon*
Salt and fresh-grated black pepper to taste

Rich Egg Glaze, page 115

1. Prepare Mushroom Ragout: Melt butter in a large sauté pan or skillet over medium-high heat. Add shallots and mushrooms; sauté until soft and liquid is evaporated. Add parsley and tarragon and stir to combine. Season to taste. Refrigerate overnight or cool completely before filling *brioche*.

2. Divide chilled dough into 2 equal portions. Refrigerate unused portion while working. On a lightly floured surface, roll dough into a 10-by-18-inch rectangle with a rolling pin.

3. Spread one-half of Mushroom Ragout over surface of dough, leaving a 1-inch border all around. Roll up jelly-roll fashion from long end. Pinch seams to seal. Repeat with second portion of dough.

4. Place on a greased or parchment-lined baking sheet and twist rolls together. Form into a ring, bringing 2 ends

together, and pinch to seal. Cover loosely with plastic wrap and let rise at a cool room temperature until doubled, about 1 hour. Do not rise over a pilot light or in a warm area as for regular bread dough, as butter will separate, making *brioche* greasy. Make diagonal ½-inch-deep snips around the top in about 8 evenly spaced places.

5. Brush egg glaze all over top of bread. Bake on center rack of a preheated 375° oven for 45 to 55 minutes, or until bread is golden and a cake tester comes out clean. Transfer from baking sheet to a rack to cool. Serve slightly warm.

OLIVE OIL BREAD WITH ONIONS AND GORGONZOLA

*T*his little bread with Gorgonzola and onions is a wonderful picnic food: crisp on the outside and soft on the inside, with the smooth, sweet flavor of caramelized onions. I also like it topped with a thin layer of thick tomato sauce, Parmesan cheese, and bits of green onion. Serve wedges of Olive Oil Bread with a glass of good Italian Chianti.

Yield: 3 small round breads

Sponge
1 package (1 tablespoon) active dry yeast
Pinch sugar, honey, or malt extract
3 tablespoons instant nonfat dried milk
1 cup hot water (120°)
1 cup unbleached all-purpose or bread flour

Dough
2 tablespoons good olive oil
1 teaspoon salt
1½ to 2 cups unbleached all-purpose
  or bread flour
Sponge, above

Onion Confit
3 medium onions
4 tablespoons unsalted butter
¼ cup olive oil
1 tablespoon balsamic vinegar

Olive oil for brushing
6 ounces Gorgonzola cheese

1. To make sponge, sprinkle yeast, sugar, dried milk, and 1 cup flour over water in a large bowl and beat well with a whisk until smooth and creamy. Let rise at room temperature 30 minutes, loosely covered, until bubbly.
2. Meanwhile, prepare *confit*: Slice onions thin. Melt butter with oil in a large skillet and cook onions uncovered over low heat, stirring occasionally, until very soft, about 30 minutes. Add vinegar towards end of cooking. Onions will be caramelized. Allow them to cool.
3. To make dough, add oil, salt, and 1 cup flour to sponge. Whisk hard for about 3 minutes, or until smooth. Add flour ½ cup at a time with a wooden spoon until a soft, sticky dough is formed.
4. Turn dough out on a lightly floured surface and knead lightly to form a springy ball, adding 1 tablespoon flour at a time as needed to make a smooth, soft dough. Do not add too much flour or dough will become too hard and dry. Form into a flattened ball. Cover and let rest 30 minutes in a warm place.

5. Divide dough into 3 equal portions and roll out to a 1-inch-thick round. Place on a greased or parchment-lined baking sheet with 2 to 3 inches between each bread. Brush with olive oil. Cover loosely with plastic wrap and let rise until puffy and doubled, about 25 to 30 minutes. Gently top each portion with one-third of onion *confit* and sprinkle with crumbled Gorgonzola.
6. Bake in a preheated 400° oven for 25 to 30 minutes, or until crisp and brown. Transfer to a rack to cool; serve at room temperature.

Hi Karen!

ONION TART

Here is a relative of the quiche: an onion custard baked atop yeasted bread dough. In Alsace Lorraine, the onions would be sautéed in goose fat, in Italy olive oil, and in Germany fresh sweet butter. This is satisfying food, and it can be eaten hot, warm, or cold as the season dictates. It is a spectacular picnic dish. Serve with Black Forest ham, fresh walnuts, and white wine. Please note that the Tart Dough makes enough for 2 tarts or 1 large 11-by-17-inch rectangular baking pan.

Yield: One 12-inch onion tart;
enough dough for 2 tarts or 1 shallow 11-by-17-inch sheet

Tart Dough
1 package (1 tablespoon) active dry yeast
Pinch sugar
1 cup warm water (105° to 115°)
2¾ to 3 cups unbleached all-purpose or bread flour
1 tablespoon sugar
1½ teaspoons salt
2 tablespoons corn oil
1 egg, slightly beaten

Filling
4 large yellow onions, sliced thin
½ cup (1 stick) unsalted butter
1 cup sour cream or crème fraîche
3 eggs
Dash salt
1 teaspoon fresh-ground black pepper

1. Sprinkle yeast and sugar over ½ cup warm water in a small bowl; stir until dissolved. Let stand until foamy, about 10 minutes.
2. Place 1 cup flour in a large bowl. Add sugar and salt. Add remaining water, oil, egg, and yeast mixture. Beat hard with a whisk for 3 minutes. The dough will form a smooth batter. Add flour ½ cup at a time with a wooden spoon to form a shaggy dough.
3. Turn dough out onto a lightly floured surface and knead until smooth, resilient, and no longer sticky, about 5 minutes, adding flour 1 tablespoon at a time as needed. Shape into a ball and place in a greased bowl, turning once to grease top. Cover with plastic wrap and let rise in a warm place until tripled, about 1 to 1½ hours.
4. To make filling, in a sauté pan or skillet, sauté sliced onions in butter over low heat until golden and soft, about 20 minutes. Let cool to room temperature.
5. Just before shaping dough, combine sour cream, eggs, salt, and pepper in a bowl; add onions.
6. Gently deflate dough, turn out onto a lightly floured surface, and divide into 2 equal portions. Freeze 1 for later use. Roll out remaining portion to fit a greased springform pan or a tart tin with a removable bottom. Pat into bottom and up sides. Fold any extra dough down. Pour onion mixture over dough.
7. Bake immediately in a preheated 375° oven for 35 minutes, or until crispy and golden. The onion filling will be delicate brown and puffy. Let stand 10 minutes before removing pan sides to cool before cutting into wedges.

SAUSAGE EN BRIOCHE

Wrap your favorite sausage in an elegant cloak for a first course. For a light lunch, serve with a glass of wine and a crisp salad dressed with a balsamic vinaigrette.

Yield: 2 free-form loaves;
serves 10 as a first course, 6 for lunch

1 recipe Brioche dough, page 36, chilled overnight
Rich Egg Glaze, page 115
2 cooked mild or spicy Italian or garlic sausages, weighing just under a pound each
Unbleached flour for sprinkling
Homemade mustards, page 122

1. Divide chilled dough into 2 equal portions. Refrigerate 1 portion and roll other on a lightly floured surface into a rectangle about 8 by 12 inches. Brush entire dough surface with Rich Egg Glaze. Place 1 sausage in center of dough. Lightly sprinkle with flour. Wrap dough tightly around sausage and pinch edges to seal. Repeat with second portion of dough.
2. Place loaves seam down on a greased or parchment-lined baking sheet. Brush with glaze. Cut 3 small holes in top of each loaf and decorate top with dough forms if desired, fastening with glaze. Let stand 15 minutes, then bake in a preheated 350° oven for 25 to 35 minutes. Let rest 15 minutes before slicing and serving with homemade mustards.

WILD-MUSHROOM CROUSTADE

*T*he morel mushroom has a loyal following of American culinary enthusiasts. Commonly known as the "sponge mushroom" for its honeycomb appearance, it is the easiest wild mushroom for hunters to identify. The stem and cap are hollow. It has a buttery eggplant-like texture and a taste that is rich and appealing beyond belief. To make this sandwich, quarter some morels, but leave small ones whole to enjoy their elongated shape and the meshy texture of the caps. This recipe calls for fresh mushrooms. Choose fresh morels that are dry and have a fresh, earthy smell. Use them within 3 days, and wash them right before cooking. Dried mushrooms, differing quite dramatically in taste and texture, simply won't do. This is another bread that is wonderful for a picnic. Serve it hot or at room temperature, cut into wedges, with a salad of fresh garden greens and white corn on the cob.

Yield: 4 to 6 servings

1 pound fresh morels, wiped with a damp cloth
1 medium onion, chopped
2 medium shallots, chopped
2 garlic cloves, minced
½ cup (1 stick) unsalted butter
¼ cup olive oil
1 pound large domestic mushrooms, quartered
2 sprigs fresh thyme, chopped,
*   or ½ teaspoon dried thyme*
½ cup chopped fresh parsley
½ cup dry white wine
¼ cup Madeira
Salt and fresh-ground black pepper
4 slices smoked bacon
1 large round French bread, page 30
Bacon drippings or olive oil

1. Quarter some of the morels, leaving most of the smaller ones whole. In a sauté pan or skillet, sauté onion, shallots, and garlic in butter and oil until soft. Add all mushrooms and thyme and cook over medium heat about 5 minutes, or until juices are exuded. Add parsley and wines and cook until liquid is reduced by half and mushrooms are cooked. Season with salt and fresh-ground pepper.

2. Lay bacon slices on a foil-lined sheet. Bake for 10 minutes in a preheated 375° oven, or until bacon is just soft. Drain on paper towels.

3. Slice off top of loaf and remove soft insides with a fork, leaving a 2-inch border of bread all around.

4. Fill loaf with mushroom mixture and cover top with bacon strips. Replace top of loaf and brush outside with a bit of bacon drippings or olive oil. Place a sheet of aluminum foil loosely over top of bread.

5. Bake in a preheated 375° oven for about 20 minutes, or until hot and crusty.

A**NY GOOD YEAST BREAD RECIPE** can be divided into smaller pieces of dough to create little breads. Displaying little breads on your table or using them to complement an array of finger foods creates an impression of abundance and is the most efficient way to serve bread to a large crowd. People delight in handling and eating an individual loaf, be it a few bites or an oversized bun designed to wrap a hamburger. The family of little breads is large: hard and soft rolls, *blini* and flat breads, yeasted pancakes and biscuits, *pita* and bagels, *calzone* and bread sticks. (There is a whole other genre of yeasted sweet little breads, the capstone of the baker's art: croissants, miniature *brioches*, cinnamon rolls, and a universe full of glazed, glossed, and embellished little sweet things—see pages 89 to 95.)

Certainly food should be loved for its taste above its aesthetic appeal, but who can resist such wonderful shapes as fantans, clover leaves, butterflies, long johns, crescents, cushions, and pinwheels? Creating imaginative little breads is an art in which formulas and tradition can be rejected or renewed, as you desire. Bakers may be austere or baroque, lovers of the crusty and dense or the soft and fluffy. No apologies are necessary if a traditionalist should scoff at your personal baking touch.

A standard loaf of bread made with 2½ to 3 cups of flour will produce 12 small dinner rolls or 6 sandwich buns. Sections of dough may be weighed out as in professional kitchens; otherwise expect your rolls to vary slightly in size and shape. Take care not to overwork the little bits of dough while shaping, to avoid a tough texture. A recipe specifically for rolls will usually leave the dough a bit softer than a regular loaf, or add eggs to lighten the texture.

After forming, give the rolls a full final rise for the best baked shapes. As with all yeast breads, cover doughs while rising to prevent the forming of a crust. For pan rolls, place in a greased round or rectangular baking dish with sides touching to create a soft-sided roll, such as Yogurt–Poppy Seed Rolls. Muffin tins also work nicely, giving a small domed shape. Otherwise, little breads need lots of space in which to bake. Place on heavy aluminum baking sheets about 1 to 2 inches apart to allow for expansion during rising and baking. Parchment paper is great, as there is no need to grease sheets or wash pans later. Do not substitute waxed paper, as it is flammable, or aluminum foil, which inhibits heat and prevents bottoms from browning evenly.

Check the recipe yield against your oven dimensions, as the rolls may need to be baked in shifts. As one sheet of rolls is baking, place the other sheet in the refrigerator to slow rising before placing in the oven. The rising and baking times are proportionately smaller for little breads in relation to larger loaves. Little breads usually bake in about 15 to 25 minutes. Oven temperature remains constant with the original recipe instructions when adjusted from a standard recipe.

WATER ROLLS

*T*his recipe produces a round roll that is crusty just out of the oven; as it cools it softens and is suitable for sandwiches. A liberal dusting of rice flour gives the rolls a finished look. Use sifted unbleached flour if you can't find rice flour, but it's worth searching out.

Yield: About 1 dozen sandwich buns
(for dinner rolls, divide into
24 equal pieces)

1 package (1 tablespoon) active dry yeast
Pinch sugar
1³⁄₄ cups warm water (105° to 115°)
2 tablespoons vegetable oil
2 teaspoons salt
2 egg whites, lightly beaten
About 5 cups unbleached all-purpose
  or bread flour
¹⁄₃ cup rice flour for dusting

1. Stir yeast and sugar into ¼ cup warm water in a large bowl. Stir to dissolve and let stand 10 minutes, or until foamy.
2. Combine remaining water, oil, salt, and egg whites into yeast mixture with a whisk. Stir in flour 1 cup at a time with a wooden spoon to make a soft dough.
3. Turn dough out onto a lightly floured surface and knead, adding flour 1 tablespoon at a time as necessary, until smooth and elastic, about 5 minutes. Place in a greased bowl, turn once to grease top, cover with plastic wrap, and let rise in a warm place until doubled, about 1 hour.

4. Gently deflate dough and turn out onto a lightly floured surface. For sandwich buns, divide dough into 12 equal pieces. Shape into balls, place about 1 to 2 inches apart on 2 greased or parchment-lined baking sheets, and flatten with the palms of your hand. Dust with rice flour. Cover loosely with plastic wrap and let rise until doubled, about 25 minutes. With the back of a knife, make a depression on top of each roll in the shape of a cross or a spoke pattern with 5 legs, pressing in no more than ½ inch. Let rest 15 minutes only.
5. Bake in a preheated 400° oven for 20 minutes, or until brown. Cool on a rack.

SESAME-WHEAT LONG ROLLS

*H*omemade soft, thick rolls are a very special treat. Whether used for blanketing hot meats at barbecue time or as a cold sandwich roll, there is nothing ordinary about them. For a young crowd, spread with Fresh Nut Butter (page 119) and raspberry jam. For a more sophisticated palate, serve with Herbed Ricotta (page 121) with sliced yellow or red plum tomatoes and layer of lettuce or *arugula*.

Yield: 16 rolls

1¹⁄₂ packages (1¹⁄₂ tablespoons) active dry yeast
2 tablespoons brown sugar
1¹⁄₂ cups warm water (105° to 115°)
³⁄₄ cup warm milk (105° to 115°)
4 tablespoons butter, melted
1 tablespoon salt
2 tablespoons raw sesame seeds
1¹⁄₂ cups whole-wheat flour
4 to 4¹⁄₂ cups unbleached all-purpose
  or bread flour
Rich Egg Glaze, page 115 (optional)

1. Sprinkle yeast and a pinch of brown sugar over water in a small bowl. Stir to combine and let stand until foamy, about 10 minutes.
2. Combine milk, butter, remaining brown sugar, salt, sesame seeds, and whole-wheat flour in a large bowl. Beat hard with a whisk until smooth, about 3 minutes. Add yeast mixture. Add unbleached flour ½ cup at a time, using a wooden spoon, until dough just clears sides of bowl. Turn out onto a lightly floured surface.
3. Knead for about 5 minutes, adding flour 1 tablespoon at a time as necessary to make a smooth, soft, slightly sticky dough. Place in a greased bowl and turn once to grease top. Cover with plastic wrap and let rise in a warm place until doubled, about 45 minutes to 1 hour.
4. Deflate dough gently and turn out onto a lightly floured surface. Divide into 16 equal pieces. Shape each piece into an oblong oval. Roll up from long end tightly and pinch seam, like a mini French loaf. Place 2 inches apart on 2 greased or parchment-lined baking sheets. Cover loosely with plastic wrap and let rest 30 minutes, or until puffy and almost doubled. Brush with Rich Egg Glaze, if desired.
5. Bake in a preheated 375° oven for 20 to 25 minutes, or until lightly browned. Remove to a wire rack to cool.

BLACK BREAD ROLLS

*B*lack breads are usually made with whole-grain flours such as rye, and darkened with coffee, cocoa, carob, molasses, toasted crumbs, or caramel. These rolls make a good sandwich, spread with Brie cheese, unsalted butter, Dijon mustard, and Black Forest ham. I like to add a few fresh leaves of *arugula* or watercress for a bit of crunch. Serve with *cornichons* on the side.

Yield: 12 round sandwich rolls

2 packages (2 tablespoons) active dry yeast
Pinch sugar
2¼ cups warm water (105° to 115°)
6 tablespoons unsalted butter, melted
3 tablespoons molasses
1 tablespoon instant coffee powder
1 tablespoon salt
1 tablespoon caraway seed
1 teaspoon fennel seed
⅓ cup bran
¼ cup unsweetened cocoa powder
2 cups rye flour
3 to 3½ cups unbleached all-purpose flour
Cornmeal for sprinkling (optional)

1. Dissolve yeast and sugar in ½ cup warm water in a small bowl and stir to dissolve. Let stand until foamy, about 10 minutes.
2. Place all remaining ingredients except white flour and cornmeal in a large bowl. Whisk until smooth and add yeast mixture. Beat for about 3 minutes.
3. Add flour ½ cup at a time and continue beating with a wooden spoon until too stiff to stir. Turn out onto a lightly floured surface and knead until smooth, elastic, and no longer sticky, about 5 minutes, adding flour 1 tablespoon at a time as needed.
4. Place in a greased bowl, turning once to grease top of dough. Cover with plastic wrap and set in a warm place to rise until doubled, about 1 to 1½ hours.
5. Gently deflate dough, turn out onto a lightly floured surface, and divide into 12 equal portions. Grease or line 2 baking sheets with parchment and sprinkle with cornmeal, if desired. Form each dough portion into a round ball and place on baking sheets seam side down. Flatten with your palm. Cover loosely with plastic wrap and let rise until doubled and puffy, about 25 minutes.
6. Bake in a preheated 375° oven on middle to lower rack for 40 minutes, or until slightly browned and firm to the touch. Place on a rack to cool before splitting.

PETITS PAINS D'OIGNONS

*T*he onion is a member of the sacred lily family; its many-layered skin symbolizes eternity. The Pharaohs of Egypt lined the banks of the Nile with onion plants. Religious significance aside, the onion has permeated our cuisine and complements every vegetable. These little onion rolls, made from a plain dough, are so good straight from the oven, it is rare for a batch to last even half a day.

Yield: 16 medium rolls

1 recipe French Bread dough, page 30
4 tablespoons unsalted butter
2 large yellow onions, chopped
¼ cup heavy cream
Cornmeal for sprinkling

1. Prepare French Bread dough; while it is rising, prepare onions. Melt butter in a large heavy skillet over medium heat. Sauté onions over medium heat until soft, stirring frequently, about 15 minutes. Add cream, increase heat to high, and reduce by half. Mixture will be very thick. Cool to room temperature.
2. Divide dough into 16 equal portions. Form each into a round ball. Place about 2 inches apart on 2 greased or parchment-lined baking sheets sprinkled with cornmeal. Using kitchen shears or a sharp knife, snip a ½-inch-deep X into the center of each roll. With your fingers, press a deep depression in the center of each X. Place 1 to 2 tablespoons of onions in center of depression on each roll.
3. Place immediately in a preheated 425° oven on the lowest rack. Bake for 15 to 18 minutes, or until golden brown and crusty. Serve immediately, if possible, or freeze for later.

BABY BUTTERMILK FANTANS

*J*ust like the Fantan showgirls, these rolls get a lot of attention. They are made of buttery layers stacked sideways and baked in a miniature muffin pan.

Yield: 2 dozen small rolls

1 package (1 tablespoon) active dry yeast
Pinch sugar
¼ cup warm water (105° to 115°)
1 cup warm buttermilk (105° to 115°)
¼ cup sugar
Grated zest of 1 lemon
½ cup (1 stick) unsalted butter, melted
1 egg
2 teaspoons salt
4 to 4½ cups unbleached all-purpose
  or bread flour

1. Combine yeast, sugar, and warm water in a small bowl and stir to dissolve. Let stand until foamy, about 10 minutes.
2. Combine buttermilk, sugar, zest, ¼ cup melted butter, egg, and salt in a large bowl. With a whisk, stir in 1½ cups flour and beat hard for 2 minutes, or until mixture is smooth and creamy. Add flour ½ cup at a time with a wooden spoon until a soft dough is formed.
3. Turn dough out onto a lightly floured surface and knead until soft, smooth, and elastic, about 5 minutes, adding flour 1 tablespoon at a time as needed. Place in a greased bowl, turn once to grease top, and cover with plastic wrap. Let rise in a warm place until doubled, about 1 hour.
4. Turn dough out onto a lightly floured surface. Divide dough into 3 equal portions. Roll or pat each portion into a 5-by-12-inch rectangle about ½ inch thick. Brush rectangle with remaining melted butter. With a sharp knife or pastry wheel, cut 3 sections lengthwise, about 1½ inches wide. Pile strips of dough into a stack. Cut into 1½-inch-square pieces (8 pieces per strip). Place cut side up in 2 greased miniature muffin pans. (It helps to alternate direction of rolls to allow room for expansion.) Dribble any leftover butter over tops of rolls. Cover loosely with plastic wrap and let rise until doubled, about 30 minutes.
5. Place in a preheated 400° oven and bake 15 to 18 minutes or until golden brown. Remove from pans and cool on a rack. Serve warm.

YOGURT–POPPY SEED ROLLS

*P*oppy seeds are the minute blue-black seeds of the poppy flower. They have been decorating cakes and breads since the days of the ancient Egyptians and Romans. Today, homemade poppy seed–studded rolls are always the first to disappear on a sandwich buffet.

Yield: 1 dozen rolls

1 package (1 tablespoon) active dry yeast
Pinch sugar
½ cup warm water (105° to 115°)
½ cup plain yogurt
1 tablespoon sugar
3 tablespoons instant nonfat dried milk
1 teaspoon salt
4 tablespoons unsalted butter, melted
3 to 3½ cups unbleached all-purpose
  or bread flour
Rich Egg Glaze, page 115
2 tablespoons poppy seeds for sprinkling

1. Sprinkle yeast and sugar over warm water in a small bowl and stir to dissolve. Let stand until foamy, about 10 minutes.
2. In a large bowl, whisk together yogurt, sugar, dried milk, salt, and butter. Add yeast mixture. Add 3 cups of flour about ½ cup at a time, using a wooden spoon, until dough just clears sides of bowl and forms a soft dough.
3. Turn dough out onto a lightly floured surface. Knead for about 5 minutes, adding as much of the last ½ cup flour 1 tablespoon at a time as needed to keep dough smooth and very soft, yet able to hold its shape. Place dough in a greased bowl, turn once to grease top, and cover with plastic wrap. Let rise in a warm area until doubled, 45 minutes to 1 hour.
4. Turn out gently onto a lightly floured surface and divide into 12 equal pieces. Form into 12 long finger-shaped rolls. Place on a greased or parchment-lined baking sheet. Lay the rolls in a circular pattern like a mandala, with one end of each roll touching in the center. Cover loosely with plastic wrap and let rise until doubled, about 20 minutes. Brush with Rich Egg Glaze. Sprinkle with poppy seeds.
5. Bake in preheated 375° oven for 25 to 30 minutes or until brown and puffy. Cool on a rack for 15 minutes and eat warm with butter and cheese.

Sandwich Buns

Divide dough into 8 equal pieces. Shape each into a ball, place on a greased or parchment-lined baking sheet seam down, and flatten with palm. Cover loosely with plastic wrap and let rise until doubled, about 20 minutes. Brush top of each roll with Rich Egg Glaze and sprinkle with poppy seeds. Bake as directed.

GARDEN FLAT BREADS

*T*he Italians are masters at baking, as is shown in these little flat breads, also known as *focaccias*, the classic peasant hearth cakes. A cross between a home-baked cracker and a roll, they are fast to bake, lending themselves to accompanying pasta, salad, or that first glass of wine before dinner. The herb combinations create colorful mosaics.

Yield: Twelve 6-inch flat breads

1 recipe French Bread dough, page 30
Cornmeal for sprinkling
½ cup olive oil
One or more herb mixtures, following

1. Prepare French Bread dough and let rise until doubled. Gently deflate dough, turn out onto a lightly floured surface, and divide into 12 equal portions. Roll out or pat each into an irregular round shape. Dough will be about ½ inch thick. Place on 2 or 3 greased or parchment-lined heavy baking sheets sprinkled with cornmeal.
2. Brush tops of dough with plenty of olive oil (the dough will soak it up). Sprinkle each with an herb mixture and press in. The breads may be slashed in a decorative or random fashion at this point, if desired.
3. Place immediately in a preheated 450° oven on the lowest shelf (or on floor of a gas oven). Bake for 12 to 15 minutes or until bottoms are nicely browned. Eat hot or at room temperature.

HERB MIXTURES

- Chopped fresh flat-leaf parsley, chopped fresh thyme, and julienned red bell pepper
- Chopped fresh rosemary or sage and coarse salt with chunks of fresh garlic
- Fresh oregano leaves, chopped fresh chives, and thinly sliced shallots
- Sliced tomatoes, chopped fresh flat-leaf parsley, chunks of sun-dried tomato, and slivers of garlic
- Chopped yellow onions sautéed in butter, walnut halves, and chopped fresh flat-leaf parsley
- Fresh leaves of basil, chunks of sun-dried tomato, and slivers of garlic
- Slices of sautéed Japanese eggplant and freshly grated Parmesan
- Prosciutto, slivers of black olives, and chopped yellow bell peppers
- Chopped fresh flat-leaf parsley and drained capers

GARLIC FOCACCIA

*S*erve a glass of Zinfindel with Garlic Focaccia cut into triangular wedges and piled into a beautiful basket. I like a heavy tin pizza pan with holes for baking *focaccia*. It gives the crust ample exposure to the hot stone, and provides easy handling and a good base for forming the dough into a circular shape. Buy garlic that is plump and firm to the touch and store at room temperature with plenty of ventilation.

Yield: One 14-inch flat bread

1 recipe Olive Oil Bread dough, page 65,
   made with 1 tablespoon dried basil
   or oregano and ¼ cup freshly grated
   Parmesan cheese
3 tablespoons olive oil
3 garlic cloves, slivered
Coarse salt (optional)

1. Prepare Olive Oil Bread dough, adding basil and Parmesan in Step 3 while mixing dough.
2. Let dough rise in a warm area until doubled, about 30 to 40 minutes. Meanwhile, preheat a baking stone in a 450° oven for at least 20 minutes, if desired. Pat dough into a greased 14-inch pizza pan with holes, or place on a greased or parchment-lined baking sheet. Brush dough with olive oil and insert garlic slivers all over top of dough. If desired, sprinkle with coarse salt.
3. Place pizza pan on hot stone, if used. Place in a preheated 450° oven, reduce heat to 400°, and bake 15 to 20 minutes, or until bottom is brown. Slide *focaccia* out of pan to cool on a rack.

CORNMEAL BLINI

*B*lini are dollar-sized whole-grain yeasted pancakes that are eaten out of hand. One of the great peasant dishes of the world, cornmeal or buckwheat *blini* get lots of attention at parties. Although *blini* are usually associated with caviar, they are different and delicious served just with sour cream and chopped hard-cooked eggs, sprinkled with chives or green onions for lunch or as a first course. To vary taste and texture, substitute an equal amount of whole-wheat or buckwheat flour for the cornmeal. Cornmeal gives a rather bland, sweet *blini*, whole-wheat a nutty wholesome *blini*, and buckwheat flour the traditional musky-flavored *blini*. Use a heavy griddle or nonstick skillet and a small spatula for most efficient handling. These pancakes can be made up to 2 days ahead and refrigerated between layers of waxed paper, or frozen for up to a month.

Yield: About 60 to 80 cocktail-sized pancakes (2 to 3 inches in diameter)

1 package (1 tablespoon) active dry yeast
Pinch sugar
¼ cup warm water (105° to 115°)
1¼ cups warm milk (105° to 115°)
4 eggs, separated
1 teaspoon salt
1 teaspoon sugar
4 tablespoons unsalted butter, melted
⅔ cup cornmeal, finely ground in blender or food processor
1⅓ cups unbleached all-purpose flour
Garnishes, following

1. Sprinkle yeast and sugar over warm water in a small bowl. Stir to dissolve and let stand until foamy, about 10 minutes.
2. With a wire whisk, blender, or food processor, blend milk, yolks, salt, sugar, butter, and yeast mixture until well blended.
3. Add cornmeal and flour, blending until mixture is smooth and consistency of heavy cream. Cover with plastic wrap and let stand at room temperature until doubled, about 1 hour.
4. Beat egg whites to firm peaks and fold into batter.
5. Heat a skillet over medium heat. Brush with a little melted butter. Spoon 1 tablespoon of batter into hot pan. Cook until golden brown on bottom and bubbles just break on surface, about 1 minutes. Flip to cook other side briefly. Stack on a dry cotton towel and keep warm in an oven on low heat until serving time, covered with aluminum foil. Brush each with a bit of melted butter, if desired.
6. Put a dollop of garnish in center of each *blini* to serve.

GARNISHES

For a cocktail party, place an assortment of your choice of garnishes in separate bowls and allow guests to choose. For a first course, serve 3 to 4 *blini*.

- Sour cream, *crème fraîche* or *aïoli*
- Golden or black caviar
- Chopped raw onion, chives, or fresh dill
- Minced smoked salmon or trout
- Chopped hard-cooked eggs
- Cream Cheese with Fresh Herbs, page 121

Little Savory Breads

CORNMEAL CRESCENTS

*T*hese little cornmeal breads have a Southwestern flair. Corn has no gluten, so cornmeal is usually mixed with all-purpose flour for a lighter texture. Cornmeal gives breads a slightly sweet flavor and crumbly texture. Serve these crescents with green and orange accent butters, Baja Chili Butter and Orange Butter, page 118.

Yield: 2 dozen crescents

1 package (1 tablespoon) active dry yeast
Pinch sugar
¼ cup water (105° to 115°)
1 cup warm milk (105° to 115°)
¼ cup corn oil
¼ cup sugar
2 teaspoons salt
1 egg
¾ cup cornmeal
3½ to 4 cups unbleached all-purpose
  or bread flour

1. Dissolve yeast and sugar in water in a small bowl. Stir to dissolve and let stand until foamy, about 10 minutes.
2. Combine milk, oil, sugar, salt, egg, and cornmeal in a large bowl. Whisk hard to make a smooth batter, about 2 minutes. Add yeast mixture. Add flour ½ cup at a time with a wooden spoon to make a soft dough.
3. Knead on a lightly floured surface to make a smooth dough, about 5 minutes. Dough will feel a bit greasy and slightly sticky. Place in a greased bowl, turn once to grease top, and cover with plastic wrap. Let rise in a warm place until doubled, about 1 hour.

4. Gently deflate dough, turn out onto a lightly floured surface, and divide into 3 equal sections. Roll or pat each into a circle about ¼ inch thick. Cut into 8 pie-shaped sections, each measuring about 2½ to 3 inches across the wide end. Roll wedges into a crescent shape from long side to point. Place, with tip of crescent down, 1 inch apart, on 2 greased or parchment-lined baking sheets. Cover loosely with plastic wrap and let rise until just doubled, about 20 to 30 minutes.
5. Bake in a preheated 375° oven 15 to 18 minutes, or until golden. Cool on racks.

PANE BASILICO

*S*erve these fragrant emerald-flecked herb rolls with sliced mortadella and steamed artichokes, or with an Italian-style antipasto platter.

Yield: 1 dozen pan rolls

1 package (1 tablespoon) active dry yeast
Pinch sugar
¼ cup warm water (105° to 115°)
1 cup warm milk (105° to 115°)
1½ teaspoons salt
2 tablespoons olive oil
3½ to 4 cups unbleached all-purpose
  or bread flour
¼ cup chopped fresh basil
6 tablespoons grated asiago *cheese*
2 tablespoons olive oil for brushing

1. Sprinkle yeast and sugar over water in a small bowl and stir to dissolve. Let stand until foamy, about 10 minutes.
2. With a whisk, combine milk, salt, olive oil, and 1 cup flour in a large bowl. Add yeast mixture and beat 2 minutes, or until smooth. Add fresh basil and 4 tablespoons of cheese. Add remaining flour ½ cup at a time with a wooden spoon to make a soft dough that just clears sides of bowl. Scrape bowl and remove dough to a lightly floured surface.
3. Knead for about 5 minutes, adding flour 1 tablespoon at a time as needed to make a smooth dough. Place in a greased bowl, turn once to grease top, and cover with plastic wrap. Let rise in a warm place until doubled, about 45 minutes to 1 hour.
4. Deflate dough and turn out onto a lightly floured surface. Divide dough into 12 equal pieces. Form each into a ball, pulling surface tight and pinching seams on bottom. Place in a greased 10-inch pie plate, springform pan, or earthenware baking dish to form a solid flat round of rolls. Cover loosely with plastic wrap and let rise until doubled, about 20 minutes. Brush with olive oil and sprinkle with remaining 2 tablespoons *asiago*.
5. Bake in a preheated 400° oven for 30 to 40 minutes, or until brown. Slide out of pan to cool on a rack. Pull apart and serve warm.

APRICOT-OATMEAL BREAD

The first commercial apricot orchard started in the Santa Clara Valley, California. Today California apricots rival the legendary apricots from Armenia and the Mediterranean coast of France. The main variety used for drying is the Blenheim from England, known for its deep orange-yellow skin highlighted with a delicate red blush. The fresh apricot is the herald of summer, but dried apricots are available all year round, adding a distinctive sunny tang to homemade bread. Apricot-Oatmeal Bread is good with sausage and eggs and makes wonderful toast.

Yield: 2 large braided loaves

1½ packages (1½ tablespoons) active dry yeast
Pinch sugar
1 cup warm water (105° to 115°)
1¼ cups warm buttermilk (105° to 115°)
¼ cup honey
2 tablespoons molasses
2 tablespoons unsalted butter
1 cup rolled oats
¼ cup hazelnuts, chopped and lightly toasted (see page 116)
1 tablespoon salt
1 cup whole-wheat flour
4 to 5 cups unbleached all-purpose or bread flour
1 egg, lightly beaten
½ cup dried apricots, minced
¼ cup currants, soaked in 2 tablespoons sherry for 20 minutes, then drained
Oats for sprinkling
2 tablespoons warm honey for glazing

1. Sprinkle yeast and sugar over warm water in a small bowl and stir until dissolved. Let stand until foamy, about 10 minutes.
2. Combine buttermilk, honey, molasses, and butter in a small bowl. In a large bowl combine oats, nuts, salt, whole-wheat flour, and 1 cup unbleached flour. Pour wet ingredients into bowl along with yeast mixture and egg. Beat hard with a whisk for 2 to 3 minutes, or until smooth.
3. Add unbleached flour ½ cup at a time with a wooden spoon until dough is thick and shaggy. Turn dough out onto a lightly floured surface and sprinkle with apricots and currants. Incorporate apricots and currants by patting the dough gently into a large rectangle about 1 inch thick. Sprinkle fruits over entire surface of dough. Fold into thirds and gently knead to evenly distribute fruit. Knead dough, adding 1 tablespoon flour as necessary to make a smooth and springy dough, about 5 minutes. Do not add too much flour or dough will become dense and hard to work.
4. Place in a greased bowl, turn once to grease top, and cover with plastic wrap. Let rise in a warm area until doubled, about 1½ hours. Gently deflate dough, turn out onto a lightly floured surface, and divide into 6 portions. Form portions into oblongs about 12 to 14 inches long with your palms. Lay 3 strips side by side and braid, pinching and tucking ends under securely. Place on a greased or parchment-lined baking sheet sprinkled with oats. Cover loosely with plastic wrap and let rise for about 30 minutes, or until almost doubled.
5. Bake in a preheated 375° oven for 35 to 40 minutes, or until brown. Brush with warm honey just out of oven. Cool on racks to slice.

HONEY-PRUNE BREAD

Prunes are sun- or oven-dried plums with their stone left intact. California's Santa Clara Valley grows the best and most varieties of plums in the United States. European and Japanese varieties range in color from a deep purple to a luminous yellow-green. T___ __ is even a red-meat, heart-shape___ _____ most prunes are made from _____ __al Samson and Pellier _____ _____ rcially treated w___ _____ ____ __tassium _____ _____ ___ _d fruit _____ _____ ___ _hese ___ _____ ____ _um vari-e___ _____ __g them in warm w___ ____ ____ af is adapted from a recipe __ ____ _llader, who writes the "Natura___ ___ __ in the *San Francisco Chronicle*. Her br__ad recipes are earthy, nutritious, flavorful, and always worth baking.

Yield: Two 9-by-5-inch loaves

1 package (1 tablespoon) active dry yeast
Pinch sugar
1 cup warm water (105° to 115°)
1 cup warm milk (105° to 115°)
3 tablespoons honey
3 tablespoons unsalted butter
2½ teaspoons salt
1½ cups whole-wheat flour
Grated zest of 1 orange
8 ounces moist pitted prunes, snipped
3 to 3½ cups unbleached all-purpose or bread flour

1. Sprinkle yeast and sugar over warm water in a small bowl and stir to dissolve. Let stand until foamy, about 10 minutes.
2. Combine milk, honey, and butter in a small bowl.
3. Place milk mixture, yeast mixture, salt, and whole-wheat flour in a large bowl. Beat hard with a whisk for 3 minutes, or until smooth. Add zest and prunes, then add ½ cup unbleached flour at a time with a wooden spoon until a soft dough is formed.
4. Turn dough out onto a lightly floured surface and knead until soft and smooth, about 5 minutes. Dough will be just past sticky, yet hold its shape. Place in a greased bowl, turn once to grease top, and cover with plastic wrap. Let rise in a warm area until doubled, about 1 to 1½ hours.
5. Gently deflate dough, turn out onto a lightly floured surface, and divide into 2 portions. Form into loaves and place in 2 greased 9-by-5-inch pans. Cover loosely with plastic wrap and let rise until just above top of pans, about 30 to 40 minutes.
6. Bake in a preheated 350° oven for about 40 to 45 minutes, or until brown and a cake tester comes out clean. Remove from pans to cool on racks before slicing.

CASHEW-DATE BREAD

Nuts and dried fruit have a natural affinity for each other. Besides the cashew and date combination, I have also used dried apples, raisins, and walnuts; dried apricots and pecans; dried pears and hazelnuts; dried peaches and brazil nuts. The dough is a light wheat and oat mixture that makes a rich, sweet morning bread when toasted. Cashew-Date Bread is also good sliced thin for a cream cheese tea sandwich garnished with sweet navel orange sections.

Yield: Two 8½-by-4½-inch loaves, or five 6-by-3½-inch loaves

2 packages (2 tablespoons) active dry yeast
Pinch sugar
¼ cup warm water (105° to 115°)
1 cup warm buttermilk (105° to 115°)
1 cup warm water (105° to 115°)
½ cup honey
½ cup rolled oats
4 tablespoons unsalted butter, melted
1 tablespoon salt
1 teaspoon ground cinnamon
1½ cups whole-wheat flour
¾ cup coarsely chopped pitted dates
¾ cup coarsely chopped raw cashews
About 4 cups unbleached all-purpose or bread flour

1. Sprinkle yeast and sugar over warm water in a small bowl and stir to dissolve. Let stand until foamy, about 10 minutes.
2. Place buttermilk, water, honey, oats, butter, salt, and cinnamon in a large bowl. Add whole-wheat flour and yeast mixture. Beat for 3 minutes, or until creamy and smooth. Add dates and cashews. Add flour ½ cup at a time with a wooden spoon to form a shaggy dough.
3. Turn dough out onto a lightly floured surface and knead until smooth, about 5 to 8 minutes, adding 1 tablespoon flour at a time as necessary to make a soft, springy dough. Take care not to add too much flour and to push any stray fruit or nuts back into dough if they fall out. Dough will have a slight dense and sticky quality. Place in a greased bowl and turn to grease top. Cover with plastic wrap and let rise in a warm area until doubled, 1 to 1½ hours.
4. Gently deflate dough, turn out onto a lightly floured surface, and divide into 2 large or 5 small loaves. Shape and place in greased pans. Cover loosely with plastic wrap and let rise until level with tops of pans, 30 to 40 minutes.
5. Bake standard loaves in a preheated 375° oven for 35 to 40 minutes, or until brown and a cake tester comes out clean. Bake mini loaves 25 to 30 minutes. Remove from pans to racks and cool completely before slicing.

OLD-FASHIONED RAISIN BREAD WITH MOLASSES GLAZE

*T*he dried fruit of the Thompson seedless grape is well loved in breadmaking. There is no better bread than homemade raisin bread. It makes morning toast in all its glory, but is also good with a bit of butter for dessert.

Yield: Six 6-by-4-inch loaves

1 package (1 tablespoon) active dry yeast
1 teaspoon sugar
2½ cups warm water (105° to 115°)
½ cup (1 stick) unsalted butter, melted
1 egg
½ cup sugar
2 teaspoons salt
5½ to 6 cups unbleached all-purpose
  or bread flour
1 cup dark seedless raisins, plumped in hot water
  15 minutes and drained
Molasses Glaze, page 115

1. Combine yeast, sugar, and ½ cup warm water in a small bowl. Stir to dissolve and let stand until foamy, about 10 minutes.
2. In a large bowl, combine remaining water, butter, egg, and yeast mixture with a whisk. Add sugar, salt, and 2 cups flour. Beat hard until smooth, about 3 minutes. Add raisins. With a wooden spoon, add flour ½ cup at a time to form a shaggy dough.
3. Turn out onto a lightly floured surface and knead until smooth and elastic feeling, about 5 minutes, adding flour 1 tablespoon at a time as needed. If any raisins fall out, push them back in. Place in a greased bowl, turn once to grease top, and cover with plastic wrap. Let rise in a warm place until doubled, about 1 to 1½ hours.

4. Gently deflate dough and turn out onto a lightly floured work surface. Divide into 6 equal portions. Form each portion into a loaf and place in a greased 6-by-4-inch loaf pan. With kitchen shears, snip the top of each loaf 5 or 6 times at a 45-degree angle a full 2 to 3 inches into the dough to make a jagged pattern on top of each loaf. Cover loosely with plastic wrap and let rise until fully doubled in volume, about 40 minutes. Gently recut snips if a more pronounced pattern is desired.
5. Brush with Molasses Glaze. Bake in a preheated 375° oven for 25 to 30 minutes, or until golden and a cake tester comes out clean. Remove from pan to cool on a rack before slicing.

BREAD WITH THREE CHOCOLATES

*T*he first bread I bought at Il Fornaio bakery in San Francisco was a yeasted Italian chocolate loaf. In my desire to duplicate that unusual flavor and texture, this special-celebration bread was born. Good brands of chocolate include Callebaut, Tobler, Perugina, and Lindt. Good brands of cocoa are Poulain, Van Houten, and Dröste. Serve as dessert or with tea in the afternoon.

Yield: 2 round loaves

1 package (1 tablespoon) dry active yeast
½ cup sugar
1 cup warm water (105° to 115°)
5½ to 6 cups unbleached all-purpose
  or bread flour
½ cup unsweetened Dutch cocoa powder
2 teaspoons instant espresso powder
2 teaspoons salt
1 cup warm milk (105° to 115°)
6 tablespoons unsalted butter, melted
2 eggs
5 ounces semisweet or bittersweet chocolate,
  chopped
2 ounces milk chocolate, chopped

1. Sprinkle yeast and a pinch of sugar over ½ cup warm water in a small bowl. Stir to dissolve and let stand until foamy, about 10 minutes.
2. Combine 2 cups flour, remaining sugar, cocoa, espresso, and salt in a large bowl. Add remaining warm water, milk, butter, and eggs. Whisk hard until smooth and add yeast mixture. Beat for about 2 minutes, or until smooth. Add chopped chocolate with a wooden spoon. Add remaining flour ½ cup at a time until mixture forms a shaggy dough. Take care not to break up chocolate too much.
3. Turn dough out onto a lightly floured surface and knead for about 5 minutes, adding flour 1 tablespoon at a time as needed to make a smooth, silky dough. Place in a greased bowl, turn once to grease top, and cover with plastic wrap to rise in a warm area until doubled, about 1 to 1½ hours.
4. Gently deflate dough, turn out onto a lightly floured board, and divide into 2 equal portions. Shape into round loaves and place in 2 greased 6-cup charlotte molds, or 8-inch-diameter ovenproof casseroles or springform pans. Cover loosely with plastic wrap and let rise to 1 inch over rim of pans, about 30 minutes.
5. Bake in a preheated 375° oven for 40 to 45 minutes, or until crusty and a cake tester comes out clean. Cool on a rack completely before cutting into wedges to serve.

Savarin with Berries and Raspberry Brandy

*S*avarin is a superb French yeast cake soaked in spirits and served as dessert after a light meal. It should be eaten the day it is made, when it is moist and quite delicate. It is an adult's dessert: simple, sophisticated, and not too sweet. *Savarin* is good by itself; if you use berries, you might want to match them with a complementary spirit, such as Grand Marnier, kirsch, Chambord, rum, or *framboise*. Serve for Mardi Gras or as a unique birthday surprise.

Yield: One 9-inch round cake; 12 servings

1 package (1 tablespoon) active dry yeast
4 teaspoons sugar
¼ cup warm water (105° to 115°)
2 cups unbleached all-purpose flour
4 eggs
1 teaspoon salt
*½ cup (1 stick) unsalted butter, cut into
  16 pieces and softened*

Orange Syrup
¾ cup sugar
¾ cup water
½ cup fresh orange juice

Apricot Glaze
1 cup apricot jam

Berries
*2½ cups any combination of fresh quartered
  strawberries, pitted cherries, raspberries,
  blueberries, or blackberries*
¼ cup sugar
¼ cup liqueur or spirit

Whipped cream
1 cup heavy cream
1 tablespoon sugar
1 tablespoon liqueur or spirit

1. Sprinkle yeast and 1 teaspoon sugar over warm water in a small bowl and stir to dissolve. Let stand until foamy, about 10 minutes.
2. Place flour in a large bowl and make a well in center. Add eggs, remaining 3 teaspoons sugar, and salt. With a wooden spoon, gradually mix a few tablespoons of flour into eggs. Add yeast mixture and stir until a sticky, soft dough forms. Beat vigorously for about 3 minutes, or until smooth.
3. Place in a greased bowl and sprinkle butter pieces over top. Cover with plastic wrap and let rise at room temperature until doubled, about 1 hour. Fold butter into dough and gently slap dough against sides of bowl until incorporated completely. Dough and butter will be about the same temperature during mixing.
4. Spoon dough into a greased 5-cup *savarin* or 9-inch metal ring mold with a rubber spatula. The mold will be no more than one-half full. Cover with plastic wrap and let rise at room temperature about 25 minutes, until level with top of pan. Remove plastic and let rise 20 minutes more. Bake in a preheated 375° oven for 30 to 35 minutes, or until a cake tester comes out clean. Cool in pan 5 minutes. Loosen edges and turn out onto a rack to cool completely. The cake may be wrapped and stored at room temperature up to 3 days at this point.
5. To make orange syrup, combine sugar and water in a small pan and heat until sugar is dissolved, about 5 minutes. Add fresh orange juice. Heat to boiling and ladle over cake until syrup is absorbed. Let stand at room temperature about 1 hour.
6. Whirl apricot jam in a blender or food processor until smooth. Heat to boiling. Brush cake with hot apricot glaze to seal in moisture. Slide cake onto a serving platter or use 2 spatulas to lift cake. It can be refrigerated at this time for a few hours before serving.
7. Combine berries, sugar, and liqueur in a medium bowl. Let stand about 10 minutes. Whip cream with sugar and liqueur until soft peaks form. To serve, spoon berry mixture into center of *savarin*. Garnish top of berries with whipped cream.

PLUM CRUMB CAKE

A yeasted coffee cake, this crumb cake is moist, tender, and an exceptional surprise. The batter is mixed in exactly the same manner as a quick bread, with the batter resting about 30 minutes before baking. Made here with luscious ripe fresh plums, you can substitute other firm seasonal or dry frozen fruit such as nectarines, rhubarb, cherries, or blueberries. During the winter, use a home- or commercial-canned fruit such as unsweetened berries or sour cherries, drained well. Serve warm from the oven with iced coffee, the scent of violets and lilacs in the air, and good friends. This is also good eaten cold.

Yield: One 9-inch cake; 8 servings

1 package (1 tablespoon) active dry yeast
Pinch sugar
1/4 cup warm water (105° to 115°)
1/2 cup warm buttermilk (105° to 115°)
1/4 cup sugar
1/4 cup vegetable oil
1 egg
1/2 teaspoon salt
Grated zest of 1 lemon
2 1/2 cups unbleached all-purpose flour
2/3 cup sour cream
1/4 cup sugar
1 tablespoon all-purpose flour
1 teaspoon vanilla extract

Crumb Topping
1/3 cup unbleached all-purpose flour
1/4 cup sugar
1/2 teaspoon ground cinnamon
Dash ground mace
4 tablespoons cold unsalted butter,
*   cut into pieces*

2 cups fresh red or French plums,
*   pitted and sliced*

1. Sprinkle yeast and sugar over warm water in a small bowl. Stir to combine and let stand until foamy, about 10 minutes.
2. Combine buttermilk, sugar, oil, egg, salt, and zest in a large bowl. Add yeast mixture and 1 cup flour. Beat well, about 3 minutes, or until smooth. Add remaining 1 1/2 cups flour and no more. The batter will be sticky and stiff.
3. Generously grease a 9-inch springform pan, or a 9-inch quiche pan that is at least 2 inches deep and has a removable bottom. With a spatula, scrape batter into prepared pan. Spread batter with lightly floured fingers to fill pan evenly. Cover with plastic wrap and let rest in a warm area for about 30 minutes. Batter will be slightly puffy.
4. Meanwhile, combine sour cream, sugar, flour, and vanilla in a medium bowl. Beat until smooth with a whisk. Set aside.
5. To make Crumb Topping, combine flour, sugar, and spices in a medium bowl. Cut in butter until mixture is consistency of coarse crumbs.
6. Pour sour cream layer evenly over batter. Gently distribute plums over sour cream layer. Sprinkle crumb mixture to completely cover fruit. Bake in a preheated 400° oven about 45 minutes, or until top is lightly browned and cake tester comes out clean. Let cake cool in pan 15 minutes, then remove from pan to cool on a rack or cut in wedges to serve warm. Store in refrigerator.

ALMOND BABKA

T he following recipe gives a choice of an almond, cheese, or a delicate chocolate-cinnamon filling in a vanilla-flavored dough. This is an exemplary coffee cake that freezes well. One recipe of filling is enough for one recipe *babka* dough. Polish and Hungarian bakers are as renowned as the French (the *croissant* was invented in a Hungarian bakery), and their exotic sweet breads are delicious. This recipe is adapted from one by Lou Pappas, the food editor of the *Palo Alto Times Tribune*. Her breads are consistently some of the finest I have ever tasted. For the best results, use a *kugelhof* mold with a nonstick coating, an angel food pan, or any other fancy tube pan with a 10- to 12-cup capacity. This recipe may also be made into two 9-by-5-inch loaves. Dust with powdered sugar or drizzle with Powdered Sugar Glaze, page 115.

Yield: One large coffee cake

1 package (1 tablespoon) active dry yeast
Pinch sugar
1/4 cup warm water (105° to 115°)
1/2 cup (1 stick) unsalted butter, melted
1/4 cup sugar
1 1/2 teaspoons salt
2 teaspoons vanilla extract
1/2 teaspoon almond extract
3/4 cup warm milk (105° to 115°)
3 eggs
About 4 cups unbleached all-purpose flour
2 tablespoons unsalted butter, melted,
*   for brushing dough*
3 tablespoons Vanilla Powdered Sugar,
*   page 116, or powdered sugar.*

Almond Filling
One 8-ounce can almond paste
1/4 cup ground blanched almonds
4 tablespoons unsalted butter, softened
1 tablespoon sugar
1 egg

1. Sprinkle yeast and sugar over warm water in a small bowl and stir to dissolve. Let stand until foamy, about 10 minutes.
2. In a large bowl, combine butter, sugar, salt, vanilla, almond, milk, eggs, and 1 cup flour. Beat until smooth with a whisk. Add yeast mixture. Beat 3 minutes, or until smooth. Add flour ½ cup at a time with a wooden spoon until a soft dough is formed.
3. Turn dough out onto a lightly floured surface and knead until smooth and silky, about 5 minutes. Be certain dough remains soft. Place in a greased bowl, turn once to grease top, and cover with plastic wrap. Let rise in a warm area until doubled, about 1½ hours. Meanwhile combine filling ingredients in a bowl, beat until smooth, and set aside.
4. Gently deflate dough, turn out onto a lightly floured board, and roll or pat into a 10-by-12-inch rectangle. Brush with melted butter. Spread with filling, leaving a ½-inch border all around dough. Roll up jelly roll fashion and pinch seams. Holding one end, twist dough about 6 to 8 times to make a rope. Form into a flat coil and place in a well-greased 10-to 12-cup *kugelhof* mold or tube pan. Pinch ends together and adjust dough to lie evenly in pan, no more than two-thirds full. Cover loosely with plastic wrap and let rise until even with top of pan, about 45 minutes.
5. Bake in a preheated 350° oven for 40 to 45 minutes, or until golden brown and a cake tester comes out clean. There will be a hollow sound when tapped. Let stand 5 minutes in the pan, then transfer from baking pan to a rack to cool completely. Let stand 4 hours to overnight, wrapped in plastic, before slicing.

CHEESE BABKA

Yield: One large coffee cake

1 recipe Almond Babka dough, page 86

Cheese Filling
1½ cups dry cottage cheese or ricotta
⅓ cup sugar
1½ tablespoons sour cream or crème fraîche
1½ tablespoons flour
1 egg
Grated zest of 1 lemon
½ teaspoon vanilla extract
*3 tablespoons currants, plumped in
    2 tablespoons rum or cognac for ½ hour*

Prepare Almond Babka dough through Step 3. Combine all ingredients until creamy. Roll out as in Step 4. Fill with cheese filling, and proceed as for Almond Babka.

CHOCOLATE BABKA

Yield: One large coffee cake

1 recipe Almond Babka dough, page 86

Chocolate Streusel
¾ cup sugar
⅓ cup unbleached all-purpose flour
*4 tablespoons unsalted butter, softened and
    cut into pieces*
3 tablespoons unsweetened powdered cocoa
1 teaspoon ground cinnamon

Prepare Almond Babka dough through Step 3. Combine all ingredients until crumbly. Roll out as in Step 4. Fill with chocolate streusel, and proceed as for Almond Babka. While cake is still warm drizzle with Powdered Sugar Glaze, page 115, using Irish cream liqueur for liquid.

APPLE BRIOCHE

*S*treusel is an old German word describing a combination of fat, flour, and sugar that is strewn over the top of pastries and breads as a crumb topping. Nuts and spices may also be added for variation. Streusel creates a delicious crisp layer or filling in breads. It also adds to a beautiful finished appearance on top of this rich apple-filled yeast bread. The variations in the proportions of streusel ingredients are endless. Use this excellent basic recipe to top any yeast or quick bread. Store leftover streusel in the freezer.

Yield: One 12-inch braid

*3 large, firm apples, such as Pippin,
    Golden Delicious, or Rome Beauty, peeled,
    cored, and sliced ¼ inch thick*
1 tablespoon fresh lemon juice
3 tablespoons Calvados or applejack
½ cup sugar
1 tablespoon water
1 teaspoon ground cinnamon
*1 recipe Brioche dough, page 36,
    chilled overnight*

Streusel
½ cup sugar
⅓ cup unbleached all-purpose flour
4 tablespoons chilled unsalted butter

Rich Egg Glaze, page 115

1. Macerate apple slices with lemon juice and Calvados for 1 hour, stirring often. Place apples, sugar, water, and cinnamon in a heavy 12-inch skillet and boil 1 minute to reduce liquid and dissolve sugar. Cool to room temperature.

2. Turn Brioche dough out on a lightly floured surface. Roll out into a 10-by-15-inch rectangle. Spread cooled apple filling down center third of rectangle. With a sharp knife, cut strips 1½ inches to 2 inches apart diagonally, almost touching filling. Starting at top, fold strips alternately over filling. If there is excess at end, tuck it under. Transfer carefully to a greased or parchment-lined baking sheet.

3. Prepare Streusel: Combine sugar and flour until blended. Cut in cold butter with a pastry blender or a food processor until coarse crumbs are formed. Brush dough with egg glaze and sprinkle with streusel.

4. Cover loosely with plastic wrap and let rise at a cool room temperature until puffy and not quite doubled, about 40 minutes.

5. Bake in a preheated 350° oven for 40 to 45 minutes, or until bread is browned and filling is bubbly. Transfer from baking sheet to a rack to cool completely. Serve, sliced, at room temperature.

HAZELNUT EGG BREAD WITH BITTERSWEET CHOCOLATE GLAZE

*T*his is an elegant bread in the rustic but sophisticated style of a *brioche*. It is adorned with a glaze of bittersweet chocolate poured over the top, making a bold presentation. This is not a particularly sweet bread. The dough is soft, yet pliable. For easiest handling, make this bread in a heavy-duty electric mixer. This recipe will adapt to being molded in any rectangular, round, or cylindrical shape or in a lovely set of 3-strand braids.

Yield: 2 free-form braided loaves, or 4 one-pound coffee cans

1½ packages (1½ tablespoons) active dry yeast
¼ cup sugar
¼ cup warm water (105° to 115°)
¾ cup (1½ sticks) unsalted butter, at room temperature
1 tablespoon salt
6 eggs
2 teaspoons vanilla extract
1 cup warm milk (105° to 115°)
1½ cups hazelnuts, finely chopped and toasted (see page 116)
About 6½ cups unbleached all-purpose or bread flour

Bittersweet Chocolate Glaze
6 ounces bittersweet or semisweet chocolate
½ cup (1 stick) unsalted butter
1 tablespoon corn syrup

1. In a small bowl, sprinkle yeast and a pinch of sugar over water. Stir to dissolve and let stand until foamy, about 10 minutes.

2. Beat butter, remaining sugar, and salt until creamy in the work bowl of a heavy-duty mixer with a paddle attachment. Add eggs one at a time and beat until smooth and fluffy.

3. Add vanilla, milk, and hazelnuts on low speed. Then add flour 1 cup at a time to make a soft dough. When dough is no longer sticky, turn out onto a lightly floured surface and knead lightly for about 5 minutes, adding 1 tablespoon of flour at a time as necessary, until dough is smooth. The dough will be soft and silky with some blisters appearing below the surface.

4. Place in a greased bowl, turn once to grease top, and cover with plastic wrap. Let rise at room temperature until doubled, about 1½ hours. Gently deflate. Turn out onto a lightly floured board and divide dough in desired portions. For a cylindrical shape, shape into 4 balls and place into 4 well-greased 1-pound coffee cans or equivalent-sized cylindrical or decorative molds. Do not fill over two-thirds full. If in doubt about mold being large enough, add a collar to mold with well-greased aluminum foil to extend it. Cover loosely with plastic wrap and let rise about 40 minutes, or until doubled or level with top of mold.

5. Bake in a preheated 350° oven for 40 to 45 minutes, or until golden and a cake tester comes out clean. Let stand in mold 10 minutes before turning out onto a rack to cool completely before slicing, as this bread is very delicate.

6. Prepare Bittersweet Chocolate Glaze: Melt ingredients together in top of a double boiler over simmering water. Stir gently with a small whisk until melted and smooth. Remove from heat and set aside at room temperature or for a shorter time in refrigerator until the consistency of a soft custard.

7. Pour glaze over slightly warm bread to cover top, and allow to run down sides to form a thin glaze. The glaze will firm up as bread cools. Let bread stand at room temperature for at least 4 hours before cutting into long wedges to serve.

MAPLE-OATMEAL STICKY BUNS

*T*his recipe calls for real maple syrup, not a maple-flavored sugar syrup, and maple sugar, which is a wonderful alternative to brown sugar. The sugar maple tree is indigenous to North America, with most good syrups coming from Vermont and Canada. It may seem like a luxury to use maple products in cooking, but as sweeteners, they have no peer.

Yield: 1 dozen buns

Oatmeal Brioche
1 package (1 tablespoon) active dry yeast
1 teaspoon maple sugar or brown sugar
⅓ cup warm water (105° to 115°)
⅓ cup warm milk (105° to 115°)
¼ cup maple syrup
3 tablespoons unsalted butter
1½ teaspoons salt
½ cup rolled oats
3 to 3½ cups unbleached all-purpose
  or bread flour
2 eggs, lightly beaten

Filling
3 tablespoons butter, melted
¾ cup maple sugar or brown sugar
1½ tablespoons ground cinnamon
¾ cup raisins (optional)

Maple Glaze
⅓ cup (5⅓ tablespoons) unsalted butter, melted
⅔ cup maple syrup

¾ cup pecans, chopped

1. Make oatmeal brioche: Sprinkle yeast and sugar over warm water in a small bowl. Stir to combine and let stand until foamy, about 10 minutes.
2. Combine milk, maple syrup, and butter in a small bowl. In a large bowl, combine salt, oats, and 1 cup flour. Add milk mixture, eggs, and yeast mixture. Beat hard with a whisk for 3 minutes, or until smooth. With a wooden spoon, add remaining flour to dough ½ cup at a time until a soft dough is formed.
3. Turn dough out onto a lightly floured surface and knead until smooth and springy, about 5 minutes, adding flour 1 tablespoon at a time as necessary. Place in a greased bowl and turn once to grease top. Cover with plastic wrap. Let rise in a warm area until doubled, about 1 hour.
4. Gently deflate dough, turn out onto a lightly floured surface, and roll out into a 10-by-14-inch rectangle. Brush dough with melted butter. Sprinkle with maple sugar, cinnamon, and lastly, raisins, if desired. Leave a 1-inch border all around the rectangle. Roll up jelly roll fashion from the long end. Cut gently with a serrated knife into twelve 1-to 1½-inch-thick portions. Cover loosely with plastic wrap while preparing glaze.
5. In a bowl, whisk butter and maple syrup to combine. Grease sides of a 9-by-13-inch baking dish, two 8-inch round cake pans, a 12-inch ovenproof skillet, or twelve 5-inch round sticky bun pans. Pour glaze in and sprinkle with nuts.
6. Set slices close together in maple glaze. Cover loosely with plastic wrap and let rise in a warm area until puffy and even with rim of pan, about 30 minutes.
7. Bake in a preheated 350° oven 25 to 30 minutes, or until top is brown. Remove from oven and let stand in pan for 5 minutes. Turn out of pan to cool on a rack placed over a jelly roll pan. Scrape out extra maple glaze from pan bottom with a spatula and place on rolls. Eat warm or reheated.

LEMON–GOAT CHEESE PILLOWS

*T*his sweet *chèvre* pastry is a surprise. The cream cheese combined with goat cheese gives the filling a rich, delicate taste and mellow tang. Use a California *fromage blanc* or Chabis or a French Montrachet log, as you prefer, as fresh as you can get from a reliable cheese shop. Fresh *chèvre* is sweet and moist, with *no* trace of sourness, mold, spoiled looks, or an ammoniated odor. Substitute ricotta or dry cottage cheese, if desired. This recipe uses the rapid mix method (see page 20). It can be made by hand rather than with an electric mixer, if you prefer.

Dust these pastries with your own Vanilla Powdered Sugar and serve them warm with *cappuccino.*

Yield: 2 dozen pastries

1 package (1 tablespoon) active dry yeast
3¼ cups unbleached all-purpose or bread flour
¾ cup hot milk (120°)
6 tablespoons unsalted butter, melted
¼ cup sugar
1 teaspoon salt
2 eggs
Grated zest of 1 lemon

Cheese Filling
6 ounces natural cream cheese at
*   room temperature*
6 ounces fresh goat cheese at
*   room temperature*
¼ cup sugar
1 egg yolk
1 teaspoon vanilla extract

Vanilla Powdered Sugar, page 116,
*   or powdered sugar*

1. Combine yeast and 1½ cups flour in bowl of a heavy-duty electric mixer.
2. In a medium mixing bowl, combine milk with butter, sugar, and salt. Add to yeast mixture and stir just to combine. Add eggs and lemon zest. Beat at medium speed for 3 minutes. Add flour ½ cup at a time at low speed to make a soft dough. Do not add any extra flour. Place in a greased bowl and cover with plastic wrap. Refrigerate 4 hours to overnight.
3. To make filling, blend cheeses, sugar, yolk, and vanilla until smooth and well combined.
4. Turn dough out onto a lightly floured surface and divide into 4 equal sections. Refrigerate all but 1 portion until ready to fill. Roll 1 portion into an 8-by-12-inch rectangle. Cut into six 4-inch squares with a pastry wheel or large knife.
5. Place a heaping tablespoonful of filling in center of each square. Bring both opposite corners to center and pinch to seal. Place pastries 2 inches apart on a greased or parchment-lined baking sheet. Repeat with remaining dough. Let rise, uncovered, for 20 minutes, or until doubled.
6. Bake in a preheated 375° oven for 15 to 18 minutes until puffy and brown. Cool on a rack and dust with sifted Vanilla Powdered Sugar.

CINNAMON BRIOCHES

A giant swirled cinnamon roll is always popular. Made with delicate *brioche* dough and a sweet, spicy cinnamon-pecan filling, this is the best morning roll imaginable. Good with fresh citrus juices, tea, and coffee. These rolls freeze well.

Yield: 1 dozen large rolls

1 recipe Brioche dough, page 36,
*   chilled overnight*
Rich Egg Glaze, page 115
¾ cup sugar, mixed with 1½ tablespoons
*   ground cinnamon*
¾ cup pecans, finely chopped

Icing
1 cup sifted powdered sugar
2 tablespoons milk
1 teaspoon vanilla extract

1. Turn cold dough gently out onto a lightly floured surface. Roll out into an 18-by-30-inch rectangle ¼ inch to ½ inch thick (dough may be rolled out in 2 portions if space is limited). Brush lightly with egg glaze. Sprinkle with cinnamon sugar. Cover evenly with nuts.
2. Roll up jelly roll fashion from long end. Brush seam with egg glaze and pinch to seal. Cut roll into twelve 1- to 1½-inch slices with a serrated knife, taking care not to squash slices.
3. Place 2 inches apart on a greased or parchment-lined baking sheet. Cover loosely with plastic wrap and let rise at a cool room temperature until doubled and puffy, 45 minutes to 1 hour.
4. Brush rolls lightly with egg glaze and bake in a preheated 400° oven 10 or 15 minutes or until golden.
5. In a medium bowl, beat powdered sugar, milk, and vanilla with a whisk until smooth. Drizzle or brush icing on hot rolls. Serve warm or reheated.

AMERICAN CHOCOLATE BREAD

*T*his Vienna-style bread is baked with a slab of good chocolate that melts while baking and is styled after the much richer *pain au chocolat* made from *croissant* dough. As you prefer, spread a tablespoonful of fine raspberry preserves under each piece of chocolate before forming the loaf. The small pans make perfect individual loaves.

Yield: Eight 4-by-2½-inch loaves

Sponge
2 packages (2 tablespoons) active dry yeast
2 tablespoons sugar
1 cup warm water (105° to 115°)
1½ cups unbleached all-purpose or bread flour

Dough
Sponge, above
1 cup warm milk (105° to 115°)
5 tablespoons unsalted butter, melted
1 tablespoon salt
4 to 4½ cups unbleached all-purpose
* or bread flour*
8 ounces semisweet chocolate
3 tablespoons Vanilla Powdered Sugar, page
* 116, or powdered sugar*

1. Make a sponge by placing yeast, sugar, water, and 1½ cups flour in a large bowl. Whisk until smooth, about 3 minutes. Cover with plastic wrap and let stand in a warm area until doubled, about 1 hour.

2. To make dough, stir down sponge with a wooden spoon. Add 1 cup milk, 3 tablespoons butter, salt, and 1 cup flour. Beat hard until smooth, about 2 minutes. Add flour, ½ cup at a time, to form a soft dough.

3. Turn dough out onto a lightly floured surface and knead for about 5 minutes, adding 1 tablespoon of flour at a time as necessary until dough just loses its stickiness. It will be soft and springy. Place in a greased bowl, turning once to coat top, and cover with plastic wrap. Let rise in a warm area until doubled, about 1 hour.

4. Grease 8 small loaf pans. Cut chocolate into 1-ounce portions. Gently deflate dough, turn out on a lightly floured surface, and divide into 8 equal portions. Pat each portion out into a 7-by-4-inch rectangle about ¾ inch to 1 inch thick. Place a 1-ounce piece of chocolate at short edge of each piece. Roll up jelly roll fashion and pinch edges to seal and completely enclose chocolate. Arrange each in a loaf pan, cover loosely with plastic wrap, and let rise for 15 minutes, or until almost doubled.

5. Brush loaves with remaining 2 tablespoons butter and sprinkle with about 1 teaspoon Vanilla Powdered Sugar to sparkle crust. Bake in a preheated 375° oven for 20 to 25 minutes, or until a delicate brown. Immediately remove from pans and cool 20 minutes on racks. Serve warm.

ANISE SUGAR BUNS

*A*sti Spumante is a popular sweet sparkling dessert wine from Italy. Made from muscat grapes, it has a fruity flavor rather like peaches, and adds a bright, flowery quality to these Italian-style buns. Homemade candied orange peel has little resemblance to commercial candied peels. It is chewy, tangy, and flavorful, giving a very special touch to sweet breads.

Yield: 1 dozen buns

¼ cup currants
¼ Asti Spumante or other sweet sparkling wine
1 package (1 tablespoon) active dry yeast
Pinch sugar
¼ cup warm water (105° to 115°)
¼ cup sugar
4 tablespoons unsalted butter, softened
1 teaspoon salt
2 eggs
¾ cup warm milk (105° to 115°)
3 to 3¼ cups unbleached all-purpose
* or bread flour*
¼ cup pine nuts
¼ cup slivered blanched almonds
¼ cup diced Bittersweet Candied Orange Peel,
* page 116*
Rich Egg Glaze, page 115
Anise Sugar, following

1. Place currants in a small bowl, cover with Asti Spumante, and let stand 1 hour.

2. Sprinkle yeast and sugar over warm water in a small bowl and stir until dissolved. Let stand until foamy, about 10 minutes.

3. In a large bowl, cream sugar, butter, and salt until light and fluffy. Add eggs one at a time until incorporated.

4. Add milk and yeast mixture. With a wooden spoon add 1 cup flour. Add currants, wine, nuts, and peel. Continue to add flour ½ cup at a time until a soft dough is formed. Turn out onto a lightly floured surface and knead until smooth and springy, about 5 minutes, adding flour 1 tablespoon at a time as necessary. Push back in any fruits or nuts that fall out.

5. Place in a greased bowl, turning once to grease top. Cover with plastic wrap and let rise in a warm area until doubled in bulk, about 1 to 1½ hours.

6. Gently deflate dough, turn out onto a lightly floured board, and divide into 12 equal portions. Form into round buns and place on 2 greased or parchment-lined sheets about 2 inches apart. Cover loosely and let rise until doubled, about 30 minutes. Brush with egg glaze and sprinkle with Anise Sugar.

7. Bake in a preheated 375° oven for 15 to 20 minutes, or until golden. Remove from baking sheets to cool on racks.

Anise Sugar
1 tablespoon anise seed
1 cup granulated sugar

Grind seed in a nut grinder, food processor, or mortar. Add sugar and grind together to combine. Store in a covered container.

HAZELNUT WHOLE-WHEAT BUTTERHORNS

A crescent is one of the most appealing and widely used shapes for a little bread, rather like a slice of the moon. It is an ancient symbol attributed to the Great Mother, the Queen of Heaven, Isis of Egypt, and the Virgin Mary. These butterhorns are delicately flavored with citrus and honey. They freeze beautifully, to be reheated for breakfast or a sweet repast. This recipe uses the rapid mix method (see page 20).

Yield: 2 dozen rolls

2 packages (2 tablespoons) active dry yeast
½ cup instant nonfat dried milk
⅓ cup brown sugar
2 teaspoons salt
½ teaspoon ground cinnamon
1½ cups whole-wheat flour
1¾ cups hot water (120°)
2 tablespoons honey
6 tablespoons butter
2 eggs
1 teaspoon lemon extract
*3½ to 4 cups unbleached all-purpose
    or bread flour*
*½ cup chopped hazelnuts, lightly toasted
    (see page 116)*
¼ cup butter, melted, for brushing

1. Combine yeast, dry milk, sugar, salt, cinnamon, and whole-wheat flour in a large bowl.

2. Combine water, honey, and butter in a small bowl. Add to dry ingredients with a whisk until smooth. Add eggs and lemon extract. Beat until mixture is smooth and creamy, about 3 minutes. With a wooden spoon, add unbleached flour ½ cup at a time to form a soft dough that clears sides of bowl.

3. Turn out onto a lightly floured surface and knead for about 5 minutes, adding 1 tablespoon flour at a time as needed to make a soft dough. Place in a greased bowl, turn once to grease top, and cover with plastic wrap. Let rise in a warm area until doubled, about 1 hour.

4. Turn dough out onto a lightly floured surface and divide into 3 equal pieces. Roll 1 piece into a 12-inch circle and divide into 8 pie-shaped wedges. Sprinkle one-third of nuts around outside border of circle. Roll from wide end of wedge to point. Repeat with remaining dough. Place on a greased or parchment-lined baking sheet, points down, 2 inches apart. Let rest 30 minutes, covered loosely with plastic wrap.

5. Bake in a preheated 400° oven for 10 to 12 minutes, or until puffy. Brush with melted butter just as they come out of oven, if desired. Cool on racks.

OVERNIGHT PECAN ROLLS

*E*veryone adores a sweet roll in the morning. The problem has always been how to get that yeast roll out of the oven early enough to still call it morning. This chewy, compact roll is a good answer to that problem, and the subsequent sighs will be a testament to the power of cinnamon and pecans! Serve warm with orange juice, coffee, and scrambled eggs.

Yield: 6 rolls

1 package (1 tablespoon) active dry yeast
Pinch sugar
¼ cup warm water (105° to 115°)
1 cup sour cream
½ cup (1 stick) unsalted butter, melted
2 tablespoons sugar
2 eggs
1 teaspoon salt
4 cups unbleached all-purpose or bread flour

Pecan Filling
2½ cups pecans, finely chopped
1 cup granulated sugar
½ cup brown sugar
3 tablespoons ground cinnamon

Rich Egg Glaze, page 115

1. Sprinkle yeast and sugar over warm water in a small bowl. Stir to dissolve and let stand until foamy, about 10 minutes.
2. In a large bowl, combine sour cream, butter, sugar, eggs, and salt with a whisk. Add yeast mixture and 1 cup flour. Beat hard for 3 minutes, or until smooth. Add flour ½ cup at a time with a wooden spoon to make a very soft dough, using no more than 4 cups flour in all. Divide into 6 balls and wrap in plastic wrap. Refrigerate overnight.
3. In the morning, combine ingredients for pecan filling. Roll out 1 ball to a 6-by-12-inch rectangle on a lightly floured surface. Sprinkle with about ¾ cup pecan filling. Roll up from long end and pinch seams and edges. Repeat with remaining dough. Place on a greased or parchment-lined baking sheet seam down. Cover loosely with plastic wrap and let rise about 60 minutes, or until puffy. Slash each roll ½ inch deep into 6 sections.
4. Brush with egg glaze and bake in a preheated 375° oven 15 to 20 minutes, or until golden. Cool 10 minutes on a rack and cut into sections.

Quick Breads

THE DISCOVERY OF BAKING SODA and baking powder during the nineteenth century made possible the sweet quick breads, biscuits, and muffins we know today. The new American brainchild was an instant success across the expanding continent.

Muffins and sweet breads graced every sophisticated tea table from the Palace Hotel in San Francisco to the Boston Ritz-Carlton. The homely biscuit was a feature of cowboy chuck wagons and gracious Southern mansions. Quick breads, traditionally made in the home kitchen fresh for every meal, became the pride and soul of each household.

Today commercial muffin shops sporting a wide variety of fluffy gems are a new fad. Guests return to their favorite bed and breakfast inns for house specialties such as Spiced Applesauce Muffins and Pear-Spice Coffee Cake warm from the oven. The new American cooking includes a variety of regional corn breads, from subtly Southern to spicy Southwestern in style.

Quick breads are easy for a beginning baker to master. They are an alternative to the time-consuming process of baking with yeast. Mixed and ready to bake in 15 minutes or less, quick breads need no rising time. They can even wait for hours in the refrigerator before baking to emerge right on time out of the oven.

The family of quick breads is divided between batter and dough breads. Quick batter breads include muffins, sweet loaves (or tea breads), corn breads, coffee cakes, pancakes, waffles, and popovers. They are baked in molds, such as loaf pans, because they are too thin to hold their own shape. Many recipes for quick batter breads are wonderfully embellished with fresh or dried fruits, nuts, and spices. Sweet loaves are best the day after they are baked, when the flavors and texture have had time to develop. Quick dough breads include biscuits, scones, soda breads, dumplings, shortcakes, and cobbler toppings. They are rich, tender, free-form cakes.

MUFFINS

WORLD TAKE NOTICE OF THE HUMBLE MUFFIN: the missing link between cake and bread, a combination of sweet and nutritious. The classic muffin with its round dome, straight sides, and slightly coarse texture can be mixed, baked, and served well within an hour.

Muffins can be made every day of the year, utilizing the season's harvest: plump blueberries or zucchini in summer, tart cranberries and lemons in the winter, persimmon and pumpkin purees all through the fall, and, of course, the first rosy apricots and red currants in late spring.

Use all-purpose flour for the best muffins, except where specifically noted. Pastry and cake flour produce a muffin that is too soft to hold its shape. I have always mixed my batters by hand, but the electric mixer and the food processor work equally well, using a very short, controlled mixing time.

The classic formula for a tender muffin is two parts flour to one part liquid ingredients. The technique most commonly used for the perfect muffin involves combining the wet and dry ingredients with a minimum amount of stirring to form a lumpy dough, which is then spooned into a greased form.

Too much mixing will result in a heavy muffin with a very coarse and stiff texture full of tunnels. Take care to combine batter only until just mixed, no more than 10 to 20 strokes. Although the muffin batter itself can vary depending on the flours and liquids used, the batter will usually not be silky and pourable, but will be coarse and fall in globs from the spoon. There are occasional exceptions, such as the Maple Bran Muffin, which has a thin batter.

Fill muffin cups about three-fourths full for thin batters and level with the top of the pan for thick batters. Use a small ¼-cup ladle, large spoon, or ice cream scoop for easiest handling. Too little batter or too low a heat in the oven makes for a flat-shaped muffin. Too much batter in the cup will cause the batter to spill over, giving an uneven shape. Practice to find the amount that gives you the size of muffin you desire. Place immediately on the center rack of a hot oven for best results. An oven that is too hot will produce a nonsymmetrical shape, with the sides of the muffin extending up out of the cup. If this is the case, decrease oven temperature by 25°. Bake for about 20 minutes, or until the muffins are lightly browned around the edges, springy to the touch, and a cake tester comes out clean. The top of the muffins will have a dry appearance. The muffins will release more easily from the cup if allowed to sit about 5 minutes. Remove and finish cooling on a rack before eating.

Muffin batter may be kept in the refrigerator and baked over a 3-day period. Much

after that, the flour breaks down and will develop a grayish tinge. Muffin batter may also be spooned into paper-lined forms and frozen. Freeze in a muffin tin. When frozen, remove to a plastic bag for storage. Place the frozen uncooked muffins in a muffin tin and bake in a preheated oven about 5 minutes longer than the required time on the original recipe.

Most recipes are geared to the standard 2¾-inch-diameter cup, unless noted otherwise. But the miniature muffin "gem" cup or oversized muffin cups give equally delicious results. The preparation of the pans and the baking temperatures remain constant, but the yield and baking times should be adjusted proportionately. Muffin cakes can be made from any muffin recipe, baked in an 8-to 9-inch soufflé dish, casserole, or charlotte mold, but I find the springform pan contributes to the easiest handling.

FRESH-LEMON MUFFINS

*T*he lemon tree is as common a sight in California as it is in Sicily, Greece, India, China, the Azores, Australia, and Andalusia, for it loves coastal habitats. As important a food as it is, the lemon is never eaten by itself, but always in combination with other foods. It gives freshness and elegance to baked goods.

This muffin is an incredible taste treat. Bake it plain, or layer 1 cup sweetened-to-taste raspberries or cranberries in the dough. It is delicious with butter and jam, but also wonderful split and served with fresh berries or peaches with whipped cream. This recipe also makes equally delicious fresh orange muffins.

Yield: 8 muffins

1¾ cups unbleached all-purpose flour
½ cup sugar
1½ teaspoons baking powder
½ teaspoon baking soda
¼ teaspoon salt
Grated zest of 2 lemons
½ cup (1 stick) unsalted butter, melted
⅔ cup fresh lemon juice
2 teaspoons lemon extract
2 eggs

Lemon Glaze
¼ cup granulated sugar
¼ cup fresh lemon juice

1. In a large bowl, combine flour, sugar, baking powder, soda, salt, and zest.
2. In another bowl, mix butter, lemon juice, extract, and eggs. Stir wet mixture into dry ingredients just until moistened. Spoon into greased muffin cups, mounding full.
3. Bake in a preheated 400° oven for 20 to 25 minutes, or until lightly browned around edges and springy to the touch. Meanwhile, make lemon glaze: combine sugar and lemon juice in a small saucepan. Heat to just dissolve sugar. Do not boil. Set aside.
4. Pierce baked muffins in a few places. Pour over warm lemon glaze. Cool in pan 5 minutes to absorb glaze before removing to cool completely on a rack.

MUFFIN CUP SIZE	BAKING TIME (375° to 400°)	YIELD
Miniature or gem (1⅝ inch diameter)	10 to 15 minutes	18 to 20
Regular size (2¾ inch diameter)	20 to 25 minutes	9 to 10
Oversized muffin (3¼ inch diameter)	25 to 30 minutes	6 to 7
Muffin cake (8-to 9-inch diameter)	55 to 65 minutes	1

FRESH-BERRY MUFFINS

This is the essential American berry muffin. The layering of the berries with the batter works perfectly to keep delicate fruits such as boysenberries, blackberries, and raspberries from being crushed during folding. It is important to sweeten the berries to taste before assembling the muffins. Each batch of berries will vary in its acidity-sweetness balance. Try fresh currants in this recipe, if you can find them. These muffins are best served warm and fresh with sweet butter.

Yield: 9 muffins

1 cup fresh boysenberries, blackberries,
  raspberries, or currants
2 to 4 tablespoons sugar
6 tablespoons unsalted butter, softened
¼ cup brown sugar
2 eggs
2 cups unbleached all-purpose flour
1 tablespoon baking powder
½ teaspoon salt
1 cup half and half

Cinnamon Sugar
¼ cup granulated sugar mixed with
1 teaspoon ground cinnamon

1. In a medium bowl, sprinkle berries with sugar to taste and let stand for 15 minutes. In a large bowl, cream butter and sugar until fluffy. Add eggs one at a time and beat until combined.
2. In a medium bowl combine dry ingredients. Add to wet ingredients alternately with half and half, mixing until just moistened. Half-fill greased muffin cups with batter and sprinkle with fruit. Cover with remaining batter level with top of pan, and sprinkle with Cinnamon Sugar.
3. Bake in a preheated 375° oven for 20 to 25 minutes. Muffins will be dry and springy to the touch. Cool in pan 5 minutes before removing to cool on a rack.

MAPLE BRAN MUFFINS

This is a moist, dark, classic whole-grain muffin. It is the perfect batter to dress up with a cup of fresh blueberries or chopped nuts in place of the raisins. Substitute an equal amount of dark molasses for the maple syrup to produce a dark iron-rich muffin. Serve with a tart berry butter or jam (see pages 119 and 123).

Yield: 18 muffins

2 cups bran
2½ cups buttermilk
1 cup maple syrup
⅓ cup vegetable oil
1 tablespoon nut liqueur, such as hazelnut
  or macadamia
2 eggs
2 cups unbleached all-purpose flour
½ teaspoon salt
1 teaspoon ground cinnamon
2 teaspoons baking soda
1 cup golden raisins

1. Combine bran, buttermilk, maple syrup, oil, liqueur, and eggs in a large mixing bowl. Whisk until smooth. Let stand 10 minutes.
2. Combine dry ingredients in a medium bowl and add to wet. Stir until evenly moistened, smooth and creamy. Batter will be quite wet. Stir in raisins. Ladle batter into greased muffin tins, filling about three-fourths full. A ¼-cup ladle or ice cream scoop works well.
3. Bake in a preheated 375° oven for 20 minutes. Muffins are done when tops are dry and springy to the touch. Sides will be golden. Cool in pans 5 minutes before removing to cool on a rack.

OLD-FASHIONED OATMEAL MUFFINS

Serve these comforting muffins with Winter Apricot Conserve (page 125) during the cold months or fold in 1 cup fresh blueberries in the summer. This is a wonderfully filling and nutritious muffin.

Yield: 8 muffins

1 cup rolled oats
1 cup buttermilk

Brown Sugar Streusel
⅓ cup unbleached all-purpose flour
½ cup brown sugar
4 tablespoons chilled unsalted butter, cut into
  slices

½ cup brown sugar
¼ cup vegetable oil
2 eggs
1 cup unbleached all-purpose flour
2 teaspoons baking powder
1 teaspoon ground cinnamon
½ teaspoon baking soda
¼ teaspoon salt

1. Combine oats and buttermilk in a large bowl and let sit 1 hour, covered, in refrigerator.
2. To make streusel, combine flour and sugar. Work in bits of butter with your fingers until consistency of coarse crumbs. (This will keep, covered, in refrigerator if any is left over.)
3. Stir brown sugar, oil, and eggs into oat mixture with a whisk. Mix dry ingredients in a medium bowl and stir into oat mixture until just combined. Batter will be lumpy.
4. Spoon into greased pans level with top of cups. Top with streusel. Bake in a preheated 375° oven for 20 to 25 minutes, or until dry to the touch and springy. Remove from pan and cool on a rack.

OLD-FASHIONED PRUNE MUFFINS

One bite is all it takes to figure out why this moist muffin is so popular. Once a standard bakery item, it has all but disappeared from the commercial scene, possibly for being too homely. A good prune muffin is worth its weight in gold.

Yield: 12 muffins

1 cup unbleached all-purpose flour
1 cup whole-wheat flour
1 cup brown sugar
1 teaspoon baking powder
1 teaspoon baking soda
½ teaspoon salt
1½ teaspoons ground cinnamon
½ teaspoon ground mace
½ cup (1 stick) unsalted butter, melted
2 eggs
½ cup buttermilk
½ cup prune juice
1 teaspoon vanilla extract
12 ounces moist-pack prunes, coarsely chopped
12 walnut or pecan halves

1. In a large bowl, combine flours, brown sugar, baking powder, baking soda, salt, and spices.
2. In a medium bowl, combine butter, eggs, buttermilk, prune juice, and vanilla extract and beat with a whisk until eggs are light. Add flour mixture and stir until just moistened. Fold in prunes.
3. Spoon into greased muffin cups, filling level with top of cups, and top each with a nut meat half. Bake in a preheated 375° oven for 20 minutes, or until a cake tester comes out clean and tops are springy to the touch. Let stand 5 minutes before turning out onto a rack to cool.

BANANA-PECAN MUFFINS

The banana is so common a sight on the American table, you would think it was grown in Southern California or Florida. But bananas grow in the damp exotic jungles of the world, and there are many varieties, from gigantic plantains to small finger bananas. The over-ripe banana has a black, mottled skin, and the fruit is very sweet and soft, just right for baking. The baked goods bananas grace are exceedingly popular and delicious, especially these muffins, which border on absolute perfection.

Yield: 10 muffins

1 cup sugar
½ cup vegetable oil
2 eggs
1⅓ cups (3 medium) mashed ripe bananas
2 cups unbleached all-purpose flour
1 teaspoon baking powder
1 teaspoon baking soda
½ teaspoon ground cinnamon
¼ teaspoon salt
¾ cup pecans, finely chopped

Streusel Topping
½ cup sugar
⅓ cup unbleached all-purpose flour
4 tablespoons chilled unsalted butter

1. Prepare Streusel: Combine sugar and flour until blended. Cut in cold butter with a pastry blender or a food processor until coarse crumbs are formed. Set aside.
2. Beat sugar, oil, and eggs until light colored and foamy with a whisk or an electric mixer. Add mashed banana and beat well. The banana will be incorporated but have a few chunks.
3. In another bowl, combine flour, baking powder, baking soda, cinnamon, and salt. Add pecans. Add banana mixture and stir with a large spatula until just moistened, about 10 strokes.
4. Spoon into greased muffin cups, level with top of pan. Place 1 tablespoon streusel on each. Place in a preheated 375° oven for 20 to 25 minutes, or until a cake tester comes out clean and tops are dry and springy to the touch. Cool in muffin tin about 5 minutes before turning out onto a rack to cool.

SPICED APPLESAUCE MUFFINS

*T*his is one of the best muffins I have ever made. Applesauce muffins are an American standard, but good recipes are scarce. Bette's Oceanview Diner in Berkeley makes a fabulous one, but I lost the recipe they generously shared with me. So I had to re-create it as best I could here. Make it with commercial applesauce or, for a truly memorable muffin, use the Apple Butter recipe in this book (page 125).

Yield: 9 muffins

1¼ cups unsweetened applesauce
¼ cup brown sugar
2 large eggs
2 tablespoons vegetable oil
2 cups unbleached all-purpose flour
2 teaspoons baking soda
½ teaspoon powdered instant espresso
½ teaspoon ground cinnamon
½ teaspoon freshly grated nutmeg
¾ cup raisins or chopped nuts (optional)

1. In a large bowl, mix together applesauce, brown sugar, eggs, and oil.
2. In another bowl, combine flour, baking soda, espresso, and spices. Add to wet mixture, stirring to just moisten. Add raisins or nuts, if desired.
3. Spoon into 9 greased muffin cups level with tops of cups. Bake in a preheated 375° oven for 20 to 25 minutes, or until a cake tester comes out clean and tops are springy to the touch. Let stand 5 minutes before turning out of cups to cool on a rack.

PERSIMMON MUFFINS WITH RAISINS AND PEAR BRANDY

*T*his is a sweet and spicy cakelike muffin. The bright orange globe-shaped persimmon is one of fall's glories. Persimmons make a spectacular centerpiece while waiting to be ripe enough to eat. The fruit is quite astringent raw, but very nice used in baking when overripe. At this point the texture will turn from hard and crunchy to gelatinous and quite gooey. They lend a beautiful, moist character to muffins, cakes, cookies, and steamed puddings. The pear brandy used here is very special, but regular brandy is also nice.

Yield: 9 muffins

½ cup golden or dark raisins
¼ cup pear brandy
2 eggs
½ cup milk
⅓ cup walnut oil
½ cup sugar
½ cup persimmon puree, following
2 cups unbleached all-purpose flour
1 tablespoon baking powder
½ teaspoon each ground cinnamon, nutmeg, and cloves
½ teaspoon salt

1. Soak raisins in brandy overnight.
2. In a large bowl, mix together eggs, milk, oil, sugar, persimmon, and undrained raisins with a whisk.
3. Combine flour, baking powder, spices, and salt in a medium bowl. Stir into persimmon mixture until just moistened.
4. Pour into greased muffin cups, filling level with tops of cups. Bake in a pre-heated 400° oven for 20 minutes, or until a cake tester comes out clean and tops are springy to the touch. Cool 5 minutes before turning out onto a rack to cool.

Fresh Persimmon Puree
A fresh persimmon feels very soft when ripe, with a jellylike consistency. Cut fruit in half and scoop out flesh with a spoon, leaving the thin skin intact. Puree pulp in blender or food processor just until smooth. Use at once or add a few drops of lemon juice to prevent discoloration. Refrigerate up to 2 days or freeze. One large ripe persimmon yields about ½ to ¾ cup pulp.

BACON AND CORN MUFFINS

*T*his corn muffin flecked with crisp, savory bacon is a real old-fashioned bread. Serve with Whipped Honey Butter (page 118) with brunch or coffee, or with soups and salads. Remember to eliminate the salt in the recipe if your bacon is quite salty. Take care not to overbake these muffins.

Yield: 9 muffins

1 cup diced bacon (about 4 to 5 slices)
2 eggs
1 cup buttermilk
1/3 cup corn oil or melted butter
1 1/4 cups unbleached all-purpose flour
3/4 cup yellow cornmeal
1/4 cup sugar
2 teaspoons baking powder
1/2 teaspoon baking soda
1/4 teaspoon salt

1. In a medium skillet, cook bacon until crisp, then remove from pan with a slotted spoon and drain on paper towels.
2. In a medium bowl, beat eggs, buttermilk, and oil until light with a whisk.
3. In another bowl, combine flour, cornmeal, sugar, baking powder, baking soda, and salt. Add buttermilk mixture and stir until just moistened. Fold in bacon. Batter will be lumpy.
4. Fill greased muffin cups level with tops of cups. Bake in a preheated 400° oven for about 20 minutes, or until a cake tester comes out clean and tops are springy to the touch. Let muffins stand 5 minutes before turning out onto a rack to cool.

SMOKED GOUDA AND PARSLEY MUFFINS

*S*moked Dutch Gouda cheese is pale tan in color, with a chocolate-brown rind. It makes a wonderful muffin with a bit of tomato and parsley. Serve with soups and salads, or in a lunchbox in place of a sandwich, with fruit.

Yield: 10 muffins

2 cups unbleached all-purpose flour
2 teaspoons baking powder
1/2 teaspoon salt
1/4 teaspoon fresh-ground black pepper
1 cup milk
2 eggs
4 tablespoons unsalted butter, melted
1/4 cup chopped seeded plum tomato
1/4 cup chopped fresh parsley
4 ounces smoked Gouda cheese, diced fine
  (about 1 cup)

1. In a large bowl, combine flour, baking powder, salt, and pepper.
2. In another bowl, combine milk, eggs, and butter with a whisk until foamy and light. Stir in tomato, parsley, and cheese. Stir into dry ingredients until just combined.
3. Spoon batter into greased muffin cups, level with top of pan. Bake in a preheated 375° oven for 20 to 25 minutes, or until a cake tester comes out clean and tops are springy to the touch. Let stand in pans 5 minutes before removing to cool on a rack.

CHEDDAR CHEESE AND MUSTARD MUFFINS

*T*he combination of green onion and red bell peppers with a dash of sharp Dijon mustard makes a very aromatic savory muffin. Take a basket of these muffins to eat at your next picnic on the beach.

Yield: 10 muffins

2 tablespoons minced green onion
2 tablespoons minced red bell pepper
4 tablespoons unsalted butter
1 cup unbleached all-purpose flour
1 cup whole-wheat pastry flour
2 1/2 teaspoons baking powder
1/2 teaspoon salt
2 eggs
1 cup milk
2 tablespoons Dijon mustard
1 tablespoon sugar
1 cup grated Cheddar cheese (3 ounces)

1. In a small skillet, sauté onion and pepper in butter until soft. Set aside.
2. In a medium bowl, combine flours, baking powder, and salt. In a large bowl, beat eggs, milk, mustard, and sugar with a whisk until foamy. Stir in cheese and onion mixture with its butter. Stir dry ingredients into wet ingredients until just moistened.
3. Spoon into greased muffin cups level with tops of cups. Bake in a preheated 375° oven for 20 to 25 minutes, or until a cake tester comes out clean and tops are springy to the touch. Let stand 5 minutes before removing from pans to cool on racks.

WILD RICE AND SHIITAKE MUSHROOM MUFFINS

S hiitakes are pine-scented umbrella-shaped mushrooms with the satisfying texture of meat. Once only available as a Japanese specialty in dried form, the demanding American market now has farms raising the fresh fungi. Paired here with the woodsy swamp grass called wild rice, the *shiitake* makes a filling, savory muffin worthy of your finest simple garden salad. It's also good served with roast chicken and spring vegetables, slathered with fresh Parsley-Herb Butter, page 119.

Yield: 8 standard muffins or 18 mini muffins

1 medium shallot, minced
¼ cup unsalted butter
1 to 2 ounces sliced fresh shiitakes *(½ cup)*
1½ cups unbleached all-purpose flour
½ teaspoon salt
2 tablespoons brown sugar
2 teaspoons baking powder
1 cup cold cooked wild rice (⅓ cup raw),
  page 116
2 eggs
1 cup milk

1. In a skillet, sauté shallot in butter until soft. Add *shiitakes* and sauté until soft and liquid has evaporated, about 5 minutes. Set aside to cool.
2. In a large bowl, mix together flour, salt, sugar, and baking powder. In another bowl, combine cold rice, eggs, milk, and sautéed mushrooms with butter. Add rice mixture to dry ingredients and stir until just moistened.
3. Spoon into greased muffin cups level with tops of cups. Bake in a preheated 375° oven for 20 to 25 minutes, or until a cake tester comes out clean and tops are springy to the touch. Let stand 5 minutes before turning out onto a rack to cool.

*M*AKING BEAUTIFUL BISCUITS is not an impossible dream. A wonderful biscuit is crisp on the outside and flaky and moist on the inside. The secret is a gentle, fast, cool touch.

Pastry flour has a low gluten content and makes the best biscuits, but all-purpose flour can also be used. The best flours for biscuits still come from Southern mills with names like White Lily and Martha White, due to their good locally grown wheat. Do not substitute self-rising flour unless it is specifically called for in a recipe.

Use very cold unsalted butter for the best flavor. Different cooks swear by such regional preferences as vegetable shortening, lard, and even bear fat as their secret ingredient. The fat is cut in with a quick motion of the fingers, a pastry blender, a fork, or two knives. Modern recipes may be adapted for the electric mixer and food processor. Combine very quickly to just break up the fat and form a mixture resembling coarse crumbs. Later, during baking, the moisture in the fat will evaporate and create a flaky texture.

Add cold liquid in the form of milk, cream, buttermilk, or water to create a soft, rather rough dough that is just moist to the touch. Any other wet ingredients, such as yeast or eggs, are also added at this time. To make drop biscuits, more liquid is added at this point. Drop biscuits are never quite as delicate as rolled biscuits due to the higher percentage of liquid. Always keep a small portion of the liquid in reserve to add at the very last so you can control the amount of moisture in the dough. Turn the dough out onto a lightly floured work surface and gently knead to smooth out the dough. This kind of kneading is a soft folding of the dough rather than the active kneading process for yeast breads. Remember, the secret to good biscuits is to handle the dough in a gentle, fast manner so it will stay as cool as possible throughout the mixing process.

Roll or pat the dough gently to the desired thickness, keeping in mind that the baked product will be about double in size. With a floured cutter, press firmly into the dough with a straight downward motion rather than a twisting motion. To make square biscuits without a cutter, cut the dough with a chef's knife into a grid, which also gives you the advantage of not having to reroll the scraps. To reroll, press the scraps together gently and keep the top as level as possible for an even biscuit.

Bake on an ungreased or parchment-lined baking sheet in the center of a very hot oven as directed by the specific recipe. For soft-sided biscuits, arrange them so their sides are almost touching on the baking sheet. For crisper biscuits, space them about 1 inch apart. Biscuits like to rest for a few minutes after being taken out of the oven to allow for some of the excess moisture to evaporate. They are best eaten hot and have a natural affinity for honey spreads or plain sweet butter. For the stray leftovers, wrap in aluminum foil and reheat at 325° for 10 to 12 minutes.

TO MAKE BISCUITS IN THE FOOD PROCESSOR

Add dry ingredients to the work bowl. Using a steel blade, pulse a few times to mix thoroughly. Add cold or frozen butter in pieces and process on and off until butter is the size of small peas. Add cold liquid. Process on and off just until ingredients are evenly moist and clumped together. Do not over-process past this point or biscuits will be tough. Immediately turn dough out of work bowl to knead gently, form, and bake.

SESAME WHOLE-WHEAT BUTTERMILK BISCUITS

Yield: 24 square biscuits

2 cups unbleached all-purpose flour
2 cups whole-wheat pastry flour
2 tablespoons sugar
2 tablespoons baking powder
1 teaspoon salt
1 cup (2 sticks) chilled unsalted butter, chopped
¾ to 1 cup buttermilk, as needed
4 eggs, slightly beaten
Rich Egg Glaze, page 115
¼ cup raw sesame seeds

1. Combine flours, sugar, baking powder, and salt in a large bowl and stir to combine evenly.
2. Cut in butter with pastry blender or 2 knives. The mixture will resemble coarse crumbs.
3. Add buttermilk and eggs and stir to just moisten all ingredients. The dough will be soft, then stiffen. The mixture will look shaggy, and flour may not be incorporated.
4. Turn dough out onto a lightly floured surface and knead gently about 10 times, just until dough holds together. Roll or pat out dough into a rectangle to a thickness of ½ to ¾ inch. Take care not to add too much flour. Cut with a sharp knife or pastry wheel to form 24 small squares. Brush gently with egg glaze and sprinkle heavily with sesame seeds.
5. Place ½ inch apart on a greased or parchment-lined sheet and bake in a preheated 425° oven for 15 to 18 minutes, or until golden. Let rest a few minutes and eat hot.

OATMEAL CREAM BISCUITS

Yield: 1 dozen biscuits

1½ cups unbleached all-purpose flour
½ cup rolled oats
2 tablespoons sugar
2½ teaspoons baking powder
½ teaspoon salt
Grated zest of 1 orange
5 tablespoons cold unsalted butter, chopped
¾ cup cold heavy cream
1 to 2 tablespoons extra cream for glazing
Additional rolled oats for sprinkling

1. In a large bowl, combine flour, oats, sugar, baking powder, salt, and zest.
2. Cut in butter with a pastry blender or 2 knives until mixture looks like coarse crumbs. There should be no big chunks of butter.
3. Add heavy cream with a wooden spoon and stir just to moisten all ingredients. The dough will be soft, then stiffen. Use a tablespoon more of cream, if necessary.
4. Turn dough out onto a lightly floured surface and knead gently about 10 times, just until dough holds together. Roll out to a thickness of about ½ inch. Cut with a floured 2-inch biscuit cutter. Reroll scraps to cut out additional biscuits. Brush tops with cream and sprinkle with rolled oats.
5. Place ½ inch apart on a greased or parchment-lined baking sheet. Bake in a preheated 425° oven for 15 to 18 minutes, or until golden. Cool about 5 minutes before serving hot.

GINGER-PUMPKIN BISCUITS

Yield: About 18 biscuits

2 cups unbleached all-purpose flour
3 tablespoons brown sugar
1 tablespoon baking powder
Grated zest of ½ lemon
½ teaspoon salt
½ cup (1 stick) cold unsalted butter, chopped
1½ teaspoons fresh-grated ginger root
½ cup half and half
⅔ cup cooked pureed pumpkin (page 61),
*   or canned pumpkin*

1. Mix together flour, sugar, baking powder, zest, and salt in a large bowl.
2. Cut in butter with a pastry blender or 2 knives until mixture looks like coarse meal or crumbs. Make sure big chunks of butter are broken down.
3. Combine ginger, half and half, and pumpkin. Stir into flour mixture to just moisten all ingredients. The dough will be stiff, but not dry.
4. Turn out dough onto a lightly floured surface and knead gently about 10 times, or just until dough holds together. Roll out to a thickness of about ½ inch. Cut with a floured 2-inch biscuit cutter or into squares with a pastry wheel. Reroll scraps to cut out additional biscuits.
5. Place ½ inch apart on a greased or parchment-lined baking sheet. Bake in a preheated 425° oven for 18 to 20 minutes, or until golden brown. Cool about 5 minutes before serving hot.

DATE SCONES

The date palm is the cultivated tree of the desert. The fruit is a deep earthy brown and intensely sweet with varying degrees of chewiness. Dates add a rich taste and texture to the breads they embellish. These delicate scones need only a dab of sweet butter to be pure pleasure on the breakfast table.

Yield: 8 scones

2 cups unbleached all-purpose flour
2 teaspoons baking powder
2 teaspoons ground cinnamon
1/2 teaspoon salt
4 tablespoons cold unsalted butter
1/2 cup chopped pitted dates (see page 116)
1/3 cup milk or cream
2 eggs
1 tablespoon sugar mixed with 1/2 teaspoon
   ground cinnamon for sprinkling

1. Combine flour, baking powder, cinnamon, and salt in a large bowl.
2. Cut in butter with a pastry blender or 2 knives until mixture looks like coarse crumbs. Add dates and stir gently to distribute evenly.
3. Add milk and eggs and stir until all ingredients are moistened. Add 1 tablespoon extra liquid if dough is too stiff.
4. Turn dough out onto a lightly floured surface and knead gently about 10 times, just until dough holds together. Divide dough into 2 equal portions. Pat each portion into a fat circle about 1 inch thick and 6 inches in diameter. With a knife, cut each circle into quarters, making 4 wedges.
5. Place wedges about 1 inch apart on a greased or parchment-lined baking sheet. Sprinkle with cinnamon sugar and bake in a preheated 400° oven for 15 to 20 minutes, or until golden. Serve immediately.

BUCKWHEAT-ORANGE BISCUITS

Serve these biscuits warm with butter and jam, with caviar and sour cream, or as an accompaniment to a deviled egg salad.

Yield: 30 to 34 cocktail biscuits

1 3/4 cups unbleached all-purpose flour
1/4 cup buckwheat flour
2 1/2 teaspoons baking powder
1/2 teaspoon salt
Grated zest of 1/2 orange
7 tablespoons cold unsalted butter, chopped
1/2 cup light cream
1/4 cup fresh orange juice

1. Combine flours, baking powder, salt, and zest in a large bowl.
2. Cut in butter with a pastry blender or 2 knives until mixture looks like coarse crumbs. There should be no big chunks of butter.
3. Add cream and orange juice and stir to just moisten all ingredients. Dough will be soft and then stiffen. Use a bit more cream if mixture seems too dry.
4. Turn dough out onto a lightly floured surface and knead gently about 10 times, just until dough holds together. Roll out to a thickness of about 1/4 to 1/2 inch. Cut with small cutters to make unusual shapes, such as hearts and half moons. Reroll scraps to cut out additional biscuits.
5. Place 1/2 inch apart on a greased or parchment-lined baking sheet. Bake immediately in a preheated 400° oven for 10 to 12 minutes, or until golden. Cool a few minutes before serving.

BASIL AND MOZZARELLA BISCUITS

These are excellent with soups and salads.

Yield: About 16 biscuits

1 3/4 cups unbleached all-purpose flour
1/4 cup whole-wheat flour
1 tablespoon baking powder
1/2 teaspoon salt
1 cup grated chilled whole-milk
   mozzarella cheese (3 ounces)
6 tablespoons cold unsalted butter, chopped
2 tablespoons chopped fresh basil
2/3 cup milk
2 tablespoons freshly grated Parmesan cheese

1. In a large bowl, combine flours, baking powder, salt, and cheese.
2. Cut in butter with a pastry blender or 2 knives until mixture looks like coarse crumbs. Add basil.
3. Add milk and stir just to moisten all ingredients. Dough will be soft and then stiffen. Use a bit more milk, if necessary.
4. Turn dough out onto a lightly floured surface and knead gently about 10 times, just until dough holds together. Roll out to a thickness of about 1/2 inch. Cut with a floured 2-inch biscuit cutter. Reroll scraps to cut out additional biscuits.
5. Place 1/2 inch apart on a greased or parchment-lined baking sheet. Sprinkle with Parmesan and bake in a preheated 425° oven for 15 to 18 minutes, or until golden. Cool 5 minutes before serving hot.

M Y VERY FIRST GIFT OF FOOD was a small loaf of moist nut bread, wrapped in colored cellophane and beribboned, given in friendship by a neighbor. Now, all nut breads I encounter are reminiscent of that cordial and thoughtful gesture. Quick loaves are a sure first step for the budding baker, and, with a good recipe, success is easily attained. A quick loaf is moist, flavorful, and dense in texture, with a characteristic top crack running its length due to expansion during baking.

Unless otherwise noted, a recipe using 2 cups of flour will fill one rectangular 8- or 9-inch standard loaf pan, pâté pan with collapsing sides, or three 5- or 6-inch baby loaf pans. Scrape the batter with a spatula into a pan brushed with melted butter. The right-size pan is important for a nice-looking bread. Fill two-thirds to three-quarters full and spread the batter to level the top. Batter quick breads will rise not quite double during baking. A variety of shapes are possible, so I keep a collection of round, 8-inch-square, rectangular, and heart-shaped pans to choose from. One recipe will also fill a 6-cup mini-bundt pan or miniature decorative or plain tube pan, a 5-cup ring mold, and 8-inch charlotte molds and springform pans, which are also nice for coffee cakes.

Wet and dry ingredients are thoroughly mixed separately. The wet ingredients will aerate and expand in volume. When creaming butter, sugar, and eggs, the mixture should be fluffy and smooth—not gritty. The salt, leavening, and spices should be distributed evenly in the flour. When combining wet and dry ingredients, the rules are consistent for most quick breads: stir until just moist. The batter should not be smooth. Any other additions, such as fresh or dried fruits and nuts, are added now just to evenly distribute throughout the batter. Toss dried fruits with a bit of the flour to keep them from sinking in the batter when added.

Bake breads on the center rack of a moderately hot oven with plenty of room for circulation until the loaf is golden and firm to the touch and the surface has lost its shiny, wet appearance. The best test for doneness is to pierce the loaf in a few places with a knife or thin cake tester about 10 minutes before the designated time is up. When the bread is done, the tester will come out clean and the bread will have pulled away from the sides of the pan slightly. Cool about 15 minutes before removing from the pan to cool completely on a wire rack before wrapping.

Quick loaves may be stored at room temperature or refrigerated for about 2 weeks tightly wrapped. They are best served the day after baking. These breads freeze beautifully for up to 3 months. Wrap first in plastic, then foil. To thaw, let stand at room temperature, completely wrapped, for a few hours.

Serve with butter, cream cheese, or just plain for breakfast, snacks, or tea. These breads are also good with fruit, seafood, or poultry salads.

ORANGE-DATE TEA BREAD

*T*his bread is moist in texture and subtle in flavor with a hint of orange: an absolutely exceptional bread that is not overly rich. Slice thin for breakfast or serve alongside a chicken salad with pecans. After baking, wrap and let stand for one day at room temperature to develop flavor.

Yield: One 8½-by-4½-inch loaf or
6-cup mini-bundt

¾ cup chopped pitted dates
¼ cup boiling water
½ cup (1 stick) unsalted butter,
    at room temperature
1 cup sugar
Grated zest of 1 orange
1 egg
2 cups unbleached all-purpose flour
1 teaspoon baking powder
1 teaspoon baking soda
¼ teaspoon salt
1 cup milk
1 teaspoon vanilla extract
½ cup pecans, finely chopped

Orange Glaze
⅓ cup granulated sugar
3 tablespoons fresh orange juice
1 teaspoon orange brandy

1. In a small bowl, cover dates with boiling water and macerate 10 minutes, or until soft.
2. In a large bowl, cream butter, sugar, and zest until fluffy. Add egg and beat thoroughly.
3. In another bowl, combine flour, baking powder, baking soda, and salt. Combine milk and vanilla in another bowl.
4. Add flour mixture alternately with milk to creamed mixture, beginning and ending with flour and beating well after each addition. Fold in pecans and soaked dates with their liquid.

5. Spoon batter into a well-greased loaf pan or 6-cup mini-bundt pan. Bake in a preheated 350° oven for 40 to 45 minutes, or until a cake tester comes out clean.
6. In a small bowl, combine sugar, orange juice, and brandy. Immediately upon removing bread from oven, slowly pour all of orange glaze over hot cake. Let cake stand 20 minutes to absorb glaze before turning out onto a rack to cool completely.

PIÑA–MACADAMIA NUT BREAD

*T*he macadamia nut is a relative newcomer to the nut world, a specialty of Hawaii along with the pineapple. Both are natives from other exotic lands, Australia and the Caribbean, respectively. Macadamia nuts need to be bought shelled, as the nut is so hard it was at one time thought to be uncrackable. For baking, use unsalted nuts, or else rinse and dry salted nuts. Fresh ripe pineapples have an intoxicating fragrance and a flavor reminiscent of other juicy fruits. Its popularity as the King Pine has also made it a top quality canned fruit. This combination of piña, macadamias, fresh ginger, and coconut makes a rich and exotic tropical fruit nut bread.

Yield: Three 6-by-3-by-2-inch loaves

4 eggs
¾ cup sugar
½ cup vegetable oil
One 8-ounce can crushed pineapple in juice
2 teaspoons grated ginger root
½ cup buttermilk
3 cups unbleached all-purpose flour
2½ teaspoons baking powder
½ teaspoon salt
½ teaspoon baking soda
½ cup sweetened grated coconut
½ cup chopped macadamia nuts

1. In a large bowl, combine eggs, sugar, and oil and beat until light colored and fluffy. Add pineapple, ginger, and buttermilk until just combined.
2. Combine flour, baking powder, salt, and soda in a medium bowl and stir to combine evenly. Mix with pineapple mixture until well combined. Fold in coconut and nuts.
3. Divide batter equally among 3 greased 6-by-3-inch pans and bake in a preheated 350° oven for 35 to 40 minutes, or until a cake tester comes out clean. Cool 10 minutes in pans. Remove from pans to cool completely on a rack before slicing.

CARROT AND TANGERINE BREAD

*T*his is a moist, heavenly loaf with a spicy fragrance and a crispy, sweet top crust. The texture is meant to be very smooth, but it can be embellished with about ½ cup shredded coconut, poppy seeds, diced dried apricots, finely chopped nuts, or raisins, if desired. If tangerines are not in season, use oranges or substitute an orange liqueur for the citrus juice required. Serve with whipped cream cheese, mango chutney, or Winter Apricot Conserve, page 125. Carrot bread is very good alongside chicken or crab salad.

Yield: 2 loaves

3 cups unbleached all-purpose flour
1½ teaspoons baking powder
1½ teaspoons baking soda
¼ teaspoon salt
2 teaspoons ground cinnamon
4 eggs
2 cups sugar
1 cup vegetable oil
1 teaspoon vanilla extract
2 tablespoons tangerine juice
Grated zest of 1 tangerine
2 cups finely grated raw carrots

1. In a medium bowl, combine flour, baking powder, baking soda, salt, and cinnamon.
2. In a large bowl, beat eggs and sugar until thick and light colored. Add oil gradually and beat hard until doubled in volume. Add vanilla, tangerine juice, and zest. Fold in grated carrots.
3. Stir dry ingredients into wet until smooth and well combined.
4. Turn batter into two greased 9-by-5-inch pans, filling no more than two-thirds full. Bake in a preheated 350° oven for 50 to 60 minutes, or until a cake tester comes out clean. Let stand in pan 10 minutes before turning bread out onto a rack on its side to cool completely. Wrap in plastic wrap and let stand at room temperature overnight before slicing.

WHOLE-WHEAT IRISH HERB BREAD

*I*rish soda breads are truly underestimated, except by the few who crave good Gaelic-style bread. The savory herbs in this bread go well with butter and a soft cheese. This is a basic recipe, enabling the baker to substitute up to 1 cup of oat flour for wheat flour, or to exchange the herbs for spices such as ground cinnamon, cardamom, or coriander. Eat crusty and warm or at room temperature.

Yield: 2 medium round loaves

2 cups unbleached all-purpose flour
2 cups whole-wheat flour
1/3 cup brown sugar
1 tablespoon baking powder
1 teaspoon baking soda
1 teaspoon salt
1 teaspoon dried basil
1/2 teaspoon dried thyme
1/2 teaspoon dried marjoram or oregano
1/2 cup raw sunflower seeds
1 cup dried currants

1 1/2 cups buttermilk
2 eggs
2 tablespoons unsalted butter, melted

1. In a large bowl, combine flours, brown sugar, baking powder, baking soda, salt, herbs, seeds, and currants.
2. In another bowl, combine buttermilk, eggs, and butter with a whisk. Beat slightly. Add wet ingredients to dry and stir with a wooden spoon just to moisten. Turn out onto a lightly floured surface and knead gently until dough comes together, about 5 times.
3. Divide dough into 2 equal portions and place on a greased or parchment-lined baking sheet, or in 2 greased 8-inch cake pans. With a sharp knife, slash tops with an X about 1/2 inch deep. Bake in preheated 375° oven for 30 to 40 minutes, or until brown and crusty.

BUTTERMILK CORN BREAD

*T*his corn bread is the best: moist and flavorful. The natural mate for a meal of poultry, game, or baked beans, corn bread is our indigenous American bread. The skill of cooking with corn was taught by the East Coast native Americans to the first settlers. Corn bread was originally made with ground meal, maple syrup, and water. There were no leavening or dairy products. It was baked on a hot stone, wrapped around a green twig and cooked over an open fire, or boiled in a husk.

Corn breads seem to complement every kind of food. Serve warm from the oven with Pecan-Honey Butter or Parsley-Herb Butter (page 119). Serve day-old wedges with butter and a small pitcher of maple syrup for breakfast. At the end of this recipe is a list of ingredients that may be added to the batter to create a wide variety of corn breads.

Yield: One 9-inch round bread; 6 to 8 servings

1 cup unbleached all-purpose flour
1 cup yellow cornmeal
1/4 cup sugar
1 tablespoon baking powder
1/2 teaspoon salt
2 eggs
1 cup buttermilk
4 tablespoons unsalted butter, melted

1. Combine flour, cornmeal, sugar, baking powder, and salt in a large bowl.
2. In another bowl, mix eggs, buttermilk, and butter. Add to dry ingredients and stir until all ingredients are just blended. Take care not to overmix.
3. Pour batter into a greased 9-inch springform pan or pie plate. Bake in a preheated 400° oven about 25 minutes until golden around the edges and a cake tester comes out clean. Let stand 15 minutes before cutting in wedges to serve.

VARIATIONS

- 1 cup finely chopped pecans
- 1 cup blueberries, raspberries, or cranberries, sugared to taste (this is excellent for breakfast)
- 1 grated medium summer squash, 1/2 teaspoon dried oregano, and 1/4 cup freshly grated Parmesan cheese
- Grated zest of 2 oranges
- 1 cup grated Cheddar cheese
- 1 cup fresh or thawed frozen corn kernels
- 1/2 cup canned or homemade pumpkin puree and 1/2 cup toasted pine nuts
- 1/2 cup diced canned peeled green chilies, 1/2 teaspoon ground cumin, and 1/2 cup grated jack cheese (nice with chili or bean dishes)
- Substitute 1/2 cup pureed cooked carrots for 1/2 cup liquid

APPLE UPSIDE-DOWN COFFEE CAKE

*C*offee cakes are usually categorized as a complement to the breakfast table, as they are less sweet than regular cakes. But they are also good late in the day with a cup of tea, or even as a dessert with gently whipped sweet cream, *crème fraîche*, or vanilla ice cream. When apples are baked under a batter, they become caramelized, which balances the tartness of the fruit. After baking, the cake is turned upside down to reveal overlapping slices of apple. The combination of baked fruit topped with a very simple yet flavorful cake has a rustic appeal. Firm fall and winter cooking apples, such as Macintosh, Rome Beauty, Golden Delicious, and Pippins, are best. Substitute pears or poached quince for delightful variations. This is best eaten warm from the oven.

Yield: One 9-inch cake, round or square; about 8 servings

3 tablespoons unsalted butter,
* at room temperature*
1/3 cup sugar
1 teaspoon ground cinnamon
1/4 cup slivered almonds or hazelnuts
2 cups unbleached all-purpose flour
3 large apples, peeled, cored, and sliced
* about 1/4-inch thick*
1/2 cup (1 stick) unsalted butter,
* at room temperature*
1 cup packed brown sugar
2 eggs
1 1/2 teaspoons baking powder
1/2 teaspoon baking soda
1/4 teaspoon salt
1 teaspoon vanilla extract
1 tablespoon rum or Calvados
1 cup buttermilk

1. Using entire amount of butter, heavily and evenly grease a 9-by-4-inch round cake or springform pan lined on the bottom with parchment. The sides should be more lightly greased than the bottom. Combine sugar and cinnamon and evenly sprinkle over bottom of greased pan. Set aside.
2. Grind nuts with 1/4 cup of flour in a hand grinder or food processor until the consistency of a fine meal. Set aside.
3. Arrange the more perfectly sliced apples neatly around outer edge of prepared pan, tightly overlapping to form a circular design. Form a second circle in center. Layer remaining apple slices evenly in pan over arranged apples, covering any openings between slices, being certain entire surface is covered completely with apples.
4. In a large bowl or with an electric mixer, cream butter and sugar until fluffy, about 3 minutes. Add eggs one at a time, beating well after each addition.
5. In another bowl, combine remaining flour, baking powder, baking soda, salt, and ground almonds. Mix vanilla, rum, and buttermilk. Alternately add dry ingredients and buttermilk, beginning and ending with dry ingredients and beating well after each addition to make a smooth, fluffy batter. Spoon batter over arranged apples and spread evenly in pan.
6. Bake in preheated 350° oven for 45 to 50 minutes, or until a cake tester comes out clean. Let cake rest 5 minutes. With a small flexible knife, separate cake from sides of pan. Invert pan onto a cake rack. Gently shake pan to loosen cake and remove pan, lifting carefully.

VANILLA–SOUR CREAM COFFEE CAKE

*T*his is the quintessential coffee cake, made with pure vanilla extract and layered with nuts. The original source for vanilla was Mexico and the beans grown there today are still considered the finest. The vanilla pod is the fruit of a flowering jungle orchid. Vanilla is among the most expensive spices in the world, as the growing and extract processing is very labor-intensive. If cake is baked in a tube pan, spoon large, fresh strawberries into the center when serving.

Yield: One 10-inch round cake or 12-cup bundt cake, or two 9-by-5-inch loaves

3 cups unbleached all-purpose flour
1 1/2 teaspoons baking powder
1 1/2 teaspoons baking soda
1/4 teaspoon salt
3/4 cup (1 1/2 sticks) unsalted butter,
* at room temperature*
1 1/2 cups sugar
4 eggs
2 teaspoons vanilla extract
1 1/4 cups sour cream
3/4 cup packed light brown sugar
3/4 cup pecans, walnuts, or hazelnuts,
* finely chopped*
2 teaspoons ground cinnamon
1/3 cup Vanilla Powdered Sugar, page 116
* or powdered sugar (optional)*

1. In a medium bowl, combine flour, baking powder, baking soda, and salt. Set aside.
2. Cream butter and sugar in a large bowl or with an electric mixer until smooth and fluffy. Add eggs one at a time, beating thoroughly after each addition. Blend in vanilla and sour cream until just smooth.

3. Gradually add dry ingredients and beat well until fluffy and light colored. There should be no lumps or dry spots.
4. Combine brown sugar, nuts, and cinnamon in a small bowl. Place about one-third of batter into a well-greased pan. Sprinkle with one-third of nut mixture. Repeat, making three layers of batter and ending with a layer of nut mixture.
5. Bake in a preheated 350° oven 55 to 60 minutes, or until a cake tester comes out clean and top of cake is not shiny. Let stand in pan about 15 minutes before removing from pan to cool completely on a rack right side up. Serve on a cake plate, dusted with Vanilla Powdered Sugar, if desired. This cake freezes well.

BLUEBERRY-BUTTERMILK COFFEE CAKE

*T*his is a fantastic blueberry cake to serve in warm wedges with butter or in a pool of Warm Lemon Sauce. Keep it in the freezer for a special brunch.

Yield: One 9-inch cake

Crumb Topping
¼ cup sugar
3 tablespoons unbleached all-purpose flour
Grated zest of ½ lemon
3 tablespoons cold unsalted butter

2½ cups unbleached all-purpose flour
2 teaspoons baking powder
½ teaspoon baking soda
1 cup sugar
¼ teaspoon salt
1 cup buttermilk
2 eggs
½ cup (1 stick) unsalted butter, melted
2 cups fresh or unsweetened frozen blueberries, rinsed and dried
Warm Lemon Sauce, following (optional)

1. Line bottom of a 9-inch springform pan with parchment and grease sides. Prepare crumb topping: mix together sugar, flour, and zest. Cut in butter until mixture forms coarse crumbs.
2. Mix together dry ingredients in a large bowl. Combine wet ingredients and stir into dry. Mix until well blended. Fold in blueberries with a few swift strokes.
3. Turn batter into prepared pan, smooth to level, and sprinkle with crumb topping. Bake in a preheated 375° oven for 50 to 60 minutes, or until a cake tester comes out clean.
4. After 15 minutes, remove sides of springform pan to cool cake before serving.

Warm Lemon Sauce
¼ cup fresh lemon juice
½ cup water
½ cup sugar
Grated zest of 2 lemons
1 tablespoon cornstarch
3 tablespoons unsalted butter

1. Combine lemon juice, ¼ cup water, sugar, and zest in a medium saucepan and heat to just dissolve sugar.
2. Dissolve cornstarch in remaining ¼ cup water. Add to hot lemon mixture. Stir constantly with a small whisk over medium heat until mixture comes to a full boil, thickens, and becomes clear.
3. Remove from heat and stir in butter.

PEAR-SPICE COFFEE CAKE

*F*resh pears have a subtle and fragile taste. Choose firm pears that are even in color. A mushy pear just won't do. Three-quarters of the American pear crop consists of the Bon Chrétien variety of the Bartlett pear, which is in its prime soon after picking in late September. This cake needs no embellishment, as the fruit is so delicate and delicious.

Yield: One 8-inch cake

Crumb Topping
½ cup brown sugar
⅓ cup unbleached all-purpose flour
½ teaspoon ground cinnamon
4 tablespoons cold unsalted butter

2 cups unbleached all-purpose flour
1 cup sugar
2 teaspoons baking powder
½ teaspoon baking soda
1 teaspoon ground cinnamon
½ teaspoon each ground nutmeg, cloves, and allspice
½ teaspoon salt
1 cup sour cream
4 tablespoons unsalted butter, melted
2 eggs
2 Bartlett pears, peeled and finely diced

1. Line the bottom of an 8-inch springform pan with parchment and grease sides. To make topping, mix together sugar, flour, and cinnamon. Cut in butter with a pastry cutter or 2 knives until mixture forms coarse crumbs.
2. Mix dry ingredients together in a large bowl. Combine sour cream, butter, and eggs. Mix wet and dry ingredients into a smooth and creamy batter. Fold pears in until evenly distributed.
3. Turn batter into prepared pan. Smooth to level and sprinkle with crumb topping. Bake in a preheated 350° oven for 55 to 60 minutes, or until a cake tester comes out clean.
4. After 15 minutes, remove sides of springform pan to cool cake completely on a rack before serving.

The Art of Glazing

A GLAZE IS BRUSHED onto a baked or unbaked yeasted loaf as a flavor and appearance enhancer. This is sometimes referred to as "the finishing touch." Appropriate embellishments also reflect the ingredients that make up the loaf: sesame seeds on a loaf made with sesame oil, rolled oats on oatmeal bread, or even just a dusting of flour. Glazing will help a pale loaf look darker and shiny. There is an appropriate glaze listed for most recipes in this book, but in reality, glazing is a personal preference and optional. Many of my loaves look beautiful to me "au naturel," but some loaves look more appealing with a shiny crust studded with seeds. Use a soft brush to gently apply the glaze, usually after slashing, and take care not to puncture or deflate the risen loaf before baking.

A simple brushing with milk or cream adds shine. A dusting of flour is beautiful on light, fluffy breads such as Buttermilk-Potato Bread or Rolls. Just sprinkle flour lightly over the unbaked surface of the bread. Often I will dust with flour and then lightly glaze the unfloured spaces for a contrast in finish.

An egg wash is typically used by bakers to produce a shiny crust and as a glue to hold on any solid embellishments such as nuts, seeds, herbs, meal flakes, and onions. The yolk alone produces a darker crust and is used on breads rich in fat and sugar. The white alone is a very shiny finish for a lean dough such as French bread.

Fats such as melted butter and oils can be brushed on a loaf at any point before, during, or after baking to keep a crust soft and shiny. Infusing warm oil with a sprig of fresh herbs gives added flavor.

Sweet glazes are brushed or poured on bread to make the crust sparkle and add a hint of dense flavor. From a sprinkling of maple or granulated sugar to a glaze of honey or molasses, the glaze can accent the sweetening used in the bread. Granulated sugar dissolved in water is the classic baker's glaze for sweet rolls. A dash of brandy or liqueur is a unique and individual touch. Warmed honey, jelly, and jam also are flavorful glazes. Brush hot loaves or rolls lightly.

EGG GLAZE

For French-style and country breads. Glaze before sprinkling with seeds.

1 egg white
1 tablespoon water
Dash salt

Whisk all ingredients together until combined and foamy.

RICH EGG GLAZE

For American-style loaf breads and *brioches*. Brush first before sprinkling with seeds.

1 yolk or 1 whole egg
1 tablespoon water, milk, or cream

Whisk all ingredients together until combined.

POWDERED SUGAR GLAZE FOR SWEET DOUGHS

A thin, shiny, and creamy colored icing for sweet breads and rolls. Choose a complementary flavor. Top with fruit and/or whole or chopped nuts while icing is moist. The garnish will adhere as the glaze dries.

1 cup sifted powdered sugar
2 to 3 tablespoons milk, cream, spirit, liqueur, or hot water

In a small mixing bowl, combine ingredients and whisk until smooth. Adjust consistency of glaze by adding liquid a few drops at a time. Drizzle over warm or cool bread in desired pattern.

VARIATIONS

Vanilla: Add ½ teaspoon pure vanilla extract.
Almond: Add ½ teaspoon pure almond extract.
Maple: Substitute maple syrup for milk.
Citrus: Substitute lemon, orange, lime, or tangerine juice for milk.
Chocolate: Add 1 tablespoon unsweetened cocoa powder.
Coffee: Add 1 teaspoon powdered instant espresso.
Spice: Add 1 teaspoon ground cinnamon or nutmeg.

CLEAR WASH FOR SWEET DOUGHS

¼ cup granulated sugar
¼ cup water

In a small saucepan, heat sugar and water until sugar dissolves and glaze is warm, about 5 minutes.

SALT WASH

To give a crisp crust to Italian and French breads and bread sticks.

1 teaspoon salt
¼ cup water

Combine ingredients in a small bowl.

MOLASSES GLAZE

Good on raisin and rye breads to give a dark sheen. Brush twice: once before baking and once during baking.

1 tablespoon molasses
2 tablespoons hot water

Combine ingredients in a small bowl.

CORNSTARCH WASH

Typically used on dense pumpernickel and rye breads to give a high gloss and harden the crust. Brush twice during baking, the last time 10 minutes before bread comes out of the oven.

½ cup water
1 tablespoon cornstarch

Place ingredients in a small saucepan and whisk over medium heat. Bring to a boil, stirring constantly until thick and translucent. Use immediately!

OIL WASH

To give a soft, shiny look to savory breads such as Tomato-Saffron or Fresh-Herb Bread.

1 whole egg
1 to 2 teaspoons olive or vegetable oil

In a small bowl, whisk ingredients together until combined and a bit foamy.

Embellishments & Special Techniques

To Cut Dried Fruit

Place dried fruit on a cutting board. Sprinkle a bit of flour from recipe onto fruit and chop with a chef's knife. Kitchen shears work well when sprayed with a nonstick vegetable spray.

To Store Nuts

Store all nuts in the refrigerator or freezer, as they turn rancid quickly and will ruin the flavor of a bread. Store nuts in refrigerator about 9 months and in the freezer no longer than 2 years.

To Toast Nuts

Toasting gives nuts a good flavor and crisp texture. Place nuts in an ungreased baking pan on the center rack of a preheated 325° oven for about 10 to 15 minutes, stirring once. The nuts will be hot and very pale golden. Do not bake until dark in color.

To Skin and Oven-Dry Pistachio Nuts

In a heatproof bowl, pour boiling water to cover shelled pistachio nuts. Let nuts stand for 1 minute, then drain. Turn nuts out onto a dish towel and rub off skins. Dry nuts in a baking pan in a preheated 300° F oven for 10 minutes. Store in an airtight container in freezer.

To Toast and Skin Hazelnuts

Place hazelnuts in one layer in an ungreased baking pan. Toast in a preheated 350° oven for 10 to 15 minutes, or until they are lightly colored and skins blister. Wrap nuts in a dish towel and let them stand for 1 minute. Rub nuts in towel to remove skins and let nuts cool.

To Cook Wild Rice

In a medium saucepan, bring ⅔ cup water to a rolling boil over high heat. Add ⅓ cup wild rice. Bring back to a rolling boil. Cover and reduce heat to lowest setting. Cook 50 to 60 minutes, or until tender and all liquid has been absorbed. Set aside to cool. Yield: 1 cup cooked rice.

Vanilla Powdered Sugar

Place a piece of whole or split good-quality vanilla bean into 2 cups sifted powdered sugar in an airtight container. Let stand 4 days to 1 week until scented as desired.

Frosted Grapes

Cut small clusters of grapes from main stem. Dip them into fresh lemon juice or slightly beaten egg white, then into superfine granulated sugar. Chill 15 minutes and repeat process once more. Pretty with a mix of varieties, such as green, red, and black grapes.

Bittersweet Candied Orange Peel

Yield: About 2½ cups

6 medium oranges (or 8 lemons or tangerines or 3 grapefruit)
1½ cups granulated sugar
½ cup water
2 tablespoons light corn syrup
About ¼ cup additional sugar for sprinkling

1. Cut peel on each orange into quarters and remove in whole sections from fruit. Reserve fruit for another use. Slice peel thin by hand or in a food processor with a ¼-inch slicing disc.
2. Place peel in a large non-corrodible saucepan and cover with cold water. Simmer over medium heat, uncovered, for about 10 to 15 minutes until tender. Drain and set aside.
3. To make syrup, place sugar, water, and corn syrup into same saucepan. Bring to a boil, immediately turn heat to low, and stir until sugar is dissolved. Add peel. Simmer about 20 to 25 minutes. The peel will be boiling gently and become translucent. Turn heat to high and reduce any remaining liquid to a thick syrup, about 3 minutes, stirring constantly.
4. Drain peel immediately in a strainer and place in a single layer on a baking sheet lined with parchment or waxed paper.
5. Let stand at room temperature to dry, 6 hours to overnight. Sprinkle peel with sugar to separate pieces. To store indefinitely, refrigerate or freeze between layers of waxed paper in an airtight container.
6. To moisten candied peel for use in baking, remove from refrigerator a few hours before needed. Toss with 1 to 2 tablespoons orange brandy or fresh orange juice for each 1 cup peel. Let stand at room temperature. Drain before use.

*E*VEN THOUGH WE HAVE BECOME more aware of the level of fat in our diet, the ubiquitous slice of bread slathered with fresh sweet butter will always be a cornerstone of the American diet. Bread itself is usually low in fat, making butter a natural complement. In many countries, olive oil is preferred to butter.

I have my favorite spreads for homemade bread, which I usually make in very small batches at whim: jams, preserves, nut butters, and spreads. This gives me control over the quality of the ingredients and allows me to adjust for special needs such as less sugar and less salt.

Any type of milk produces enough cream to be churned into butter. The flavor and aroma of commercial butter is the result of fermentation that is set into motion by a butter "starter." No starter is needed for homemade butter. The color of butter will vary with the season, depending on the diet of the animal. Buy fresh butter, salted or unsalted (sweet) as preferred. It should be pale, sweet smelling, and creamy. Do not buy butter that is streaked, cheesy smelling, or greasy. Butter may be stored in the refrigerator or freezer. Homemade butter is easily made with a blender or a food processor, and a recipe follows.

Compound butters are sweet creamery butters combined with one or more of a variety of chopped herbs, spices, garlic, vinegar, a dash of spirits, citrus rinds, or ground nuts in small proportions to produce a savory or sweet spread. Included here are a good variety of compound butters designed to complement a wide array of yeast and quick breads.

A *jam* is crushed fresh fruit cooked with sugar or honey until all the free liquid is evaporated, leaving a thickened puree. A *jelly* is fruit cooked and strained to make a clear juice that is thickened and flavored with sugar. Some fruits need added pectin to produce the glittering, wobbly jellied state. *Preserves* are whole pieces of uncrushed fruit cooked with sugar in the same fashion as jam. *Conserves* are fruits cooked in the same fashion as jam, with the addition of dried fruits or nuts. *Marmalade* is a soft jelly that contains fruit pulp and peel. A *fruit butter* is a fruit cooked with sugar or honey until very thick. A *fruit honey* is stewed, dried fruit that is pureed and then mixed with a proportion of honey to taste. *Nut butters* are purees made from flavorful oily nuts and can be used as a substitute for butter.

HOMEMADE BUTTER

Making butter in the food processor or blender is fast, clean, and very efficient. No more standing on the porch for hours with the churn. Homemade butter has a fresh flavor and melts smoothly on hot bread. There will be about 1 cup whey, the watery part of the milk, drained from the newly coagulated butter. It is rich in vitamins and minerals and can be used in baking. Store newly made butter in a covered container in the refrigerator. Let stand 20 to 30 minutes at room temperature to soften before using.

Yield: 6 ounces (¾ cup) butter

2 cups cold heavy cream (not sterilized)
¼ to ½ teaspoon salt to taste (optional)

1. Chill blender container or bowl and blade of food processor in freezer for 15 minutes.
2. Place cream and salt in chilled container or bowl with blade in place. Process for 2 minutes. Scrape sides. Process again until liquid and solids separate, about 3 minutes.
3. Pour off liquid. Line a sieve with 3 layers of cheesecloth and place in sink. Scrape butter into sieve and squeeze cheesecloth to remove excess liquid. Place in a covered container and store in refrigerator or use immediately.

ORANGE BUTTER

Yield: ½ cup

½ cup (1 stick) unsalted butter, cut into pieces and at room temperature
Grated zest of 1 orange

Mix butter and zest with back of a spoon or in a blender or food processor until fluffy and well combined. Store, covered, in the refrigerator. Bring to room temperature before serving.

MUSHROOM BUTTER

Yield: About 1 cup

2 shallots, minced
1 cup (2 sticks) unsalted butter, cut into pieces and at room temperature
1 pound domestic or wild mushrooms, sliced
2 tablespoons soy sauce
¼ cup brandy, Madeira, or water

Sauté shallots in half of butter in a large sauté pan or skillet until limp. Add mushrooms and cook over medium-high heat about 10 minutes. Add soy sauce and liquid. Cook on high heat to evaporate liquid. Remove from heat and puree in a blender or food processor while hot. Cool to room temperature and refrigerate to firm. Combine remaining butter with chilled mushroom puree until smooth, using a wooden spoon, blender, or food processor. Will keep, refrigerated, up to 1 week. Serve at room temperature with *croissants*, *brioches*, vegetables, broiled meats, and pastas.

MUSTARD BUTTER

Yield: ½ cup

½ cup (1 stick) unsalted butter, cut into pieces and at room temperature
2 tablespoons Dijon or grainy mustard
2 tablespoons finely chopped fresh parsley

Combine all ingredients until well blended and smooth.

BAJA CHILI BUTTER

Yield: ½ cup

½ cup (1 stick) unsalted butter, cut into pieces and at room temperature
2 tablespoons minced canned peeled green chilies
½ teaspoon ground cumin

Blend thoroughly with back of a spoon, blender, or food processor until fluffy and well combined. Store, covered, in the refrigerator. Bring to room temperature before serving.

WHIPPED HONEY BUTTER

Yield: ¾ cup

½ cup (1 stick) unsalted butter, cut into pieces and at room temperature
¼ cup mild local honey

Beat butter until creamy and light. Add honey and beat until fluffy. Serve at room temperature. Store, covered, in the refrigerator.

BERRY BUTTER

Yield: About ¾ cup

1 to 2 tablespoons sugar, to taste
½ cup fresh raspberries, strawberries,
*   boysenberries, or blueberries*
½ cup (1 stick) unsalted butter, cut into pieces
*   and at room temperature*

Sprinkle sugar over berries and let stand 5 minutes. Blend butter and berries in a blender or food processor until just combined. Store, covered, in the refrigerator. Let stand at room temperature ½ hour before spreading on warm muffins. (Note: frozen berries may be used; thaw and drain before pureeing.)

SEAFOOD BUTTER

Yield: About 1 cup

4 tablespoons unsalted butter, cut into pieces
*   and at room temperature*
2 to 3 ounces flaked smoked salmon
*   or cooked bay shrimp*
1 teaspoon fresh lemon juice
2 sprigs fresh parsley or dill

Combine all ingredients in a blender or food processor and blend together until smooth. Serve chilled. This butter is very good with thin slices of crisp plain French or whole-wheat melba toast. It may be stored in the refrigerator, covered, for 2 days.

PARSLEY-HERB BUTTER

*A*n all-purpose green butter, taking on the different flavors of the herbs used. Good with simple breads and rolls, or toss with fresh hot pasta or vegetables.

Yield: 1 cup

¼ cup loosely packed fresh parsley
1 tablespoon chopped fresh herb, such as dill,
*   basil, or tarragon*
1 cup (2 sticks) unsalted butter, cut into pieces
*   and at room temperature*

In a blender or a food processor, chop parsley and herb. Add butter and process until smooth, scraping sides as necessary. Pack into a crock and serve at room temperature. Herb butter keeps 1 week refrigerated, or it can be frozen.

PECAN-HONEY BUTTER

*G*round toasted nuts, honey, and butter are a perfectly luscious combination. This spread is good on corn breads, pancakes, and waffles, and is also excellent made with hazelnuts.

Yield: 1 cup

½ cup (1 stick) unsalted butter, cut into pieces
*   and at room temperature*
¼ cup honey
¼ cup pecans, lightly toasted (see page 116)

In a blender or food processor, blend butter, honey, and pecans until smooth. Stop to scrape down sides of bowl as necessary. May be stored, covered, in the refrigerator up to 1 week. Serve at room temperature.

PINE NUT BUTTER

½ cup (1 stick) unsalted butter, cut into pieces
*   and at room temperature*
¼ cup toasted pine nuts (see page 116)
Grated zest of ½ orange

Combine butter, pine nuts, and orange zest in a blender or a food processor. Process until combined and nuts are ground. Store covered in the refrigerator until ready to use.

FRESH NUT BUTTER

Yield: About 1 cup

1 cup unsalted mixed nuts, raw or toasted
*   as preferred*
½ cup (1 stick) unsalted butter, cut into pieces
*   and at room temperature*

Chop nuts coarsely in a blender or food processor. Add butter and process just until smooth. Store, covered, in refrigerator; serve at room temperature.

SESAME-PEANUT BUTTER

*S*esame-Peanut Butter is very high in protein. It will keep, covered, in the refrigerator for about 1 month.

Yield: About 1 cup

¼ cup raw sesame seeds
2 cups unsalted dry-roasted peanuts
1 to 2 tablespoons vegetable oil, as needed

1. Spread sesame seeds in a sauté pan or skillet over medium heat and toast for about 5 minutes, shaking the pan to toast evenly and prevent burning. Let cool. (These will keep indefinitely, covered.)
2. Place 1 cup peanuts and 1 tablespoon oil in a blender or a food processor. Blend until smooth, scraping down sides as needed.
3. Add rest of peanuts and sesame seeds. Blend until smooth, adding oil as needed to achieve desired consistency.

TAPENADE

*T*apenade is a Mediterranean olive spread that has a good-sized following. It can be made from any type of black olive and a varying amount of anchovy with a bit of olive oil for balance. This is a simple paste to make very quickly with ripe pitted California olives.

Combine equal portions of *tapenade* and softened unsalted butter for a nice compound butter.

Yield: 1¼ cups

1 cup pitted black California olives, drained
3 tablespoons olive oil
1 tablespoon anchovy paste
1 tablespoon fresh lemon juice
1 garlic clove, chopped
2 teaspoons capers, drained, for garnish

Combine all ingredients in a blender or food processor and process until blended and just smooth. Let stand at least 1 hour. Garnish top with capers. Serve alongside a crock of sweet butter.

SWEET CHESTNUT PÂTÉ

Yield: 1½ cups

One 8¾-ounce can sweetened chestnut spread (crème de marrons)
4 ounces natural cream cheese, at room temperature
2 tablespoons unsalted butter, at room temperature
1 tablespoon brandy, or orange or nut liqueur
¼ cup bittersweet or semisweet chocolate, finely chopped or in chips
¼ cup pecans, hazelnuts, or walnuts, chopped

In a blender, food processor, or electric mixer, combine chestnut spread, cream cheese, butter, and liqueur until blended and fluffy. Fold in chocolate and nuts. Can be stored, covered, in the refrigerator up to 1 week. Let stand at room temperature 1 hour before serving.

CREAM CHEESE WITH FRESH HERBS

*W*hen a recipe calls for cream cheese, use natural cream cheese if possible rather than the kind stabilized with gelatin. It is fluffy and somewhat of a delicacy. This herbaceous mixture is delightful on a buffet surrounded by fresh breads or as a sandwich spread.

Yield:

*8 ounces natural cream cheese,
    at room temperature
1 tablespoon olive oil
1 tablespoon Calvados or pear brandy
1 shallot, minced
3 tablespoons chopped fresh herbs: parsley,
    chervil, dill, oregano, sage, or tarragon
1 cup heavy cream
Dash salt and white pepper*

Using a wooden spoon, electric mixer, blender, or food processor, blend cheese, olive oil, and Calvados until fluffy. Add shallot and herbs. Whip cream with salt and pepper. Fold into cheese. Line a 2- to 3-cup porcelain or straw mold or colander with 3 layers of cheesecloth, letting cloth hang over edges. Lay a whole sprig of herb decoratively on bottom of lined mold. Spoon cheese into mold. Fold cloth over top and press gently to pack mold. Cover with plastic wrap and place in refrigerator to drain overnight. To serve, unfold cloth and invert onto a serving dish. Remove cheesecloth and discard.

HERBED RICOTTA

Yield: 1 cup

*8 ounces whole-milk ricotta
¼ cup finely chopped fresh dill
1 teaspoon capers, drained*

Mix together until evenly blended and store, covered, in the refrigerator.

BAKED MARINATED GOAT CHEESE

*1 teaspoon dried thyme
1 teaspoon dried savory
½ teaspoon dried oregano
½ teaspoon fresh-cracked black pepper
11 ounces aged French or domestic goat cheese,
    such as Montrachet
½ cup good Italian olive oil*

1. Mix herbs and pepper together and press into cheese, covering entire surface. Use more herbs, if needed.
2. Place in a container and pour olive oil over cheese. Cover tightly and refrigerate 1 to 2 weeks.
3. To serve: Remove log from oil and slice cheese into 6 equal pieces. Place in a low baking dish. Cover with the oil.
4. Bake in a preheated 400° oven for 5 to 8 minutes, or until hot.

FETA CREAM BUTTER

Yield: 1¼ cups

*½ cup feta cheese, rinsed
½ cup (1 stick) unsalted butter, cut into pieces
    and at room temperature
2 ounces natural cream cheese,
    at room temperature
Green onion tops for decoration
Fresh mint leaves for serving*

Combine feta, butter, and cream cheese with back of a spoon or in a blender or food processor and blend until just smooth. To serve, garnish with strips of green onion. Excellent on dark ryes. Serve on a bed of fresh mint. Can be stored, covered, in the refrigerator up to 1 week. Let stand at room temperature ½ hour before serving.

ST. ANDRÉ BUTTER

*S*t. André is a relative newcomer to the sophisticated world of semisoft cheeses. It has a delicate, buttery flavor and consistency. Try this butter with Country Bread with Golden Raisins and Walnuts, page 45.

Yield: About 1½ cups

*½ cup (1 stick) unsalted butter,
    at room temperature
4 ounces St. André cheese at room temperature,
    rind removed
¼ cup walnuts, lightly toasted (see page 116)
3 tablespoons Asti Spumante*

Cut butter and cheese into chunks and blend until smooth in a blender or food processor. Add walnuts and wine. Process until just smooth. Spoon into a crock and store in the refrigerator. Let stand at room temperature an hour or so before spreading on fresh bread.

Mustard is a paste of ground mustard seeds, salt, and white wine or vinegar. It is a popular condiment, adding a hot spicy accent to food. Mustard can be sharp and pungent, such as the popular French Dijon style, or mild and sweet like most American types. Grainy mustards, such as *moutarde de Meaux*, have an earthy and aromatic nature. Add a small proportion of a savory or pungent accent ingredient, such as dill or horseradish, to a good plain mustard to create your own uniquely flavored or grained mustards.

DILL MUSTARD

Yield: ½ cup

½ cup Dijon or grainy mustard
1 teaspoon champagne vinegar
1 teaspoon dried dill weed

Combine ingredients until well blended and smooth.

HORSERADISH MUSTARD

Yield: ½ cup

½ cup Dijon or grainy mustard
1 tablespoon creamy prepared horseradish

Combine ingredients until well blended and smooth.

HERBES DE PROVENCE MUSTARD

Yield: ½ cup

½ cup Dijon or grainy mustard
¾ teaspoon herbes de provence

Combine ingredients until well blended and smooth.

TOMATO MUSTARD

Yield: About ½ cup

½ cup Dijon or grainy mustard
2 tablespoons tomato paste or
    pureed sun-dried tomatoes
1 teaspoon Worcestershire sauce
1 small garlic clove, pressed

Combine all ingredients until well blended and smooth.

*T*HE COMBINATION OF JAM, bread, and butter is one of the most satisfying of eating pleasures. Americans have always loved the simmered fruit and sugar combination called jam. Once a product relegated to home production, the commercial market has a full-scale business keeping us in a variety of excellent to downright awful fruit butters, jams, marmalades, and the like. It has become a great American cottage industry, capitalizing on our very sweet tooth. You may be lucky enough to find a good product to suit your palate, but if you like the fresh, tart nature of the fruit itself to be your first taste sensation and want to avoid the cloying sweetness of too much sugar, consider making your own. The interest in home jam making has grown, sparked by the abundance of beautiful, ripe fruit available through the year. There are many wonderful recipe books entirely devoted to mastering the traditional techniques of jam and jellies.

You can puree fruit butters with a blender, food processor, or by hand through a sieve. Look for a soft, rather creamy texture rather than a solid gelatinous mass characteristic of high amounts of sugar and pectin.

Spirits naturally complement the flavor of fruit. Use them in place of any liquid, dictated by your own taste preferences. For a very mild accent flavor, add the spirit in the initial stage of cooking to evaporate most of its alcohol. For a more pronounced adult flavor sensation, add the spirit at the end of the cooking, stirring just to combine. The heat of the fruit mixture will do the rest to meld the flavors.

BERRY JAM

Yield: About 1 cup

1½ cups fresh raspberries, strawberries,
*   boysenberries, or blueberries*
⅓ cup sugar or honey
1 tablespoon fresh lemon juice

Follow directions for Apricot Jam, page 125.

FIG JAM

Yield: About 1 cup

2 cups chopped fresh ripe black or green figs
4 thin slices lemon with peel, chopped
½ cup sugar or honey

Follow directions for Apricot Jam, page 125.

APRICOT JAM

Yield: About 1 cup

2 cups coarsely chopped fresh apricots
1/3 cup sugar or honey
2 tablespoons cognac, apricot brandy,
    or fresh orange juice

In a heavy saucepan, mix fruit, sugar, and liquid. Bring to a boil over high heat, stirring frequently. Reduce heat immediately to a simmer and cook, uncovered, until thick, 15 to 20 minutes. Transfer to a jar and cool at room temperature before covering and storing in the refrigerator.

Microwave Instructions: Combine coarsely crushed fruit, sugar, and liquid in an 8-cup microwave proof bowl. Microwave on high 8 to 10 minutes, uncovered. Cool one-half hour; jam will thicken as it cools. Transfer to a covered container and refrigerate.

BRANDIED LIME MARMALADE

Yield: About 1 cup

4 medium limes
3/4 cup sugar
2 teaspoons brandy

Peel and quarter 3 limes. Remove all seeds and puree limes in a blender or food processor. Leaving peel on remaining lime, cut lime in thin slices, then cut slices into quarters. Proceed as in recipe for Apricot Jam, above.

FRUIT HONEY

This is a good spread to make in the dead of winter for bread, muffins, and scones.

Yield: About 2 cups

1/2 pound best quality dried fruit, such as pears, apricots, prunes, peaches, or mixture
1 1/4 cups mild honey, such as wildflower, star thistle, or clover

Place fruit in a medium saucepan and add water just to cover. Bring to a boil, then simmer uncovered over low heat until water is absorbed and fruit is soft, about 20 minutes. Remove from heat and cool completely. Puree in food processor until smooth. With motor running pour in honey. Store in a tightly covered jar at room temperature.

APPLE BUTTER

Yield: About 2 cups

4 large firm tart green apples
1/4 cup water
1/4 cup sugar, or to taste
4 tablespoons unsalted butter
2 teaspoons ground cinnamon

Peel, core, and coarsely chop apples. Place in a heavy medium saucepan with water, sugar, butter, and cinnamon. Cook over low heat until soft, about 15 to 20 minutes. Puree until smooth. Cool 1/2 hour, transfer to a covered container, and refrigerate up to 2 weeks. Note: This recipe is also delicious made with half fresh pears or apricots.

CHAMPAGNE PRUNE BUTTER

Yield: About 2 cups

1 pound pitted dried prunes
1/2 cup sweet champagne, such as Asti Spumante
1/2 cup water
4 tablespoons unsalted butter
1/4 cup sugar
2 tablespoons fresh orange juice
1 teaspoon ground cinnamon

Place prunes in a large saucepan, add champagne and water, and cook covered 15 to 20 minutes, or until soft. Add butter, sugar, orange juice, and cinnamon. Puree until smooth. Cool 1/2 hour, place in covered container, and refrigerate.

WINTER APRICOT CONSERVE

Yield: About 2 cups

12 ounces dried apricots
1/3 cup sugar
3 tablespoons fresh lemon juice
2 tablespoons unsalted butter
1/3 cup dark seedless raisins
1/3 cup slivered blanched almonds

Place apricots in a large saucepan and add water to cover. Simmer, uncovered, until soft, about 20 minutes. Add sugar, lemon juice, butter, raisins, and almonds. Stir to combine. Transfer to a jar and let cool. Cover and store in the refrigerator.

LEMON CURD

Yield: About 2 cups

4 tablespoons unsalted butter
3/4 cup fresh lemon juice
Grated zest of 2 lemons
1 cup granulated sugar
4 whole eggs
2 egg yolks

Melt butter in top section of double boiler. Beat together remaining ingredients with a whisk or in a blender or food processor. With water at a simmer, slowly add egg mixture, stirring constantly with a whisk. Cook over medium heat, stirring constantly, until thickened, a full 10 minutes. Pour into a jar and let cool before storing in refrigerator.

The Art of Melba

APRACTICAL AND DELICIOUS use of day-old bread is melba toast, or twice-baked bread. Melba toasts, rusks, *crostini*, and croutons are all variations of the same process. Melba toast is any size sliced bread that has been dried slowly in an oven, sautéed in a skillet, toasted under a broiler, or even grilled over an open fire. Do not underestimate melba toasts as a companion for dips and meat or vegetable pâtés or as a crisp complement to soups and salads. They are very tasty piled in a basket as a crisp hors d'oeuvre or floating atop a bowl of soup. Melba toasts may be topped with cheeses, herbs, garlic, or spreads. They can be in the form of slices or cut with a biscuit or cookie cutter into squares, rectangles, diamonds, or hearts. Leave crust on or off.

Made ahead of time for convenience, plain melba toasts will keep in an airtight container for up to 1 week or frozen in plastic bags for up to 1 month.

PLAIN MELBA

Perfect for accompanying pâtés or to spread with sweet butter and caviar.

Cut 1 loaf firm day-old or frozen French bread into slices ¼ inch to ½ inch thick. Bake in a preheated 300° oven on an ungreased baking sheet on the center oven rack for 45 minutes to 1 hour, or until crisp and evenly golden. Can be made the day ahead and stored in an airtight container at room temperature.

BUTTER CROUTONS

Plain croutons are wonderful floating in a soup bowl, or alongside sliced cheese and fruit. One of my favorite combinations is a hard roll split in half and grilled, served with cold smoked trout, horseradish sauce, and a few stalks of asparagus. And that is just the beginning…

Cut day-old bread into slices ½ inch to ¾ inch thick or split day-old rolls in half. In a sauté pan or skillet, sauté them over medium heat in butter, olive oil, or an equal combination of the two. Turn them as necessary, until crisp and golden brown. Remove with tongs to drain on paper towels.

HOMEMADE SALAD CROUTONS

Any good bread, such as egg, pumpernickel, or whole-wheat, makes good salad croutons. Cut day-old bread, including the crusts, into 1-inch cubes. Sauté lightly in olive oil and pressed garlic until just golden, stirring constantly; or drizzle with melted butter and bake until dry at 375°. Stir every 8 minutes or so to keep from burning. Remove when just golden and drizzle with more melted butter, squeezed fresh garlic, a few tablespoons of grated Parmesan, and chopped fresh parsley. Serve tossed in a good salad.

CROUSTADES

A croustade is a serving vessel made from a large loaf of bread. The top crust is removed and the inside crumb cut out, leaving a shell at least 1 inch thick all around. Brush the insides with melted butter or good oil. Dry the *croustade* in a 350° oven until crisp. Usually *croustades* are made from day-old rounded or rectangular *brioche* loaves, a good *pain de mie* or pullman loaf, large round French loaves, or little rolls, which are nice for individual servings. *Croustades* are especially good filled with creamed wild mushrooms, deviled seafood, or chicken.

FRENCH ROLLS STUFFED WITH HAM PÂTÉ

*H*ere is an elegant and deliciously different picnic or out-of-pocket sandwich that is quick and easy to prepare. Serve with a variety of mustards (page 122), bean vinaigrette, and a white wine.

Yield: Serves 12

1 pound cooked ham: honey-baked, smoked, or Westphalian style
½ cup heavy cream
3 tablespoons brandy
2 teaspoons Worcestershire sauce
1 tablespoon Dijon mustard
2 tablespoons chopped fresh parsley
3 tablespoons capers, drained
12 small French bread rolls

1. Trim fat and outer skin from ham and cut into cubes. Place in a blender or food processer and grind until chunky. Add all remaining ingredients except bread and process until smooth. Refrigerate until firm, about 30 minutes.
2. Slice a small section off end of each French roll. Remove insides with a fork or by pulling with your fingers, leaving a hollow shell about ½ inch thick. Reserve insides for homemade bread crumbs.
3. Stand rolls on one end and stuff with pâté, taking care to fill shell completely, leaving no holes. Smooth ends. Wrap rolls in aluminum foil or plastic wrap. Refrigerate for several hours before serving.

BRIE EN CROUSTADE

*T*his is a memorable and delicious hot appetizer for a small crowd. Remember that the *croustade* itself is meant to be torn apart and eaten. It is also excellent made with St. André cheese.

Yield: Serves 8

1 medium round loaf French bread
½ cup (1 stick) unsalted butter or olive oil
2 to 3 garlic cloves, pressed
1 pound Brie cheese
½ pound soft jack cheese
1 French baguette
2 fresh Pippin or Macintosh apples, peeled, cored, and cut into thin slices

1. Hollow out French loaf to an even thickness of about ½ to 1 inch. Make slashes around rim of shell, if necessary, to open up top. Cube leftover insides of bread for dipping or reserve for fresh bread crumbs.
2. In a small saucepan, melt butter and add garlic. Brush inside and outside of shell with garlic butter. Place on a greased or parchment-lined baking sheet and bake in a 375° oven until crisp, about 10 to 15 minutes.
3. Meanwhile, cut cheese into cubes, leaving rind on Brie. Remove crisped shell from oven and fill with cheese cubes. Bake until cheese is melted, about 15 to 30 minutes. Cover with aluminum foil to protect crust from excessive browning until cheese is melted.
4. Slide hot *croustade* onto a serving platter or bread board. Surround with thin-sliced baguette and apple slices.

HOMEMADE BREAD CRUMBS

*C*ut day-old bread into pieces. Place on an aluminum foil-or parchment-lined baking sheet. Bake in a preheated 300° oven until dry and golden, 30 minutes to 1 hour. Cool. Grind in small batches in a blender or food processor to desired degree of fineness. Make sure container is completely dry. Bread crumbs will keep 2 months in an airtight container. Do not refrigerate. They can also be frozen in an airtight container.

For Italian-style seasoned bread crumbs, add 2 tablespoons grated Parmesan cheese and ½ teaspoon *each* dried savory, basil, and tarragon to every cup of fine dry bread crumbs.

For fresh bread crumbs, cut thick slices of bread and remove crusts. Cut into cubes and process to degree of fineness desired in a blender or food processor, as for dried bread crumbs. Use within 2 days.

DESSERT MELBA

S imilar to a *biscotti* or a rusk, dessert melba is good with tea or as an accompaniment to *sorbets* and fresh fruits. Slice day-old egg bread, *brioche*, sweet breads with fruits and nuts, or *savarin* into ½- to 1-inch-thick slices. Sprinkle with sugar and a spice such as nutmeg, cinnamon, or cardamom, if desired. Place in a single layer on an ungreased baking sheet. Bake at 300° until golden, crisp, and dry, about 45 minutes to 1 hour. Remove from sheets to cool on a rack. Store in an airtight container. These are also good spread with fresh apple butter, flavored cream cheese, or Sweet Chestnut Pâté, page 120.

SESAME MELBA

½ cup (1 stick) unsalted butter,
   at room temperature
1 garlic clove, pressed (optional)
1 loaf day-old white, whole-wheat,
   or French bread
¼ cup raw sesame seeds

1. Cream butter and garlic together.
2. Slice bread ½ inch thick. Spread with garlic butter. Place sesame seeds on a flat plate. Lay bread, buttered side down, into seeds to coat entire surface. Place on an ungreased baking sheet, buttered side up.
3. Bake in a preheated 325° oven until crisp, about 15 minutes.

BRIE CROUTONS

These are large croutons to serve alongside butter lettuce dressed with vinaigrette.

1 large round loaf day-old French
   or peasant bread
½ cup Dijon mustard
1 pound Brie
¼ cup chopped fresh parsley

1. Cut bread into horizontal slices. Spread with mustard. Cut slices of Brie and lay on top. Sprinkle with fresh parsley, if desired.
2. Place under a broiler until melted and bubbly.

MOZZARELLA TOAST

4 garlic cloves, pressed
⅔ cup olive oil
2 loaves French bread
½ pound whole-milk mozzarella cheese

1. Combine garlic and olive oil. Slice bread ¾ inch thick. Brush both sides of bread lightly with oil.
2. In a sauté pan or skillet, fry bread slices on both sides until just crisp. Place a slice of cheese on top of each toast and place in a preheated 375° oven just until cheese melts, about 5 minutes.

LARGE GARLIC CROUTONS

Serve in large baskets with soups and salads.

½ cup olive oil
½ cup (1 stick) unsalted butter
Small whole head of garlic, center root
   and outside excess paper removed and cloves
   broken apart but unpeeled

3 tablespoons water
3 French baguettes

1. Melt oil and butter together in a small saucepan. Place garlic in a blender or food processor with water and process until pureed. Pour into warm butter and stir until combined.
2. Cut baguette into slices ¼ inch to ½ inch thick. Using a pastry brush, brush garlic butter on one side of bread slices. Place on an ungreased baking sheet and bake in a preheated 450° oven for 5 to 7 minutes, or until crisp. Serve immediately, or when cool. Store in a plastic bag or airtight container.

PUMPERNICKEL TOAST

Serve with egg salad and caviar.

½ cup (1 stick) unsalted butter
2 garlic cloves, pressed
1 loaf thin-sliced pumpernickel or black bread
½ cup freshly grated Parmesan

1. Melt butter in a small saucepan and add garlic. Brush on pumpernickel bread that has been sliced ½-inch thick and cut into diamonds. Place on an ungreased baking sheet and sprinkle with cheese.
2. Bake in a preheated 300° oven 15 to 20 minutes, or until crisp.

HERBED MELBA

Serve with potato-leek or fresh tomato soup.

1 loaf white, whole-wheat, or French bread
½ cup (1 stick) unsalted butter, melted
2 to 3 tablespoons finely chopped mixed
   fresh herbs: parsley, thyme, and chives

1. Slice day-old bread about ½ inch thick.
2. Brush one side of bread with butter. Place on an ungreased baking sheet. Sprinkle with fresh herbs.
3. Bake in a preheated 325° oven until dry and crisp, about 15 to 20 minutes.

GOAT CHEESE TOAST

1 French baguette
½ cup (1 stick) unsalted butter,
*   at room temperature*
Baked Marinated Goat Cheese, page 121,
*   prepared through Step 2*

1. Slice baguette into ½-inch-thick slices. Toast lightly.
2. Spread each side with a bit of butter. Spread with marinated goat cheese.
3. Broil just until cheese softens and is golden brown. Serve warm or at room temperature.

PESTO TOAST

1 French baguette
¾ cup pesto sauce
¼ cup fresh-grated Parmesan cheese
¼ cup pine nuts

1. Slice baguette into ½-inch-thick slices. Lightly toast one side under the broiler.
2. Spread untoasted side with pesto, sprinkle with a bit of Parmesan, and top with a few pine nuts.
3. Broil just until cheese melts and nuts are toasted. Serve immediately.

Bread and Spirits

To Accent and Heighten Flavors in breadmaking, use alcoholic spirits. A little goes a long way. For example, less than a tablespoon per 6 cups flour of real vanilla, almond, anise, or lemon extract will give a simple loaf a hint of the exotic and lavish. Rustic country-style breads do not boast liqueur or sugar, as these items were at one time too expensive for use on a daily basis. Hence, embellished breads became synonymous with holidays and special occasions. Except for the ritual plumping of raisins, spirits are associated most often with quick rather than yeasted breads. Yet yeasted breads are greatly enhanced by the expressive character of spirits, and it is worthwhile to experiment boldly. Add spirits as a flavoring directly into the mixing of the dough; soak or sprinkle hefty additions such as fresh and dried fruits; or use as a glaze. Your palate may also find a combination of two or more spirits exciting. There are no rules, but the ingredients should be a guide to which spirit is appropriate, an obvious choice being hazelnuts or almonds paired with the hazelnut liqueur Frangelico, or, more unusual, persimmons with pear brandy or blueberries with bourbon. Also remember the fruits used in yeast breadmaking should be of a firm nature (such as apples, pears, and dried fruit) or pureed, unless they are sprinkled over the surface to create an open effect. Delicate fruits, such as berries or pears, find their place in quick breads, as they would lose their shape and flavor in a kneaded dough.

Use fine-quality alcoholic-based extracts, as imitation extracts cannot come close in flavor after being baked. Beyond extracts, choose from brown and white spirits, brandies, beer, wine, and liqueurs. Brown spirits include bourbon and rum, and both retain a good strong flavor and aroma after baking. White spirits, such as gin and vodka, are quite harsh and are not generally used in baking, although vodka can be successfully added to cake batters in combination with a liqueur. Brandies are made from grapes, unless the label notes otherwise. The family of fruit brandies includes apple, pear, raspberry, apricot, plum, and cherry, to name a few. Brandies meld with any fruit or nut flavor perfectly. Beer and wine can be added to dough in place of the liquid. Liqueurs are sugar-based infusions and are exceptional in baking, giving a deeper or counterpoint flavor of fruits, nuts, spices, barks, coffee, and even chocolate.

Bourbon, a whiskey predominantly made from corn, is as American as apple pie, with a very strong tang suited to nuts, especially pecans. Rum is made from distilled sugarcane. Dark rum is excellent for plumping fruit or as an addition to cheese or nut fillings. It accents apples and plums, pairs naturally with maple, and is always good for glazing. White rum is usually combined with acid fruits, such as pineapple.

There are many grades of brandy from California and France, appealing to all tastes and pocketbooks. Cognac and Armagnac are famous brandies named after the regions of

France from which they hail. Armagnac is very full bodied and pungent. Brandy is excellent for glazing. All dried and fresh fruits are enhanced by brandy, as are even carrots and zucchini when used in sweet doughs. Brandy is a must in every serious baker's pantry, and if you buy one all-purpose spirit, brandy should be it.

In France, fruit brandies are called *eau de vie*, or "water of life." They are strongly aromatic and have no added sweetening as do liqueurs. Travelers to the Continent are well advised to shop for these unique clear-colored brandies made from peaches, apricots, pears *(poire)*, strawberries *(fraises)*, yellow plums *(mirabelle)*, cherries *(kirsch)*, and even figs. Many of these brandies are produced only with regional fruits and are never exported. California is producing kiwi, quince, and pear brandies. They tend to be expensive, but worth the price. A favorite fruit brandy is the clear *framboise*, made from raspberries, which highlights the flavor of all berries. Calvados is an apple brandy from the legendary orchards of Normandy. American applejack can be used as a substitute. This brandy is perfect with apples, quince, pears, and cinnamon. Maraschino, a cherry brandy, is truly a celestial spirit, having no relationship at all to the dyed cocktail garnish of the same name. It is made from the European Marasca cherries, which are small, quite bitter, and black. It has a more pronounced cherry taste than kirsch and is worth searching out. The best Maraschino comes from Italy. Kirsch and Cherry Marnier are often easier to find on local shelves.

Beer, white wines, and champagne find their way naturally into doughs. Used in place of other liquids, they give a pronounced yeasty flavor, as in Italian-Style Herb Bread. Use sweet sparkling wines such as Asti Spumante in spreads or with fruits in sweet rolls. Red wines are too strong and dark to be used in doughs, but if you wish to plump fruit in a favorite mellow burgundy, there are no rules. Fruit wines, a California specialty, range from apricot, pomegranate, and pear to mead, a honey wine. Japanese plum wine is also quite sweet and delicate. Other mellow, fruity wines usually served as dessert, such as Madeira, port, cream sherry, and Black Muscat, are good in baking.

The sphere of liqueurs was once purely medicinal, but these strong, intense elixirs have made their way into a social sphere and now baking. Liqueurs are usually thick, smooth in texture, and colorful, as they are a mashed infusion and sugar added to a spirit rather than a distillate of fruit juice and yeast, as are brandies.

In a pinch, make your own fruit liqueur by covering fresh or dried fruit mixed with a small handful of crushed almonds with a neutral spirit such as vodka. Let sit for at least a month, tightly capped. Strain to use, and pour fruit over ice cream or pound cake. These brandies were made to be used in food!

Every Mediterranean country makes a liqueur out of anise, such as Pernod, the earthy juice from the sun-baked South of France. Pernod is a wonderful licorice-flavored addition to doughs calling for anise or fennel seeds, such as *panettone* and ryes. There is a sweet caraway liqueur called Kümmel, which is also spiked with cumin and coriander.

The Scandinavian countries specialize in wonderful berry liqueurs like the deep-purple blackberry. Cassis, from France, is made from red currants. Farm-grown berry liqueurs are quite sweet and fragrant, complementing all berries, cherries, and dark fruits.

Citrus spirits abound, with the romantic Grand Marnier in the lead. That combination is true French cognac and bitter orange peels, and is wonderful with all fruits and nuts. It is an absolute classic in the kitchen. All Mediterranean countries make some spirit from citrus, even a lovely Italian sweet lemon that is not exported. Cointreau is a lighter citrus liqueur from the West Indies.

Coffee- or chocolate-based liqueurs, such as Tia Maria, *crème de cacao*, and Kahlúa, give a warm accent to deep and dark breads such as black ryes or chocolate bread. Bailey's Irish Cream is a combination of Irish whiskey, cream, and chocolate. It is sweet, smooth, and absolutely luscious, making an excellent glaze for sweet breads. Store cream-based liqueurs in the refrigerator after opening.

Wherever there is an abundance of nut trees grown, a nut liqueur is made, such as hazelnut Frangelico or Italian *nocino*. These spirits have a luscious, sensuous nature that accents any bread made with nuts or winter fruits such as pears and pumpkins. Macadamia nut liqueur from Hawaii is wonderful in muffins.

Unusual fruit-based liqueurs include the Italian Amaretto, which is a combination of apricot, bitter almond, and crushed apricot pits, and the American Southern Comfort, which is a combination of bourbon, oranges, peaches, exotic fruits, and spices. I use these spirits interchangeably with brandy, rum, and bourbon for a spicier addition.

I find the mint- and herb-based spirits refreshing, but usually too sharp and heady for breadmaking.

Buy the best-quality spirit you can afford, and store, tightly capped, at room temperature. Spirits keep indefinitely.

Bread and Food

An Evening of Wine, Bread, and Cheese, that most time-honored of trinities, is a feast that has been enjoyed for centuries. As an auxiliary vehicle to a meal, bread occupies a place of importance. Its appearance is dramatic enough alone, needing no garnish. It complements the rustic as well as the elegant. A simple bread enhances the flavor, texture, and aroma of a varied array of foods from entrees to snacks.

Consider bread in the context of how you wish your meal to be served: buffet style, served in courses, off large platters butler style, or plated all at once in the kitchen. Will there be one or more different kinds of bread served? Can guests slice or tear off portions, or will the bread be served alongside an individual plate?

Presentation is as important as good ingredients, although there are no firmly established rules. Look for usual as well as unusual receptacles for presenting bread at the table, teasing the eye and reflecting your own style of entertaining. Whether a free-form country loaf, oblong, baguette, or the predictable rectangular loaf, serve bread on a bread board with a serrated knife to be cut into thick slices at the table. Other ideas are bread in a napkin-lined basket, nestled alongside a salad, or perhaps on a pedestal cake plate. Bread may be wrapped in a napkin, like a surprise. Garnish a flat basket with edible flowers that reflect the loaf's basic ingredients: squash, lemon, or herb blossoms. The earthy colors of bread are paired well with simple flowers such as nasturtiums or marigolds. Culinary fashion comes and goes, but bread presented simply on a starched white tablecloth, to be broken and spread with a bit of butter or cheese, never loses its wholesome appeal.

I think that the colors that best display food are stark white and cobalt blue, and I like to highlight homemade breads with a simple background of cotton cloth, stoneware tiles, wood, porcelain, and handwoven basketry, using contrasting colors and textures.

Bread complements cheese, fruit, and nuts, creating a substantial repast any time. Provide a simple table setting of appropriate knives, spreaders, and a nutcracker. Some favorite combinations are Country Bread with Golden Raisins and Walnuts, Roquefort cheese, Comice pears, and pistachios in the shell; Rain and Sun (a buckwheat and cornmeal bread) with butter, jam, and juicy navel oranges; or thin-sliced American Chocolate Bread alongside a bowl of sweet berries and cream.

With a simple soup or salad, bread can assert whole-grain flavor or a range of additional ingredients. Different breads can give thick-or thin-sliced sandwiches of cold meat, cheese, and vegetables new interest and variety. Picnic breads combine all the elements of a sandwich; with pickles and bit of wine you have a full meal. Serve at room temperature to heighten flavors.

Thin-sliced bread can be cut into diminutive shapes reminiscent of a deck of cards, such as the diamond, for cocktails or tea. To garnish salads, dip one point of a cut shape into melted butter and then into finely chopped parsley.

Pair hearty meats, bean dishes, and rich and creamy foods with French-style breads. Sauces command a quick wipe, with bread soaking up excess oil, salt, and acidity. Bland-flavored foods such as potatoes can be balanced with savory rolls. Sweet breads are popular for breakfast, brunch, afternoon tea, and dessert.

Menu Suggestions

Elegant, casual, whimsical—let the season and your palate be your guide.

Breakfast for the Children

Fresh orange-strawberry juice
Sliced bananas
Cashew-Date Bread/orange kefir cheese

Spring Breakfast in the Sunroom

Old-Fashioned Raisin Bread with
   Molasses Glaze and fresh sweet butter
Earl Grey tea
Strawberries and whipped *crème fraîche*

Sandwiches

Bacon, lettuce, and tomato
   with Whole-Wheat Egg Bread
Thin-sliced smoked ham and watercress
   with Gruyère Pullman Loaf
Fresh chicken salad with Pistachio-Honey
   Oat Bread
English Cheddar cheese and chutney with
   thin-sliced Honey Whole-Wheat Bread
Cold meatballs in marinara sauce
   with Water Rolls
Herbed ricotta and tomatoes with
   Sesame-Wheat Long Rolls
Sautéed mushrooms, turkey, and mozzarella
   with Red Pepper–Semolina Bread
Monterey jack cheese and green chilies
   with Yogurt French Bread

Summer Barbecue

Miso-grilled prawns, trout, and chicken
Cold tortellini with sun-dried-tomato
   vinaigrette
Fresh greens with creamy herb dressing
Italian Peasant Bread with Parsley-Herb
Butter
White corn on the cob roasted in foil
Iced tea with sliced oranges, limes,
   and lemons

Picnic in the Woods

Wild-Mushroom Croustade
Potato salad with watercress
Fresh ripe cherry tomatoes
Champagne/butter cookies/fresh fruit

Thanksgiving Afternoon for 20

Apricot-and-honey-glazed roast turkey
Corn bread and apple stuffing
Nutted wild rice
Carrot and rutabaga puree
Roast sweet red onions
Cranberry-cassis jelly
Taos Pumpkin Bread with Pine Nut Butter
Challah braids with poppy seeds
Whipped sweet butter

Saturday Luncheon

Sausage en Brioche
Variety of homemade grainy mustards
Cold cucumber mousse
Radicchio and butter lettuces with
   shallot vinaigrette

Elegant Late Supper

Butter lettuce with lemon and olive oil
Brie Croutons
Wild rice paella with chicken, shellfish,
   and dried mushrooms
Cucumber-cilantro relish
Water Rolls with sweet butter
Raspberry brûlée
Coffee
Cognac

activating yeast, 20
active dry yeast, 9, 20
all-purpose flour, 6, 22
almond babka, 86–87
American chocolate bread, 92
anise sugar buns, 92–93
apple: brioche, 87–88
    butter, 125
    upside-down coffee cake, 112
applesauce muffins, spiced, 102
apricot: conserve, winter, 125
    glaze, 84
    jam, 125
    -oatmeal bread, 79
Arborio rice, 8
Asti Spumante, 92

babka: almond, 86–87
    cheese, 87
    chocolate, 87
baby buttermilk fantans, 73
bacon and corn muffins, 103
baguettes, 30
    olive, 57
Baja chili butter, 118
baked marinated goat cheese, 121
baker's paddle, 14, 15
baking: biscuits, 105–7
    dish, *cloche,* 45
    little breads, 69
    muffins, 97
    quick loaves, 109
    sheets, 14, 16
    stone, 14, 15
    yeasted breads, 25
baking powder, 9, 10, 96
baking soda, 9–10, 96
banana-pecan muffins, 101
barley, 7
basil: bread, whole-wheat, 55
    and mozzarella biscuits, 108
    rolls, 78
basmati rice, 8
bâtards, 32
batter bread: yeasted, 20
    quick, 96
beehive ovens, 15, 60
berry(ies): butter, 119
    jam, 123
    muffins, fresh-, 100
    rye, 7, 15
    with *savarin,* 84
Bette's Oceanview Diner, 102
biscuits, 105-8
bittersweet: candied orange peel, 116
    chocolate glaze, 88

black bread: rolls, 72
    Russian, 53
bleached flour, 6
blini, cornmeal, 76
blueberry-buttermilk coffee cake, 113
bolting, 7
boules, 32
bran, 6
    -molasses sunflower bread, 38
    muffins, maple, 100
brandy: in lime marmalade, 125
    pear, persimmon muffins with
        raisins and, 102
    raspberry, *savarin* with berries and, 84
bread(s): boards, 16
    crumbs, homemade, 127
    flour, 22
    and food, 132–33
    knife, 14, 25
    quick, 96–113
    and spirits, 130–132
    sticks, 34
    with three chocolates, 83
    yeasted, 27–95
Brie: croutons, 128
    en croustade, 127
    with pumpernickel bread, 64
brioche, 36, 88
    apple, 87–88
    champignon, 64–65
    cinnamon, 90
    large, *à tête,* 37
    oatmeal, 89
    sausage in, 67
    spinach, 63
brown rice, about, 8
    bread, 38
buckwheat, about, 8
    -orange biscuits, 108
    in rain and sun bread, 49
bulgur, 7, 46
buns: sandwich, 73
    see also little savory breads, little
sweet breads
butter(s): compound, 117–19
    croutons, 126
    homemade, 118
    see also fruit butters, nut spreads
butterhorns, hazelnut whole-wheat, 93
buttermilk: biscuits, sesame
whole-wheat, 107
    coffee cake, blueberry-, 113
    corn bread, 111
    fantans, baby, 73
    -honey bread, 28
    potato bread, 54

Cadwallader, Sharon, 79–80
cake flour, 6
cake yeast, *see* compressed yeast
candied orange peel, bittersweet, 116
carrot: and poppy seed bread, 61
    and tangerine bread, 110–11
cashew-date bread, 80
Celeste's sunflower-oatmeal bread, 47
cereals, mixed-grain, 7
challah, 28
    cinnamon, 30
champagne prune butter, 125
champignon(s): brioche, 64–65
    French bread, 30
Cheddar cheese: in herb bread, 55
    and mustard muffins, 103
cheese: babka, 87
    biscuits, 108
    bread, herb and, 55
    spreads, 121
    see also specific cheeses
chestnut pâté, sweet, 120
chèvre, 90
    see also goat cheese
chili butter, Baja, 118
chocolate: babka, 87
    bread, 83, 92
    glaze, bittersweet, 88
cinnamon: brioches, 90
    challah, 30
    sugar, 100
clay tiles, unglazed, *see* baking stone
clear wash, 115
cloche baking dish, 45
coffee cake(s): quick, 112–13
    yeasted, 86–88
compressed yeast, 9
confit, onion, 65
conserve, winter apricot, 125
convection ovens, 15
converted rice, 8
cooling: yeasted breads, 25
    quick loaves, 109
cool rise method, 23
corn: about, 7
    bread, buttermilk, 111
    muffins, bacon and, 103
cornmeal: about, 7
    blini, 76
    crescents, 78
    -honey bread, 41
    in rain and sun bread, 49
cornstarch: about, 7
    wash, 115
country bread: with golden raisins and

walnuts, 45
    round French, 30
    rye, 50
couronne, 37, 64–65
couscous, 7
cracked wheat: about, 7
    bread, 46
cream: biscuits, oatmeal, 107
    butter, feta, 121
cream cheese with fresh herbs, 121
crescents: cornmeal, 78
    hazelnut whole-wheat, 93
croustade(s), 37, 127
    wild-mushroom, 68
croutons: Brie, 128
    butter, 126
    homemade salad, 126
    large garlic, 128
crumb: cake, plum, 86
    topping, 86, 113
currant bread, pumpernickel-, 64
cutting dried fruit, 116

dark rye: flour, about, 7
    bread, 53, 64
    see also pumpernickel
date: bread, cashew-, 80
    scones, 108
    tea bread, orange-, 110
deflating dough, 23
dessert melba, 128
Dijon rye bread, 52
dill: mustard, 122
    rye, seeded, 60
doneness, testing for: in quick
loaves, 109
    in yeasted breads, 16, 25
dough: hook, 21
    scraper, 14, 22
dried: fruit, cutting, 116
    yeast, instant, 9
dry yeast, 9
drying pistachios, 116
durum wheat, 7, 56, 59
Dutch crunch topping, 38

egg (s): about, 10
    bread, 43
        hazelnut, 88
    see also brioche, challah
    glaze, 115
    rich, 115
    wash, 114
embellishments, 116
    adding to dough, 24, 109
endosperm, 7
equipment, 13–16

fantans, baby buttermilk, 73
farina, 7
fats, 10
    as glazes, 114
    for greasing pans, 24
fennel-orange rye bread, 52
feta cream butter, 121
ficelles, 30
fig jam, 123
filling(s): almond, 86
    cheese: for babka, 87
        for lemon pastries, 90
    olive, 57
    pecan, 95
    see also confit, ragout
flat breads: garden, 75
    garlic, 75
Fleischmann Yeast Test Kitchens, 20
flour(s): all-purpose, 22
    amount to use, 6, 97
    barley, 7
    bleached, 6
    bread, 6, 22
    cake, 6
    corn, 7
    gluten, 7
    graham, 7
    grinding, 6
    millet, 8
    pastry, 6, 105
    rice, 8, 70
    self-rising, 6
    semolina, 7
    soy, 8
    specialty, 6
    stone-ground, 6
    triticale, 7
    unbleached, 6
    variations in, 6
    water-ground, 6
    wheat, 6–7
    whole-grain, 6
focaccia: herb, 75
    garlic, 75
food with bread, 133
food processors: making biscuits in, 107
    making butter in, 118
    making French bread in, 32
    making yeasted breads in, 21–22
freezing, 25, 99, 109
French bread, 30–32
    nut, 42
    rolls, 30
        with onions, 72
        stuffed with ham pâté, 127
    yogurt, 33

fresh: -berry muffins, 100
    herb bread, 57
    -lemon muffins, 99
    nut butter, 119
    persimmon puree, 102
    tomato juice, 60
frosted grapes, 116
fruit: butters, 125
    dried, cutting, 116
    honey, 125
    see also specific fruit

garden flat bread, 75
garlic: croutons, large, 128
    focaccia, 75
ginger-pumpkin biscuits, 107
glazes, 52, 88, 89, 110, 114–15
glazing, 24, 25, 114
gluten, 6, 7, 22, 23, 24, 25, 105
    flour, 7
goat cheese: baked marinated, 121
    pastries, lemon-, 90
    toast, 129
Gorgonzola, olive oil bread with, 65
graham: bread, 47–49
    flour, 7
Graham, Sylvester, 7
grains, 6–8
grapes, frosted, 116
greasing pans, 24
grinding flour, 6
grits, 7
gros brioches à tête, 37
Gruyère pullman loaf, 34

ham pâté with French rolls, 127
hard wheat, 6
hazelnut(s): egg bread, 88
    in French nut bread, 42
    skinning, 116
    toasting, 116
    whole-wheat butterhorns, 93
heavy-duty electric mixer, 21
herb bread, 55, 57, 60, 75
    cheese and, 55
    Irish, whole-wheat, 111
    Italian-style, 63
    see also specific herbs
herb(s): butter, parsley-, 119
    cream cheese with fresh, 121
    in garden flat breads, 75
    with melba, 128–29
    mustard, 122
    with ricotta, 121
    rolls, 78
    see also specific herbs
Hiken, Barbara, 28

homemade: bread crumbs, 127
    butter, 118
    salad croutons, 126
hominy, 7
honey: butter, 118, 119
    bread, buttermilk, 28
    bread, cornmeal-, 41
    fruit, 125
    oat bread, pistachio-, 41
    -prune bread, 79–80
    and seed bread, 34
    substituting for sugar, 10
    whole-wheat bread, 46
horseradish mustard, 122

instant dried yeast, 9
Il Fornaio bakery, 83
Irish herb bread, whole-wheat, 111
Italian: peasant bread, 32–33
    -style herb bread, 63
    whole-wheat bread, 42–43

jams, 123–25

kneading breads, 20
kugelhof, 37, 86

large: *brioche à tête,* 37
    garlic croutons, 128
Larsen, Judy, 47
leaveners, 9–10, 96
lemon: curd, 125
    glaze, 99
    goat cheese pillows, 90
    muffins, fresh-, 99
    sauce, 113
l'épis, 32
lime marmalade, brandied, 125
liquids, 10, 105
little breads: savory, 32, 34, 36, 69–78
    sweet, 89–95
loaves: forming, 24
    quick, 109–11

macadamia nut bread, piña-, 110
maple: bran muffins, 100
    -oatmeal sticky buns, 89
marmalade, brandied lime, 125
masa harina, 7
medium rye flour, 7
melba, 126–28
menu suggestions, 135
micro-rise method, 15
microwave ovens, 15, 25, 125
millet, 8
mixed-grain cereals, 7
mixing dough: for biscuits, 105
    for muffins, 97
    for quick loaves, 111
    for yeasted breads, 20, 21–22

molasses: sunflower bread, bran-, 38
    glaze, 115
morels, in wild-mushroom *croustade,* 68
"mother," 32
mousselines, 37
mozzarella: biscuits, basil and, 108
    in herb bread, 63
    toast, 128
muffins: about, 97–99
    savory, 103–4
    sweet, 99–102
mushroom(s): butter, 118
    in *croustade,* 68
    muffins, *shiitake,* with wild rice, 104
    ragout, in brioche, 64
mustard(s), 122
    butter, 118
    glaze, 52
    muffins, cheddar cheese and, 103

nine-grain cereal, 7
nut bread: French, 42
    piña-macadamia, 110
nut(s): butter, 119
    spreads, 120
    storing, 116
    toasting, 116
    see also specific nuts

oat(s): about, 7
    bread, pistachio-honey, 41
    see also oatmeal
oatmeal: bread, apricot-, 79
    brioche, 89
    Celeste's sunflower-, 47
    cream biscuits, 107
    muffins, old-fashioned, 100
    sticky buns, maple-, 89
    see also oats
oil wash, 55, 115
old-fashioned: oatmeal muffins, 100
    prune muffins, 101
    raisin bread, 83
olive: baguettes, 57
    spread, 120
olive oil bread, 65
onion(s): *confit* in olive oil bread, 65
    in French bread rolls, 72
    tart, 67
orange: biscuits, buckwheat-, 108
    butter, 118
    -date tea bread, 119
    glaze, 110
    peel, bittersweet candied, 116
    rye bread, fennel-, 52
    syrup, 84

oven spring, 25
ovens, 15, 25
overnight: pecan rolls, 95
  sponge, 20

pain: de campagne, 30
  de mie, 34
  de seigle, 51
  ordinaire, 30
pane basilico, 78
pan(s): about, 14
  greasing, 24
  for little breads, 69
  for muffins, 97, 99
  pullman, 34
  for quick loaves, 109
Pappas, Lou, 86
parchment paper, 14, 69
parsley: -herb butter, 119
  muffins, smoked gouda and , 103
pastries, lemon-goat cheese, 90
pastry: brushes, 14
  flour, 6, 7, 43, 105
peanut butter, sesame-, 120
pear brandy, persimmon muffins with
  raisins and, 102
pear-spice coffee cake, 113
pearl barley, 7
pecan: -honey butter, 119
  muffins, banana-, 101
  rolls, overnight, 95
pelle, 14
persimmon: muffins, 102
  puree, fresh, 102
pesto toast, 129
petits: brioches à tête, 36, 37
  pains, 32
    d'oignons, 72
picnic breads, 63–68
pina–macadamia nut bread, 110
pine nut butter, 119
pistachio(s): drying, 116
  -honey oat bread, 41
  skinning, 116
plain melba, 126
proofing yeast, 20
plum crumb cake, 86
polenta, 7
poppy seed: bread, carrot and, 61
  rolls, yogurt-, 73
potato: bread, buttermilk-, 54
  rolls, 54
  water, 50, 51
powdered sugar glaze, 115
prune: bread, honey-, 79–80
  butter, champagne, 125
  muffins, old-fashioned, 101
pullman: loaf, Gruyère, 34
  pan, 34

pumpernickel, about, 7
  bread, 53
  -currant bread, 64
  toast, 128
pumpkin: biscuits, ginger-, 107
  bread, Taos, 60–61
  puree, 61

quarry tiles, *see* baking stone
quick: breads, 96–113
  -cooking oats, 7
  loaves, 109–11
  -rise yeast, 9

ragout, mushroom, 64–65
rain and sun bread, 49
raisin(s): bread, old-fashioned, 83
  golden, country bread with, 45
  persimmon muffins, with, 102
rapid-mix method, 20, 57
raspberry brandy, *savarin* with berries
  and, 84
red pepper–semolina bread, 59
refrigerator method of rising, 23
reheating, 25, 105
rice: about, 8
  flour, 8, 70
  see also brown rice, wild rice
rich egg glaze, 115
ricotta, herbed, 121
rising dough, 23, 24
Robin Hood Consumer Test Kitchen, 23
rolled: bread, 20
  oats, *see* oats, oatmeal
rolls: black bread, 72
  cinnamon, 90
  crescent, 78, 93
  French, 32
  with ham pâté, 127
  herb, 78
  onion, 72
  potato, 54
  sesame-wheat, 70
  water, 70
  yogurt–poppy seed, 73
  see also little savory breads, little
  sweet breads
Russian bread, black, 53
rye, about, 7
  bread: country, 50
    dark, 53
    Dijon, 52
    fennel-orange, 52
    pumpernickel-currant, 64
    rolls, 72
    seeded dill, 60
    sour, 51
    Swedish, 52

saffron bread, tomato-, 59–60
St. André butter, 121
salt, 10
  wash, 115
sandwich buns, 73
sausage(s): *en brioche,* 67
  in herb bread, 63
savarin with berries and raspberry
  brandy, 84
savory little breads, 32, 34, 36, 69–78
seafood butter, 119
second rise, 24
seed bread, honey and, 34
seeded dill rye, 60
self-rising flour, 6
semolina, 7
  bread, red pepper-, 59
  flour, 6, 7, 59
sesame: melba, 128
  -peanut butter, 120
  -wheat long rolls, 70
  whole-wheat buttermilk biscuits, 107
scones, date, 108
shiitake mushrooms muffins, wild rice
  and, 104
skinning pistachios, 116
slashing loaves, 24, 114
slicing bread, 25
smoked gouda and parsley muffins, 103
soda bread, 111
soft wheat, 6
sour cream coffee cake, vanilla-, 116–17
sour rye bread, 51
soy flour, 8
special techniques, 116
specialty flours, 6, 7–8
spice coffee cake, pear-, 113
spiced applesauce muffins, 102
spinach brioche, 63
spirits: in bread, 130–132
  in glazes, 114
  in jams, 123
  see also specific spirits
sponge method: about, 20
  in recipes, 32, 33, 42, 50, 51, 59, 65, 92
spreads, 117-25
steel-cut oats, 7
sticky buns, maple-oatmeal, 89
storing: muffins, 97–99
  nuts, 116
  quick loaves, 111
  yeasted breads, 25
streusel, 87, 100, 101
sugar: anise, 93
  cinnamon, 100
  glaze, powdered, 115
  powdered, vanilla, 116
sunflower: bread, bran molasses, 38
  -oatmeal bread, Celeste's, 47

Swedish rye bread, 52
sweet chestnut pâté, 120
sweet yeasted breads, 79–95, 89–95
sweetening, 10

tangerine bread, carrot and, 110–11
Taos pumpkin bread, 60–61
tapenade, 120
tart, onion, 67
tea bread, orange-date, 110
techniques: biscuits, 105–7
  little breads, 69
  muffins, 97–99
  quick loaves, 111
  yeasted breads, 25
temperature: for activating yeast, 20
  for rising dough, 23, 24
three-grain bread, wild rice and, 50
toast: goat cheese, 129
  mozzarella, 128
  pesto, 129
  pumpernickel, 128
toasting nuts, 116
tomato: juice, 59, 60
  mustard, 122
  -saffron bread, 59–60
topping: crumb, 86, 113
  Dutch crunch, 38
  streusel, 101
tools, 14
triticale flour, 7

unbleached flour, 6
unglazed clay tiles, quarry tiles:
  see baking stone
vanilla: powdered sugar, 116
  -sour cream coffee cake, 112–13
vegetable breads, 54, 57, 59–61, 63–65,
68, 72
  see also specific vegetables

walnuts, country bread with
  golden raisins and, 45
warm lemon sauce, 113
washes, *see* glazes
water-ground flour, 6
water rolls, 70
wheat, 6–7
whipped honey butter, 118
white: breads, 28–37
  flour dough, 22
  pastry flour, 43
whole-grain: breads, 38–53
  dough, 22
  flour, 6
  muffins, 100

whole-wheat: bread, 42, 43, 46, 55, 111
    butterhorns, hazelnut, 93
    buttermilk biscuits, sesame, 107
    flour, 6, 7, 43
    in three-grain bread, 50
wild-mushroom *croustade,* 68
wild rice, 8
    cooking, 116
    and *shiitake* mushroom muffins, 104
    and three-grain bread, 50
winter apricot conserve, 125
wood ovens, 15
work space, 16
work surface, 14

yeast: about, 9
    activating, 20
yeasted bread(s), 27–95
    adding embellishments, to, 24
    baking, 25
    coffee cakes, 86–88
    cooling, 25
    deflating dough, 23
    doneness, testing for, 16, 25
    equipment for, 13–16
    glazing, 24
    little, 69–78, 89–95
    mixing dough, 20, 21–22
    reheating, 25
    rising dough, 23, 24
    slashing loaves, 24
    slicing, 25
    storing, 25
    sweet, 79–95
    white, 28–37
    whole-grain, 38–53
yogurt: French bread, 33
    -poppy seed rolls, 73

*This book was
composed in Granjon types by
On Line Typography,
San Francisco*

*It was printed
and bound by
Toppan Printing Co., Ltd.,
Tokyo, Japan*

*Design & production by
Thomas Ingalls + Associates,
San Francisco*